D1264196

CHEYENNE AUTUMN

BY MARI SANDOZ

Introduction to the Bison Books
Edition by Alan Boye

UNIVERSITY OF NEBRASKA PRESS   •   LINCOLN

© 1953 by Mari Sandoz
Introduction © 2005 by the Board of Regents of the University of Nebraska
Reprinted by arrangement with the Estate of Mari Sandoz, represented by McIntosh
and Otis, Inc.
Manufactured in the United States of America

∞

First Nebraska paperback printing: 1992

Library of Congress Cataloging-in-Publication Data
Sandoz, Mari, 1896–1966.
Cheyenne autumn / Mari Sandoz; introduction to the Bison Books edition by Alan
Boye.
p. cm.
Originally published: New York: McGraw-Hill, 1953.
Includes bibliographical references and index.
ISBN-13: 978-0-8032-9341-0 (pbk.: alk. paper)
ISBN-10: 0-8032-9341-0 (pbk.: alk. paper)
1. Cheyenne Indians—Kings and rulers—Biography.   2. Cheyenne Indians—History.
3. Cheyenne Indians—Government relations.   I. Title.
E99.C53S2   2005
978.004'97353—dc22   2005009164

ALAN BOYE

Introduction

Under cover of darkness on the night of September 9, 1878, a band of Northern Cheyenne Indians fled U.S. Government captivity in Oklahoma to begin a bitter and tragic but ultimately triumphant journey to their Montana homeland. That night about three hundred men, women, and children were able to slip away from their standing shelters so silently that one hundred soldiers camped nearby and positioned to prevent their escape from Indian Territory continued to sleep, unaware. For the next several months these Cheyennes struggled northward toward their ancestral lands, all the while evading capture and engaging the military in several battles.

The bloody century of war with the Native peoples of the West was reaching its climax. Only two years earlier many of these same Cheyennes had helped wipe out George Armstrong Custer at the Battle of the Little Big Horn. Since then the U.S. Government had been conducting an all-out offensive against Indians of the northern plains. As a part of this campaign, a Northern Cheyenne village—located in what is now Wyoming—had been destroyed in a surprise attack during the winter of 1876. More than a thousand people abandoned their belongings and fled into the mountains with nothing more than the clothes on their backs.

The following spring, destitute and on the brink of starvation, these same Northern Cheyenne people agreed to be taken south to Indian Territory, with the understanding that they would be able to return to their northern homelands if they did not like it there. Once they arrived in the south, however, their misery only worsened. They were forced to compete with their southern cousins for each bite of government-issued beef. Malaria, whooping cough, and measles killed their children. Deprivation was everywhere. After suffering for a year, the Northern Cheyenne people said they were going to return to their homeland in the north as they had been told they could. The U.S. Government refused to let them go, and instead had them watched day and night.

The Cheyennes left anyway.

Under the leadership of a brilliant warrior named Little Wolf, and guided by the wisdom of an old chief named Morning Star (or Dull Knife), the Indians fought a thousand-mile running battle in order to regain their homeland. Before it ended, tens of thousands of U.S. Army troops were called in to help search for the small band of Cheyennes.

While in Nebraska the band separated into two groups. Roughly half of the refugees, including Dull Knife, Wild Hog, and other leaders, were apprehended in late October when, blinded by a snowstorm, they stumbled upon a group of soldiers. The soldiers disarmed the Cheyennes and then marched them to imprisonment at a military post at the southern edge of the Dakota Badlands. Held in a room roughly the size of a basketball court, the 149 refugees spent the next six weeks in relative comfort, until—thanks to bureaucratic squabbling and inadequate leadership—the government ordered them to return to the south.

The Cheyennes refused to go. They said they preferred to die in their homeland rather than return to the sickness and misery they had known in captivity. The doors and the windows of the building were sealed shut; first the food was taken away, then the water. A few days later, on the bitterly cold night of January 9, 1879, the Cheyennes smashed their way out of the building. Within moments dozens of men, women, and children were dead or wounded from soldiers' gunfire. The rest escaped into the nearby hills. After being trailed for weeks, almost all of them were slaughtered in a shallow pit not far from the South Dakota border.

Little Wolf and the other half of the Cheyennes evaded capture. They spent the winter hiding out in northwestern Nebraska before making their way northward in the spring. They made it to Montana, where eventually they were given a small reservation in the southeast corner of the state. This reservation today continues as the home of the Northern Cheyenne people.

The most masterful and authentic retelling of the Cheyenne exodus is Mari Sandoz's *Cheyenne Autumn*. Intimate, lyrical, and moving, Sandoz's book stands as the most informed account of that dark time. Having been born less than twenty years after the events, and raised on a frontier homestead not far from the site of the final massacres, Sandoz was in a perfect position to tell the story. As a child she listened to the Cheyenne survivors who often stopped by her father's place to talk. As a professional writer later in life she conducted extensive interviews with the Northern Cheyenne people and spent over a decade researching the historical record for details of the story.

In 1930, before she had gained wide recognition as a writer, the thirty-four-year-old Sandoz and a friend spent three weeks driving a Model T through the Dakotas, Wyoming, and Montana. Her friend was interested in anthropology, and Sandoz saw the trip as a way to generate ideas for new writing projects. In particular, Sandoz wanted more information about the events of 1878–79 and the slaughter at Fort Robinson. She visited the Northern Cheyenne Reservation and spent several days talking to old-timers who had been part of the exodus. She took extensive notes but made no transcript of her interviews.

By 1936 Sandoz's first book, *Old Jules* (a biography of her complex and sometimes difficult father), was gaining fame and being more widely read. The book's financial success allowed Sandoz to begin work on the Cheyenne story. She returned to the Northern Cheyenne Reservation to conduct more interviews and continue her research of archival records. She began writing a manuscript she initially called *Flight to the North* while living in her New York City apartment.

In 1940 Sandoz was forced to set aside the project when she learned that a competing publisher was about to release a new Howard Fast novel based on the incidents. After World War II and several intervening writing projects, she finally returned to her Cheyenne book. She once again visited the reservation and other key locations of the story, trampling over prairie, rimrock, and badlands, manuscript in hand. According to Sandoz's biographer, Helen Stauffer, by that point Sandoz had gathered so much information about the Cheyennes that every square inch of her Greenwich Village apartment was filled with research materials. "The only spot not covered with boxes and files was the kitchen sink," Stauffer wrote (174). When some of the original archival material was later lost in a fire, the importance of Sandoz's work became clear. Because she had talked to survivors of the ordeal and had kept notes based on missing documents, she knew that her book contained information that could be found nowhere else. She said that, good or bad, her writing was unique in the field and that those who came after her would have to depend upon it (Nicoll 36).

By 1951 Sandoz's manuscript was complete enough for her to begin seeking a publisher. Several companies hesitated at the unusual story, told so vividly from the Indians' point of view, before McGraw-Hill agreed to publish it. The appearance of the book was briefly stalled one final time when Sandoz worried that the Cheyenne story too closely paralleled news reports of women and children fleeing the brutality of soldiers in the war then raging on the Korean peninsula. When she realized that the Korean War might continue indefinitely, *Cheyenne Autumn* was published in 1953.

Sandoz's remarkable ability to combine accurate historical research with the skills of a novelist made the book appealing not only to anthropologists and historians but to thousands of general readers as well. Nearly every review was positive, and the *New York Times* listed it as one of the best books of the year. The book has never been out of print.

Cheyenne Autumn is the work of a master writer at the peak of her craft. Told almost exclusively from the point of view of the Northern Cheyennes, we can see the tragedy as if we were the oppressed, not the victors. Her no-holds-barred description of battles is shocking, sad, and tragic, but always written in a brilliant, sparkling, prose-poetry of words.

One by one Sandoz sets the full drama of each historical event, drawing the narrative tension of the book as tight as a bowstring. We are swept up by the events, from the beginning when Little Wolf sits by a cold fire, his finger on the trigger of a rifle, to the horror and grief of those huddled-together moments before the final massacre. Still, the book is rich in humor, romantic intrigue, and the details of ordinary life. Despite the horrific conditions, Sandoz shows us calm and even joyful moments among the Cheyennes.

Readers will immediately sense the book's distinctive style. Not so much a literal transcription of the Cheyenne language, the story is told in rhythmic phrases and uses English idioms and figures of speech to replicate the sound of spoken Cheyenne. Sandoz knew that the Cheyennes seldom raised their voices, even in anger. Her muted, understated dialogue creates a wonderfully accurate translit-eration of the soft, downy tones of Cheyenne speech. The "voice" of this book remains soft and calm, too, despite its fearful topic.

While never straying far from the central story of the heroism of Little Wolf and Dull Knife, Sandoz nevertheless is able to weave an incredible number of cultural details into her narrative. We learn that in summertime Cheyennes used bear grease to help keep gnats away, for example, or that when there was no tobacco to be had, Cheyenne men smoked a mixture of the ash from their pipes with red willow bark. More important, we learn many fine points of Cheyenne cosmological and spiritual beliefs, including the idea that "all things that ever happened in a place were always of the today in the Cheyenne pattern of time." The book's most interesting revelations, however, can be found in the small, ordinary details of the life of Cheyenne women. We watch as they perform their daily rituals during the most trying of times. We see them "hurry to the lake with their waterskins," and listen while they teach the younger girls about "the plants they would need to know as good Cheyenne women: cures for painful periods and the purification." We learn how women pounded chokecherries, plums, and sand cherries into freshly roasted meat, which made the meat "easy to carry in half and quarter bladders dipped in hot tallow, and easy to divide when [the people] must scatter." We glimpse courting rituals, wedding ceremonies, and the story of how one woman divorced her husband, "as was her right," simply by throwing his belongings out of the shelter.

In the real life stories of these women and men we see the reflection of our own ordinary stories. Sandoz understood the struggle of the Cheyenne people was universal and embodied the strengths and weaknesses of all humankind. She knew that everyone clings to the same dream: that over the next hill we will reach what she called "the green pastures of our desire." She said, "I looked about me in life and in history and literature and I saw that there were two kinds of men, the defeated and the undefeated, and that surely the last was the first" (Nicoll 35).

Cheyenne Autumn is not a story about victory or defeat but about survival. The tale of these American refugees, of Native people who died trying to gain the fundamental human right of a home, still strikes a deep and timely chord.

WORKS CITED

Nicoll, Bruce. "Mari Sandoz: Nebraska Loner." *The American West* 2.2 (Spring 1965): 32–36.
Stauffer, Helen Winter. *Mari Sandoz—Story Catcher of the Plains*. Lincoln: University of Nebraska Press, 1982.

Preface

IN MY CHILDHOOD OLD TRAPPERS AND INDIAN TRADERS OR their breed descendants still came to visit around our fire on the Niobrara River, men with such names as Charbonneau, Provost, Dorion, Richard, Bordeaux, Bent, and Merrivale. Some of them had hunted with my father for twenty-five years—deer and antelope and sometimes big-horn sheep and grizzly as far away as the Big Horn Mountains. Some of them knew Old Jules from his months at Fort Robinson in 1884, only five years after the Cheyennes of this book broke out of the barracks there and fled for their lives over the winter bluffs.

The old-timers talked long and late hours about those days, and about the earlier years, when their ancestors came as free trappers or with the fur companies into what they called the trans-Missouri country, the region stretching from the bend of the Missouri to the headwaters of the east-flowing streams in the mountains. This region, the Great Plains, sticking like a great thumb from Canada down deep into Texas, was the old buffalo and Indian country.

Sometimes the old-timers told stories of their forerunners, the early Spanish and French who brought the first iron and gunpowder to the Indians of the region. Perhaps while they talked, their Sioux and Cheyenne relatives were sitting back from our fire sucking their long pipes, making the agreeing sign and their *"Hou!" "Hou!"* These Indians told stories, too, of their old buffalo-hunting life and of the first real encounter with the United States Army in the Grattan fight of 1854. At that time the white men in the region were only a few little islands in a great sea of Indians and buffaloes. Twenty-three years later, in 1877, the buffaloes were about gone and the last of the Indians driven to the reservations—only a few little islands of Indians in a great sea of whites.

This exploit of modern man is unrivaled in history: the destruction of a whole way of life and the expropriation of a race from a region of 350,000,000 acres in so short a time. It entailed first of all a tremendous job of public conditioning. In the 1830s and 1840s the buffalo Indians were considered the most romantic of peoples, drawing visitors from everywhere. Such men as Prince Paul of Württemberg, Prince Maximilian, Sir William Drummond Stewart, Catlin, Parkman, and hundreds of others came to ride in the surrounds, to eat roast hump ribs, to study and become one with this great Red Hunter.

But that was before the white man wanted these Indian lands. The discovery of gold and the rise of economic and political unrest over much of the civilized world, with millions of men hungry for a new start, changed that, and suddenly the romantic Red Hunter was a dirty, treacherous, bloodthirsty savage standing in the way of progress, in the path of manifest destiny. By 1864, with the nation at war ostensibly to free the black man from slavery, the public had been prepared to accept a policy of extermination for the red. The policy was actually initiated as early as 1854 and 1855. It was given such impetus by General "Squaw Killer" Harney's unprovoked attack on Little Thunder's peaceful Sioux village in 1855 that there was no really serious objection to the massacre of the Cheyennes at Sand Creek, Colorado, in 1864. Not even from Lincoln, the Emancipator. Perhaps he remembered his few days burying dead from the Black Hawk War. As President he paid off some election favors by turning Indian agencies over to petty politicians, one man at least accumulating a fortune from his $1,200-a-year job. The Emancipation Proclamation was almost two years behind Lincoln, the Gettysburg Address a year and a week old when the Cheyenne men, women, and children were killed at Sand Creek. The next summer under President Johnson, General Connor issued sweeping orders to his Powder River expedition against the Sioux and Cheyennes: "You will not receive overtures of peace or submission from the Indians, but will attack and kill every male Indian over 12 years of age." The aggravating Indians did not waste much scarce ammunition fighting Connor's men. They were herded back to the Platte unharmed, in barefoot humiliation. Custer had better luck against the Cheyennes on the Washita in 1868. He brought in many captives but not one male over ten. Under Grant's administration Henely took no captives at all on the Sappa in 1875, and threw the bodies of the Cheyennes, even the smallest children, upon the fires of their goods and lodges.

All this time a few humanitarians were complaining against such treatment of the Indian, but no voice was loud enough to be heard above the drumbeaters for the railroads, the cattlemen, the miners, and the army contractors. There were some generals who protested these war tactics and regretted the entire Indian extermination policy, men like Pope and Crook, but their voices too were like the wind on the buffalo grass.

After this period of twenty-three years that turned a free hunting people into sullen agency sitters, there was a short series of rebellions. With the buffalo gone, the starving Indians, dismounted and disarmed, were easily shuffled off to land on which no white man could conceivably make a living. Congress now felt free to initiate more cuts in the appropriations for their helpless wards, dropping them far below the treaty stipulations, often to actual starvation levels. By midsummer, 1877, the quiet and peaceful Nez Perce were making their desperate break for survival. The next year the Sioux, Bannocks, Arapahos, Poncas, and others rebelled too, hoping to return to their old homes where the children were healthy and the cooking pots once held meat.

Of all these heroic attempts to preserve their people from starvation and disease, none outshines the 1,500-mile flight of the Northern Cheyennes from Indian Territory back to the Yellowstone country, through settled regions netted with telegraph, across three railroads, and straight through the United States Army. It is the story of a people with much that is difficult to say in white-man words. The old Cheyennes, even more than their High Plains neighbors, had a rich and mystical perception of all life as a continuous, all-encompassing eventual flow, and of man's complete oneness with all this diffused and eternal stream. It was a stream of many and complex dimensions, one in which man, the tree, the rock, the cloud, and all the other things were simultaneously in all the places they had ever been; and all things that had ever been in a place were always in the present there, in the being and occurring. To convey something of these deep, complex, and patterned interrelationships which I myself sense only imperfectly, I have tried to keep to the simplest vocabulary, to something of the rhythm, the idiom, and the figures of Cheyenne life, to phrases and sentences that have flow and continuality.

This flight of the Cheyennes is the epic story of the American Indian, and one of the epics of our history. I hope that I have not failed my friends, both the Cheyennes and the whites, too greatly in the telling here.

—M. S.

Acknowledgments

First of all I am indebted to Old Cheyenne Woman, who was one of those pulled wounded and bereaved from the Last Hole below Hat Creek bluffs. She lived with the Sioux of Pine Ridge and the neighboring whites and liked to talk in her pidgin English of the good Cheyenne way to a small girl on the upper Niobrara, particularly when the sun eased the old wounds received at Sand Creek, the Sappa, and above Robinson. She was the aunt of the sweet-singing Little Finger Nail and believed that he would have discovered the good new road for his people. But it was all blown away as by the wind, and so she lived out her days among strangers. She nursed many white children through the diphtheria epidemics and finally died, a pauper and alone, in a little white-man town.

Acknowledgment, too, is due all the other Indians, Sioux and Cheyenne, who helped with this book, and to the Nebraska State Historical Society; the War Records Offices, the Indian Records Offices and the Cartography Division, United States National Archives; the Colorado State Historical Society; Western History Room, Denver Public Library; American History Room and Sylvester Vigilante, and the Maps and Newspaper Divisions, New York Public Library; Old Records Files, Northern Cheyenne Reservation; the Museum of the American Indian, Heye Foundation; the American Museum of Natural History; Mrs. Rella Looney, Archivist, Oklahoma Historical Society; Kansas State Historical Society; Wyoming Historical Department; H. D. Wimer for much Sappa material; Caroline Sandoz Pifer, Boris Kicken, Flora Sandoz Kicken, and Jules Sandoz for help in locating the lost Little Wolf winter camps and the Dull Knife flight routes; and many, many other persons.

—M. S.

Contents

List of Illustrations

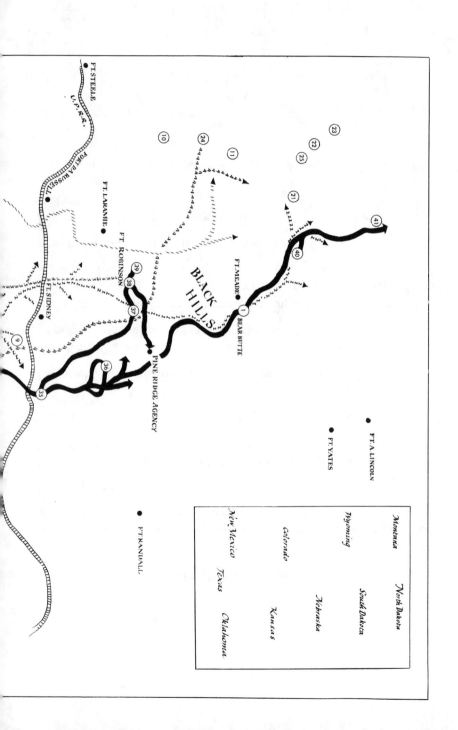

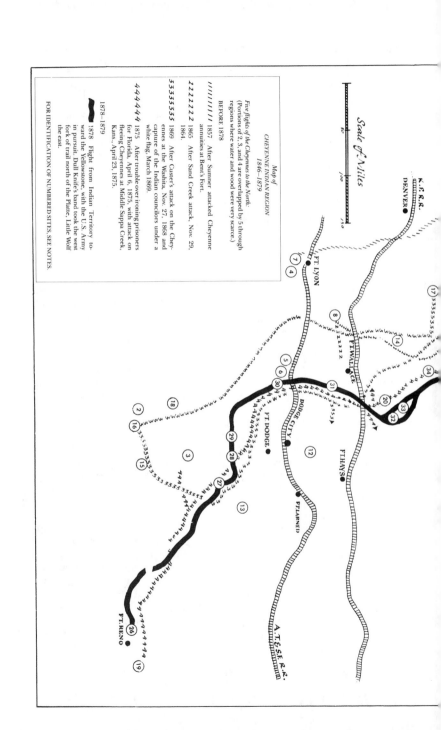

Map of
CHEYENNE INDIAN REGION
1846–1879

Five flights of the Cheyennes to the North:
(Portions of 2, 3, and 4 are overlapped by 5 through
regions where water and wood were very scarce.)

BEFORE 1878

////////// 1857 After Sumner attacked Cheyenne
annuities at Bent's Fort.

2222222 1865 After Sand Creek attack, Nov. 29,
1864.

3333333333 1869 After Custer's attack on the Cheyennes at the Washita, Nov. 27, 1868 and
capture of the Indian councilors under a
white flag, March 1869.

4444444 1875 After trouble over ironing prisoners
for Florida, April 6, 1875, with attack on
fleeing Cheyennes at Middle Sappa Creek,
Kans., April 23, 1875.

1878–1879

▬▬▬ 1878 Flight from Indian Territory toward the Yellowstone, with the U.S. Army
in pursuit. Dull Knife's band took the west
fork of trail north of the Platte, Little Wolf
the east.

FOR IDENTIFICATION OF NUMBERED SITES, SEE NOTES.

Scale of Miles
50   100   150

K.P.R.R.
DENVER ●

FT. LYON

FT. WALLACE

FT. HAYS ●

FT. LARNED ●

DODGE CITY ●

FT. DODGE ●

A.T.&S.F. R.R.

FT. RENO ●

Region of Cheyenne Resistance, 1846–1879

Background (SITES NUMBERED ON MAP)

1. Bear Butte, sacred to Cheyenne religion.
2. Annihilation of Cheyenne Bowstring warriors by Kiowas, 1837.
3. Wolf Creek fight, revenge on Kiowas, 1838, Little Wolf with pipe.
4. Yellow Wolf predicted end of buffaloes, 1846, at Bent's Fort.
5. Chief Tobacco killed by soldier, 1846. Dull Knife prevented general war.
6. Cholera decimated Cheyennes, 1849.
7. Cheyenne goods seized by Sumner at Bent's New Fort, 1857, caused first concerted flight north.
8. Sand Creek attack by Chivington, Nov. 29, 1864, starting second Cheyenne flight to north.
9. Attack on Julesburg, Jan. 7, 1865, during Cheyenne-Sioux march to Powder River country.
10. Sioux-Cheyenne attack on Platte Bridge, July 25–26, 1865.
11. Fetterman Massacre near Ft. Phil Kearny, Dec. 21, 1866.
12. Hancock burned Cheyenne village, mid-April, 1867.
13. Medicine Lodge Treaty, 1867.
14. Beecher Island fight, Sept. 17–25, 1868.
15. Washita fight, Cheyenne village destroyed by Custer, Nov. 27, 1868.
16. Custer council with Medicine Arrow, March, 1869, followed by third movement north.
17. Battle of Summit Springs against Tall Bull by Carr, July 11, 1869.
18. Adobe Walls, June 27, 1874, Indian attempt to drive out buffalo hunters.
19. Sandhill fight, Apr. 6, 1875, outbreak while ironing prisoners, beginning fourth flight to north.
20. Sappa fight, Medicine Arrow camp destroyed by Henely and buffalo hunters, Apr. 23, 1875.
21. Cheyennes under Two Moons and Sioux under He Dog struck by Reynolds, Mar. 17, 1876.
22. Rosebud fight, Sioux and Cheyennes vs. Crook, June 17, 1876.
23. Custer battle, June 25, 1876.
24. Dull Knife village destroyed by Mackenzie, Nov. 25, 1876.
25. Running fight, Miles vs. Sioux and Cheyennes, Jan. 1–8, 1877.

In 1878–1879 Outbreak

26. Dull Knife and Little Wolf departure from Cheyenne and Arapahoe agency, Indian Territory, Sept. 9, 1878. Fifth flight of Cheyennes north.
27. Fight at Turkey Springs, Sept. 13–14, 1878.
28–29. Fights, Sept. 16–22, 1878.
30. Cheyennes cross Arkansas night Sept. 23–24, 1878.
31. Lewis fight, Sept. 27, 1878.
32. Killing on the Sappa.
33. Killing on the Beaver.
34. Mauck's pursuit of Cheyennes till across Frenchman, Oct. 2, 1878.
35. Parting of Little Wolf and Dull Knife on White Tail creek.
36. Lost Chokecherry valley, Little Wolf winter camp.
37. Capture of Dull Knife on Chadron Creek, Oct. 23–25, 1878.
38. Outbreak of Dull Knife, Fort Robinson barracks, Jan. 9, 1879.
39. Last of fights in Dull Knife outbreak, Jan. 22, 1879.
40. Capture of Little Wolf by Lt. W. P. Clark, Mar. 25, 1879.
41. Fort Keogh, and a reservation.

Map redrawn by H. Lawrence Hoffman from original by the author.

The People and the Time

The Indians

Little Wolf, one of the Old Man Chiefs of the tribe, was bearer of the Sacred Chief's Bundle of the Northern Cheyennes, carrying with it the highest responsibility for the preservation of the people. He was also the tribe's fastest runner at fifty-seven, and soft-spoken but like a wounded grizzly in anger. His reputation as a bold warrior started back around the 1830s, in the intertribal conflicts of the time, given up temporarily in 1851 when the Cheyennes signed away their rights to the Overland Trail and to the joys of the warpath for annuities and an Indian agency to administer their tribal business with the government.

Although the agency was never established and the goods seldom came, the Cheyennes tried hard to remain at peace with the encroaching whites. Little Wolf did almost no warring against the troops, except during the one year of 1865—to avenge the unprovoked attack on the Cheyennes at Sand Creek the fall before. Since then, he had asked many times for the promised agency and the goods that were their due. He had even gone to Washington and received a big peace medal from President Grant. And next there was an order that they must all stay at Red Cloud, the Sioux agency in northwest Nebraska, where even the Sioux were hungry and the Cheyennes unwelcome interlopers.

In 1876 Little Wolf took his starving followers out on the regular treaty-sanctioned summer hunt. He was too late for the Custer fight, but in time for the Army's pursuit of the Indians afterward, and their destruction of Dull Knife's village on the Powder, where the Wolf helped the women and children escape and received seven bullets before it was done. They fled on through the hungry winter snows of the Yellowstone country until they finally had to listen to the promises of good treatment and an agency in their north country from the emissaries of both General Miles on the

Yellowstone and General Crook down in Nebraska. Little Wolf and Dull Knife surrendered at Red Cloud, where the promises that Crook had made to them in good faith were all broken, although the Wolf had enlisted as a scout for Crook's troops immediately. The Indians were told they could not have the promised agency and that there would be no more food for their families until they started to the hated Indian Territory far to the south. When they still refused to go, they were told that, if they did not like it, they could return—one more promise that was like the wind on the grass.

Little Wolf had two warrior sons along: Pawnee and the Woodenthigh who was named for the strong legs that were characteristic of the family. The daughter was called Pretty Walker, as also seemed fitting. The Wolf's two wives were Quiet One and Feather on Head, with a guest following them, an uninvited guest—the Thin Elk that Little Wolf had warned away from his wives twenty years ago. Now once more the Elk sat at his fire, but as an Old Man Chief and the bearer of the Sacred Bundle, he must think only of the good of the people and not see a man there with his women.

Dull Knife, also an Old Man Chief, had been a famous Dog soldier in his youth, but as early as 1846 he had talked for peace to preserve the tribe. Although his band was closely tied to the Red Cloud Sioux by marriage, Dull Knife did little fighting against the whites except in 1865. He went to Washington with Little Wolf and Hog and the rest to ask for an agency, and when nothing came, he took his people north to the buffalo herds of the Crazy Horse Sioux. Then in November the troops destroyed his village, killing many Cheyennes, including his son and son-in-law, two of the family that the troops had called the Beautiful People.

Now they were all here in Indian Territory, his northern tribesmen dying of malaria with no quinine, and of dysentery and starvation. But to this old-time Cheyenne the promise of the officers in the north was like iron, and so he was going home. With him were his two wives, Pawnee Woman and Short One, and two sons. The elder, Bull Hump, was a prominent Dog soldier, and his wife Leaf was one of the bravest, boldest young women of the tribe. The younger son was nicknamed Little Hump because he followed the elder brother in everything. The five handsome young daughters were called the Princesses by the troops, two of them probably nieces, but beautiful too.

Wild Hog, one of the headmen under the two chiefs, was a big broad man with a broad humorous face. He had his sickened Sioux wife along, a young son nicknamed Little or Young Hog, and a daughter, a quiet girl, beautiful in the reserved Cheyenne way, who was called Hog's Daughter.

The camp finder was, as usual, old Black Crane. He was a patient, judicious man who knew the vast country between them and the Yellowstone: Indian Territory, Kansas, Nebraska, Dakota Territory, Wyoming, and southern Montana. He could soothe the weary querulous women at the end of a hard day of travel and perhaps preserve peace and good humor among the hotheaded, frustrated young warriors. No one had given him real trouble except the young subchief Black Coyote, a very prominent fighter whose wife was Buffalo Calf Road, the Cheyenne warrior woman who had charged her horse into the thick of the battle in the Rosebud fight, to save her brother who was set afoot among Crook's firing troops. Of all the angry agency-hating Cheyennes, Black Coyote was the worst, and while old Crane sympathized with such fine hot anger, he realized that violence now would only bring destruction upon them all.

There were many younger people along too—the future of the tribe. One of the finest was the warrior Little Finger Nail, the artist and sweet singer of the Cheyennes. Then there was a light-haired boy called Yellow Swallow, the Cheyenne son of General Custer.

The *warrior societies,* sometimes called soldier societies, were the organized military and police force of the Cheyennes, and carried out the orders of the council chiefs. The society chiefs, without a place in the council as such, led the members in their duties and in any social and religious activities centered about the warrior lodge. The societies cut across the Cheyenne bands and beyond; there were strong Dog soldier lodges among the Sioux. A general war party, a concerted hunt, or a village camped or moving was always in charge of a designated warrior society. But the Dog soldiers had a permanent duty. They could never move until all the village was safely started. Because they were the perpetual rearguard of the people, their reputation for bravery and desperate last-ditch stands grew tremendously during the years of pursuit by the troops, and their membership vastly reduced.

The Elks, Little Wolf's society, took great pride in their war strategy and their scouting. Even in Dull Knife's village on the Powder, they had reported the coming attack and were caught only because some Fox society men came in with scalps and insisted on making a scalp dance instead of letting the people flee.

The warrior societies included most but not all of the able-bodied ambitious men of the tribe. When a prominent old chief explained to General Miles that he had never joined one, the general laughed. "I'm not a West Point man myself."

The Indian Agent

John A. Miles, of the Cheyenne and Arapahoe Agency, Indian Territory, was one of the Quakers appointed as Indian agents after years of scandal and graft in the Indian service, particularly under Secretary of War Belknap in the Grant administration. But honesty was not the sole requirement for dealing with the proud, independent element of a nomadic hunting people suddenly pushed upon an agency with nothing to do or to eat.

The Military Departments

The path of the Cheyennes fleeing from Indian Territory to the Yellowstone crossed two military departments, the Missouri and the Platte, and entered the Department of Dakota. Troops pursuing the Indians out of their own command were dependent upon the host department for supplies and support, both often unavailable or not graciously given. No department commander welcomed the capture of Indians in his area by troops from the outside.

The Military Men

Gen. George Crook commanded the Department of the Platte, which included Fort Robinson, in northwest Nebraska. He had taken the field against the Sioux and the Northern Cheyennes in the spring of 1876, with a notable encounter on the Rosebud in Montana, on the seventeenth of June. That fall and winter he and General Miles, who operated on the

Yellowstone, each maneuvered to get as many Sioux and Cheyenne Indians to surrender within his department as possible. Some of the Northern Cheyennes went in to Miles, but Little Wolf and Dull Knife were among the chiefs who listened to the bidding of Crook's emissaries and went down to Fort Robinson, where their few goods had come in the past.

Gen. Nelson A. Miles was at Fort Keogh on the Yellowstone, keeping Sitting Bull's Sioux from coming down out of Canada, and in charge of the Cheyennes not yet transferred to Indian Territory. His relentless pursuit of the Sioux and the Cheyennes the winter of 1876–1877 had helped to reduce them so near to nakedness and starvation that they finally had to surrender.

Col. Caleb H. Carlton, Third Cavalry, was ordered to Fort Robinson, Nebraska, and through the sandhills to intercept the fleeing Cheyennes when it was plain they were eluding the troops through Kansas.

Gen. George Armstrong Custer was given command of the Seventh Cavalry when it was created in 1866, to provide positions, it was said, for some of the surplus officers of the Civil War—Custer, in particular, because he campaigned with President Johnson in the off-year election. The fall of 1867 Custer was suspended on charges that included desertion of his post. When restored to his command in the fall of 1868, he was determined to make a showing and fell upon the Cheyennes camped on the Washita where the military agent had told the Indians, just the day before, their families would be safe. Among the captive women and children was a young girl, Monahsetah, whom he kept with him all winter and spring and who bore him a son in the fall—the Yellow Swallow along in the flight north.

In 1874 Custer was sent into the Black Hills where no white man had the treaty right to go. He was to locate gold and thereby stimulate financing for the stalled railroad illegally coming up the Yellowstone. In 1876 he attacked the great Indian camp on the Little Big Horn and died there. The first Indians to open fire on his column were four Cheyennes, one of them now with Little Wolf. Some of the Custer guns were still hidden among them; a carbine, taken down, hung under the buckskin dress of one of the women.

The Time

After the Civil War and through the depression years of the 1870s, there was a great push of white men into the Indian country, the land hunger augmented by the gold rushes, the buffalo-hide bonanza, the expanding railroads, and the cattle business. The demand to clear the Indians out grew louder: tear up the treaties, bribe and drive the treacherous redskins to small restricted reservations that were set up on land no white man would ever want, at least not until oil and uranium were discovered. There they would be supervised by an Indian agent, a political appointee with absolute power. Often he had the help and connivance of some government-elevated nonentity made the agency chief. Normally the Indian Bureau was under the Department of the Interior, but whenever there was serious trouble with the Indians, the civilian agents were replaced by army officers, perhaps the whole Bureau moved to the War Department, and then back when it was argued that the military was really not equipped to make good citizens of the aborigines. "The bureau on wheels" the newspapers called it.

During the Grant administration the grafting in the Indian appropriations was at its height, first in contract letting (pants that went to pieces like blotting paper in water, sugar that was half sand) and then through actual thievery by both the contractors and the agency employees. The resultant starvation fell with particular weight upon the Northern Cheyennes, always stepchildren on the hungry Sioux agency. Now they were thrust upon the most shaming dependence of all—upon the hospitality of their relatives, the Southern Cheyennes, with a cut below the appropriations that those people had last year just for themselves. But they were all helpless, as all the western tribes were helpless. Congress knew this and took the occasion to grow economical, cutting appropriations far below treaty stipulations, and with much encouragement from army contractors, who made millions out of all the starvation flights of 1877 and 1878.

But Little Wolf and Dull Knife knew only that there was not a lodge free of sickness and the keening for death. So the chiefs decided they must take the people home. When they were told they would be whipped back by the troops, they started anyway, and some of them made it through.

Gone Before

EARLY IN THE SPRING OF 1877 NEARLY A THOUSAND hungry and half-naked Northern Cheyennes came in from the Yellowstone country to Red Cloud Agency in northwest Nebraska. They surrendered to the promise of food and shelter and an agency in their hunting region. But almost before the children were warmed on both sides, they were told they must go to Indian Territory,* the far south country many already knew and hated. The two Old Man Chiefs,¹ as the tribal heads were called, listened to this command in silent refusal, but some lesser men shouted the *"Hou!"* of agreement almost before the white men got their mouths open. These Indians were given horses and fine blue blankets, and the meat and coffee and tobacco for a big feast that would build their power and following in the tribe.

"It is a trick of the spider," the chiefs protested. "The *veho* † has long spun his web for the feet of those who have wings but are too foolish to fly. . . ."

Yet even after the feasting there were barely as many as one has fingers who wanted to go south, so the Indian agent announced that he would issue no more rations to the Cheyennes here. While the Sioux women moved in their long line, holding their blankets out to receive their goods, the Cheyennes were kept off on a little knoll, their ragged blankets flapping empty in the wind, the children silent and big-eyed, watching.

Then Little Wolf and Dull Knife were told by the coaxing interpreters that the officials had said, "Just go down to see. If you don't like it you can come back. . . ." ² Finally they agreed, for meat for the kettles, and so, with blue-coated troopers riding ahead and behind, they pointed their moccasins down through Nebraska and Kansas toward their southern relatives who were already hungry.

---

* Now the state of Oklahoma.
† Cheyenne word for spider, and after the white man's coming, for him also.

The chiefs rode ahead, old Dull Knife on his yellow and white spotted horse, Little Wolf beside him on a strong, shaggy black with patches white as winter snow. At the ridge south of the agency the Indians stopped, in spite of all the urging against it, looking back toward the country that had fed and sheltered them long before one white man's track shadowed the buffalo grass. The women keened as for death, and water ran down the dark, stony faces of old Dull Knife and the rest.

It wasn't that these Cheyennes had not seen years ago that their hunting life must pass as certainly as summer died. Back in 1846, Little Wolf heard his cousin Yellow Wolf say that the buffalo was angered by the chasing with gun and bullet and by his carcasses left to rot on the prairie, and so was turning back to the place of his coming, leaving the Indian to die. Yellow Wolf spoke of this before an army officer at Bent's fort, earnestly offering to hire a man to build the Indians a fort too, and teach them to plow the earth and grow cattle to eat. The soldier chief listened, but the wind of laughter from Bent and many of the Indians blew the words away, and when Yellow Wolf, the prophet and man of peace, was shot down at Sand Creek almost twenty years later, nothing had been done.

Through Little Wolf's boyhood the Cheyennes had been very friendly to all the whites except those of the whisky wagons that carried the brown water of violence and death. In those days these Indians ranged as far southwest as the Staked Plains of Texas, but mostly they still returned to the traders of the Platte River and up toward the Black Hills. Then, by 1832, William Bent established a trading post on the upper Arkansas River and married a Cheyenne woman. After that her relatives and their adherents no longer made the long journey by pony drag to the northern traders.

All this time more and more blue-coated troopers came riding, and the emigrants began to run on the trails like dark strings of ants hurrying before the winter, bringing strange sicknesses, eating up the grass of the pony herds, killing the buffalo until the wind stank and the bleaching bones lay white as morning frost on the valleys of the Platte and the Arkansas.

The leaders of those who still traded around the Overland Trail, like Dull Knife, had held the angry young men from attack, but the pock-marked face of Little Wolf grew dark as any in the hooding blanket of the warriors as they watched the white man come. The Cheyennes were famous for their reckless war charges, their pony herds like clouds over the hills, their painted villages, and their regalia and trappings that were as handsome as their country under the October sun. They had been a rather small tribe even before the new diseases scattered their dead over the prairie, but while no one owned the earth and the buffalo herds, any people who fought well and worked to keep the parfleches full of meat could live.

As more hungry Indians were pushed westward and the encroaching whites grabbed the earth in their hands, the Cheyennes of the north began to move closer to the powerful Sioux. With bold warriors and handsome straight-walking women among both peoples, there was considerable intermarriage. Warrior societies like the Dog Soldiers set up lodges in both tribes and often fought their red enemies together. Then, in 1851, the whites called a great conference at Fort Laramie to bring peace forever to the land west of the Missouri, with wagon trains of goods to pay for the emigrant trails and for giving up the glories of the warpath. More goods would keep coming, and government agencies would be established, with an agent, a Little Father, perhaps to live there much of the year to enforce the treaty on the Indians and to distribute the annuities. The agency for the Southern Cheyennes, as the whites called them now, was at Bent's fort, but the Northern Cheyennes had to go to the Sioux agency far up the Platte.

The first big break in the peace came three years later from the whites themselves. A few whisky-smelling soldiers under Grattan killed the leading chief of the Sioux with a cannon. It was after this that the Cheyenne chiefs showed their first real anger in the government council. They wanted no more drunken soldiers shooting into peaceful camps, or emigrants scaring their buffalo. It was then that one spoke of something new, so quietly that his soft Cheyenne was barely to be heard. "We want a thousand white women as wives," he said, "to teach us and our children the new life that must be lived when the buffalo is gone. . . ." [3]

The chiefs saw the bearded dignity of the white men break into anger at this. Plainly they did not understand that the children of Cheyennes belong to the mother's people and that this was a desperate measure to assure the food and the survival of their descendants, although in a few generations there might be not one left to be called Cheyenne anywhere under the blue kettle of the sky.

The white women did not come, and the Indians received little or nothing of the treaty goods for the lands and privileges they had sold. In 1856, some restless young men went to beg a little tobacco at the Oregon trail and got bullets instead. They fired arrows back, hit a man in the arm, and troops came shooting. For months General Sumner chased them around their south country. Angry that they got away, he went to Bent's fort, where Yellow Wolf was waiting peacefully for his treaty goods stored in the fort. Sumner took what he wanted for his troops and gave the rest to the Arapahos while the Wolf's young men had to look on, their empty fingers creeping toward the trigger. But their women and children were surrounded by troops like those who had killed Little Thunder's peaceful Sioux on the Platte last summer, so the chiefs fled with their people up beyond the North Platte, where their relatives lived in peace.

Little Wolf had watched them come, and a spark of anger to smolder a lifetime was lit in his breast. He had never heard of Cheyennes running from anybody, but he lived to see it again, for this was only the first of many times.

Perhaps because the tribe seemed too few to make much trouble, they got very little of their treaty goods, and never an agency of their own. The chiefs had even been to Washington, where Little Wolf smelled the hated whisky on the general who was the Great Father, and yet they had to beg him to pity their hungry children. But his promises were like the others—no more than the shimmering mirage lakes on the summer horizon.

For most of the twenty years since that first flight north, the Cheyennes had tried to keep peaceful, but repeatedly starvation drove them out to the shrinking buffalo herds, up north to the roving Sioux, in the south to the Kiowas and the Comanches. Everywhere their strong warriors were welcomed. Yet when the Army was sent to punish Indians for making trouble, there seemed always a camp of peaceful Cheyennes near, where some agent had told them was a safe place to go. So Chivington had found them at Sand Creek in 1864, Custer on the Washita in 1868, and who could say how many times more?

By 1876, Little Wolf, long a peace man, and Dull Knife, who had worked for peace half his life, were starved off the hungry Sioux agency of Red Cloud once more. They slipped away north for their treaty-given summer hunt. Most of them were too late for the Custer battle but not for the soldiers who came chasing the Crazy Horse Sioux afterward, driving the Indians indiscriminately over their snow-covered treaty grounds with cavalry and cannon. In one of the fights Dull Knife lost three warriors from his family and Little Wolf got six wounds. Constantly fleeing, they could not hunt the few buffaloes left, and so to save their people, they surrendered while some of the strong young men still lived, and the fine young women like the daughters of Dull Knife and the Pretty Walker of Little Wolf. They came in on the good promise of friendship and peace, of plenty of food, warm clothing, and a reservation in their own country, with wagons and plows, and the cattle they had wanted so long. But instead they were dismounted and disarmed, except for a few guns they managed to hide, and now, with blankets drawn in sorrow to the eyes, they had to start far south, the 980 Indians going quietly, morosely, mostly afoot. Seventy days later 937 arrived at the Cheyenne and Arapahoe * Agency in the Territory, and no one mentioned the missing who had slipped back northward along the road, some perhaps left dead by the pursuing soldiers.

There had been a little trouble on the way. It was after they saw that the buffalo trails through their old hunting grounds were edged with sun-flowers. Bleaching bones lay all around, the ribs standing naked as the wagon bows of the settlers who drove their shining plows where the great dark herds had grazed even two years ago. Then one day a leader among the women was found hanging from a cottonwood, a noose made of her long braids.

Lieutenant Lawton came to see about the women keening as for a warrior dead. "Our sister had three husbands, all famous chiefs," the wife of Little Wolf told him. "One after the other was lost to the soldiers, the last in the Custer fighting. Now the same bluecoats are riding around us here, and just ahead is the place where many of her relatives died from their guns."

When the long string of Indians reached the Sappa Creek where the Cheyennes were killed under a white flag of surrender two years ago, the warriors stopped, their faces covered with the blankets of sorrow and anger. Men who were crippled here or compelled to leave their dead harangued for a fight, and when the lieutenant galloped back to see, he was surrounded by stripped and painted warriors, singing, ready to die empty-handed. They jerked away his pistol and were knocking him off his horse when the angry Little Wolf charged in, striking to both sides with his fork-tailed pony whip.

"Will you have all the helpless people here killed?" he roared out. "Your hearts are as empty as your hands. This is not the time!"

The warriors broke before the chief's fury, the officer escaped, and the

* *Arapahoe* preferred spelling at the time.

ringleaders were put into irons and thrown on the supply wagons. But their followers slipped away in the night.

On the North Fork of the Canadian the chiefs were led to the wide agency bottoms, the earth already worn bare by too many Indians. The soldiers set up their tents close by to watch. That night the Southern Cheyennes made the customary feast for the newcomers, with a small circle for the headmen, and for others farther out—such a thin feast as Little Wolf had never seen before. Plainly the people here were very poor with no horses or guns allowed them.

"Ahh-h, game is very scarce for the bow," the agency chief Little Robe said meaningfully. "But hungry men have good eyes and the fast moccasin, is it not true, my friends?"

Dull Knife and Little Wolf and the rest looked down into the water soup of their bowls, as their warrior sons and wives did in other circles. It was an embarrassment to eat from the kettles of the hungry, and hard to pretend the great appetite that was good manners. But the northerners would not stay to divide the little of this poor country. They would go back immediately, where there was game, good water, tolerable heat, and clean air. They said this over their moving eagle-wing fans, sitting in grass smoke that burned the eyes but kept some of the swarming mosquitoes away.

Later Little Robe carried these words to the agency, and a light bloomed in a window there until morning. Then Standing Elk was sent for, the Elk who had said *"Hou!"* to coming south. As Little Wolf watched him go, he pressed his arm against the sacred bundle of chieftainship under his shirt, the bundle that made him keeper of the people. Trouble had already begun, and so with Dull Knife he went to tell the agent that they did not like anything here and were starting home right away, before the snows fell on the Yellowstone.

But the Quaker agent said they could not go. He was a man of peace, but if the Indians left, the soldiers would whip them back.

Soon a cold wind blew up between the younger Indians too. The newcomers were full of stories of the fighting up north only a few moons ago, some from the killing of Custer, the man who had left the southern chiefs dead down here on the Washita in 1868. They showed a few Custer trophies, even a carbine that had been hidden under a woman's skirts all the way through the disarming and the road here.

The southern chiefs moved their turkey-wing fans. Killing the Long Hair Custer was a strong thing, they said, even though he was a relative to some here, the man who took their Monahsetah as wife and became the father of her son, the Yellow Swallow.

Many listening ones drew in their breath and wished to ask more about this Custer son, but the southern faces seemed turned away, and soon the tauntings against them as agency sitters came out bold as spring snakes when the rocks grow warm. So Little Wolf and the others tried to talk of the old-time victories against Pawnee and Kiowa and Comanche, where no southerner need look bad-faced. But his younger men talked of the soldier victories over these tame southern relatives, victories which ended with the survivors always running north for refuge. Finally an agency sitter matched their rudeness. Was it not, he asked, the wise and wily old Dull Knife himself who let his village be destroyed last winter?

"Ahh-h, yes, but the soldiers were led by Cheyenne scouts, our own relatives," one of the northern warriors defended.

"Relatives of the Sioux led soldiers against them the same way, but Crazy Horse was never caught!"

So it went, Dull Knife sitting, a silent gray rock in his blanket, the angry words washing over him as he remembered all those left with their faces turned up to the cold winter light that morning on the fork of the Powder.* It was Old Bear and the blunt, outspoken Hog who finally answered the southerners. Everybody knew soldiers were close that time. The horses were saddled for flight, the lodges coming down fast under the direction of Little Wolf's Elks. But some Fox soldiers brought in two Crow scalps and demanded that a dance be made. Last Bull, their warrior society little chief, had the cinches of the saddles cut, the goods scattered—a small, stubborn man feeling big that he could do this because none must shed Cheyenne blood, even to stop him. So Last Bull held the people for a late dancing, and at dawn the soldiers struck. That could not have happened when the Cheyennes were a larger people. "But now we must make the war leader too big a man, bigger than our oath-bound Old Man Chiefs or our wise and holy men. And still they have not saved us. Today we are only a

* Mackenzie attack on Dull Knife village, November 25, 1876.

crumbling sand bar in the spring Platte, with the flood waters rising all around. . . ."

In two months the newcomers were even fewer. Seventy had died of the measles and of the starvation that was everywhere except in the lodges of the agency yes-sayers like Standing Elk, whose women walked proud and plump in their new dresses. General Pope wrote to Washington, asking that the Cheyenne issues be increased to cover the new people from the north. It was important, "both in view of the safety of this new frontier and in the interest of humanity and fair dealing that all these Indians be far better fed than they are now or have been."

Nothing was done except that the agent complained against rising beef prices, cuts in appropriations, and grafting contractors. The winter was the worst Little Wolf had ever seen, with the coughing sickness in the hungry lodges and nothing for the idle hands. So the Cheyennes took on the white man's quarreling ways. Some even whipped their women and children, a shocking, paleface thing to do. Families were broken, men threw away the mothers of their children, wives slipped out the side of the lodge at night, daughters hung up their chastity ropes and became the pay women of the soldiers, a thing never seen before among these people, whose women General Crook called the most chaste he had known. And always the soldier guns were there, long shadows across the moccasin toe. Yet many young southerners were drawn to the camp of the visitors.

Then Little Wolf heard that Crazy Horse was killed up at Fort Robinson. He carried the news like gall in the mouth to Dull Knife's lodge. Their friend had led the roaming Sioux of the Powder and Yellowstone country since Red Cloud moved to the agency eight years ago. A fiercely brave man with the simple ways of his fathers, who were holy men, many Cheyennes had gladly fought beside him. Later some joined him against the whites too, the time Fetterman was destroyed, in 1866, and when he whipped General Crook on the Rosebud and the next week cut off the retreat of Custer on the Little Big Horn. But with the buffalo going he came to the agency under the same promise given the Cheyennes: food, safety, and an agency for his people. Now he was dead, killed by a soldier in an attempt to take him away to a Florida prison because some agency Indians were jealous and lied about him.

Dull Knife sat bleak-faced. Here, too, the agency chief was jealous because his young warriors strayed, and men like Standing Elk were hot to be Old

Man Chiefs. But for that Little Wolf and the Knife would have to be sent away or, like Crazy Horse, die.

So the chiefs went to the agent. "You are a good man," the Wolf said. "You can see that in this small hungry place we must stand on the moccasins of our brothers. Let us go before something bad happens."

First the agent tried to content the Wolf with a pretty southern girl for his bed. The chief refused, but the girl was sent anyway, and turned out to be his fifteen-year-old granddaughter through the wife of his youth who had died of cholera. Next the agent tried making policemen of some Southern Cheyennes just back from prison for causing trouble in 1874. Fifteen of them were given soldier coats and guns and set to walk the angry village. But no Cheyenne could take the life of a fellow tribesman, even in self-defense, so the agent gave the jobs to the Arapahos, old-time allies of the Cheyennes, who, like the whites, could kill anybody.

Summer brought Indian trouble all through the West. The Northern Cheyennes were shaking with malaria, and there was none of the bitter white powder the agent had promised. There was dysentery too, and very little food, but they were not allowed to go on their authorized summer hunt. They must remain quiet, foment no trouble, husband the issues carefully, and till the earth, the Quaker man told them.

"Make the issues last, when there was too little even before we were brought here? Till the earth with plows that never come—make no trouble, while our people die?" Dull Knife demanded, with the warriors so noisy and threatening against the whites that Little Wolf had to rise in his shaking chill to roar out his anger against them. It was too late for anything now, the Wolf said. The people were too sick, with someone carried to the burial rocks every day. They longed for their mountain and pine country, where there was no sickness and few died. If the agent would not let them go, he could telegraph the Great Father or let a few see him again.

Now the agent roared too. He wanted the young men who had already started north. Little Wolf said he knew of no one gone except to hunt stolen horses or try to get a deer or some rabbits for the sick. But still the agent demanded ten young men as hostages until everybody was back.

Hostages—for prison, for the irons on hands and feet—this was something the chiefs could not decide. They must go ask the people.

Anger broke out that night against Standing Elk, riding in with a fine new blanket and another new horse. Yes, he had talked for coming down here and was now talking strong for staying. Otherwise they would all be killed. Any man who advocated leaving now should be broken, even if it was the bundle-bearing chief, Little Wolf. For his bad counsel the Wolf should be thrown from his high place.

Ahh-h, now it was out—Standing Elk wanting to be head chief! There was a roaring as of battle, red shots cut through the air, and the women ran toward the dark hills with the children. But the peace pipe was hurried in and before it the silence came back. Then Standing Elk folded his new blanket and moved from the camp, his followers along, never to return.

Afterward Little Wolf went across the night to the north ridge, to sit alone as in other times of hard decision. As the chief began to sing his old-time medicine song, there were moccasin steps in the dry darkness. He did not stop the song or move, for if his place was to be emptied by death, that too he must accept by his oath.

It was the Keeper of the Sacred Buffalo Hat, old, and sick too. Little Wolf must not think of giving himself up as hostage for the young men. Several chiefs had done that here and had been killed. "You cannot let yourself be turned from what seems right, not by gun or knife or the wounded pride and weakness of doubt. We made you the bearer of our Medicine Bundle, our leader."

"But if I have lost the vision of the good way?"

"No Cheyenne can be compelled to do anything, nobody except our Selected Man. You must lead even if not one man follows, not even a village dog—if any had escaped the hungry pot," the Keeper added ruefully.

Afterward they went back down to the camp, silent, with no drumming, no singing from the young people. The hot, still air was thick with mosquitoes and the stink of a village too long unmoved, one full of the running sickness. And now there was the stench of dissension too.

In the morning they went a day's pony drag up the river for wood and grass and air. The agent called for soldiers. Two companies of cavalry with a howitzer took up the trail, and troops were readied northward to the Yellowstone, the telegraph wires humming with the demand for extermination. Then the Indians were discovered just above the fort inside a little horseshoe of reservation hills, the men trying to snare rabbits and gophers, the women digging roots. Still the howitzer was set to look down into the camp, and the red-faced captain galloped into the lodge circle, his double line of troopers close behind, their guns shining. The women and children fled but were ordered back, to hear the officer announce that, until they all returned to the agency and sent the children to school, there would be no rations—not just a little as before, but nothing, not even the moldy flour.

The women trembled in their rags as they shielded the sick and the young, remembering the guns that had killed so many helpless ones before. The soldiers stayed and the howitzer too. Finally, on the eighth of September the agency doctor came. With the chiefs silent beside him he walked among the lodges, past all the sick ones, the women turning the kettles upside down in the symbol of emptiness as he came, or holding out bowls of roots and grass for his eyes.

"This is a pest camp, a graveyard!" the doctor exclaimed.

But he had no medicine, no food, and besides, everything was already settled. The chiefs had gone to the last conference at the agency with their few guns hidden on their warrior guard, for surely now the protesting ones would be killed. It was a tumultuous meeting, and one of the young warriors forgot himself enough to speak out in the council. "We are sickly and dying men," the slender young Finger Nail told the agent there in his soft Cheyenne. "If we die here and go to the burial rocks, no one will speak our names. So now we go north, and if we die in battle on the way, our names will be remembered by all the people. They will tell the story and say, 'This is the place.' "

There had been a roaring of *"Hous!"* from many of the young southerners too, and to the agent's angry order to draw the troops closer Dull Knife rose with a hand lifted for silence. He spoke of the many Indian complaints: peaceful people shot by soldiers, the buffalo destroyed, the lands taken, with too little of the pay promised in the white papers, and now nothing at all. No food, no houses, no cattle or wagons or plows. So they were going back north while some were still alive.

This too brought a roaring of approval from many of Little Robe's warriors. The agency chief had once been dragged back wounded from a Pawnee war charge by Dull Knife, but that was long ago, and now he rose and knocked the old chief into the dust with the butt of his leaded saddle whip.

In that moment every warrior was up, scarred breast against breast,

knives and pistols against panting bellies, the white men pale as old paper
in the silence that waited for the one thrust, the one shot to start the massacre, the soldier guns up, ready.

But almost at once Dull Knife was on his feet and the warriors were
ordered back, all going except one who gashed himself and held up his
bloody knife, shouting, "Kill! Kill the white-man lovers!" As Little Wolf
had him dragged away, Dull Knife shook the dust from his blanket and,
with it folded about himself, looked down at the agent, his lips curling
proud.

"My friend," he said, "I am going."

Slowly, majestically, the man feared by Crow and Shoshoni and Pawnee
for forty years walked from the council, his warrior son and his band chiefs
around him. Afterward Little Wolf talked very earnestly for peace, for
permission to go home in peace as they had been promised. He could not
give the young men as hostages never to be returned, and if the agent loved
their food too much to give them any, he must keep it all. "I have long been
a friend of the whites. The Great Father told us that he wished no more
blood spilled, that we ought to be friends and fight no more. So I do not
want any of the ground of the agency made bloody. Only soldiers do that.
If you are going to send them after me, I wish you would first let me get
a little distance away. Then if you want to fight, I will fight you and we can
make the ground bloody on that far place."

1   Sixty Lodges Standing

NOW IT WAS THE NIGHT, BUT THERE WERE NO FRIENDLY clouds to run before the face of the climbing moon. Little Wolf sat alone at the deserted council fire, the big silver peace medal given him by the President in Washington shining softly on his breast. But under his shirt hung the Cheyenne Chief's Bundle and across his knee was his rifle, ready.

With his finger on the trigger the Wolf listened, looking out beyond the spread of smoky, cone-shaped lodges that stood about him, so quiet and remote in the moonlight. Here and there the diffused glow of a little fire showed through the old skins, or a few coals lay red inside a lifted lodge flap—fires that had been kept alive all through the hot summer against the chills of the shaking sickness and starvation.

Somewhere a ground owl hooted, and Little Wolf wondered how it had escaped the empty soup kettle so long, here where hunger sharpened the oldest teeth. But the owl called only once. Otherwise everything seemed to sleep except Young Eagle, blowing his love flute up on a hillside, softly, mournfully. Once more his people needed every warrior, no matter how old or how young. So he must go with them, leaving his beloved one here in the south, go even if his blood was to be spilled in a red blanket on the ground somewhere between the Fork of the Canadian, flowing so quietly back below him, and that other river, the Yellowstone, that cut its valley deep along their home country.

The Cheyenne village lay in a small pocket surrounded on all but the south by the sandy hills rising in a wall against the moon-paled sky. The new cavalry encampment was vague whitish rows of tents out of sight beyond the ridge from the Indians, but soldiers were posted along the crest of the encircling ridges, the guns ready, the cannon waiting to boom out, to burst its shells down among the smoky lodges.

No matter what happened now, this was the last night of the Cheyennes here, Little Wolf knew. All the delaying that the Indians could make was done, and tomorrow the soldiers would attack if the camp was not moving early, to be settled back at the agency. It was hard to understand these things, for the earth here was the same as that under the black coattails of the soft-speaking agent, all the same reservation set aside for their southern relatives by the treaties to which the white man had also touched the pen. Everybody except the Northern Cheyennes, who never agreed to live anywhere here at all.

A dog barked several times in a distant Indian village, where such friendly, noisy animals could still be tolerated because there was no secret movement to betray. Up along the hillside the flute still rose and fell like a sad-winged bird, but it no longer spoke of rejected love. Now it signaled to Little Wolf that the strong men selected to watch the soldier sentinels were finally all in place, ready with war ax and knife, and with arrow poised for the silent song of death if any departure was detected. They were young men but strong-hearted enough to stay their weapons if nothing was seen by the watching soldiers, no alarm given, and then to slip away behind their fleeing people, leaving the sentinels to watch the husks of the village, the sixty empty lodges standing.

For this, too, the Cheyennes must have good luck, and Little Wolf looked out to the moonlit knoll where Bridge, the medicine man, had lain for three days fasting, although he was already thin as a shin bone from all the hungry time. Bridge worked hard with his cloud ceremony, but surely the Great Powers had turned their ears from the Cheyennes, for this night laid naked every living thing. Yet the people must go, and as the flute lifted its thin cry, one figure after another crept from the quiet lodge fires, Dull Knife and the way finders going first, then Little Wolf's wife, Feather on Head, and the women after her, moving like smoke from shadow to shadow toward the little pass in the hills. They moved carefully, keeping from the moon's rounding face so no white-man eyes could see the going, nor the Indian policemen the agent had made.

Humped as buffaloes with their burdens, the Cheyennes passed, the men with their poor arms—bows or perhaps a rifle or a pistol—and the regalia that they could carry, the warbonnets, the shields, and a few other medicine things. All who had saddles or saddle pads of antelope hair took them along. The women were bent too, with the weight of the babies on their backs and with the few goods they managed to gather for the long road north. With a hand out to keep the older children close, they tried to hurry, some stumbling a little in weakness or from the contagion of anxiety.

Behind these women came the young Singing Cloud helping her father who had lifted himself from his bed of dying so his daughter need not remain behind. In her lay the last seed of a great warrior family. If this was to be lost, it must not be to ignominious hunger and shaking in a cannon-darkened lodge of a prisoner people but in a fight for life. Somewhere on the long run northward the old man would slip down and return to the grass. Then, in his vanishing the daughter would be free, free to go to the bold young Dog soldier Little Finger Nail, the sweet singer of the Cheyennes, the one who drew the finest pictures of the feats of his people.

Ahead of the Cheyennes and all along the chosen path through the watching soldiers was a thin scattering of warriors, men who would fight to the end, if they must, as so many of their brothers had died in other places from other soldiers while protecting the women and children. Leading this departure was old Dull Knife, carrying the pipe, with three good men close in the old Cheyenne way. He was sick with malaria and dysentery too, his warrior days as a leading Dog soldier only heroic tales around the evening fires now, but on his breast was the beaded lizard of his medicine dreaming that he wore whenever the people had to be saved. Not the grasping hawk or even fire can kill the big-eyed lizard so long as it is watchful. Nothing except the call of the years can bring its bones to molder in the earth. So, with this protection and because the frightened women and children would surely follow him, Dull Knife went ahead, although there would be soldiers coming from that direction too, as from behind and the sides. If not in this loud throb of the drumming heart or the next, then certainly when the sun bared the lodges standing empty.

Far back, to see that the families all got away, Little Wolf watched; then he began to move too, slipping from one shadowed spot to another up along the edge of the hills, looking down—the Wolf, the one the Cheyennes called their Brave Man. Soft-spoken and gentle, he could whip any unruly Elk warrior to his duty and still, at fifty-seven, lead him in any battle. The Wolf had fought so hard when the soldiers struck the Cheyennes up on the Powder Fork two years ago that it stopped the heart. He had been like a great wounded bear in his fury and fearlessness that time, even the soldiers said, and when it was over, he lived to carry away all the lead the whites and their Indian scouts could send into his flesh, as he carried the pockmarks of the stinking, alien disease on his face. Perhaps this was because under his arm he bore the bundle brought to the Cheyennes by Sweet Medicine very long ago, and so was selected as the dedicated one of all the tribe, the man who must always forget himself, as their culture hero had done, and remember only the people.

Behind Little Wolf came Tangle Hair with some of his older Dog soldiers, the warrior society whose duty it was never to start until all the village was moving—a perpetual Cheyenne rear guard but greatly diminished in their stands against the army attacks on the villages during the last fourteen years. Now once more this was not just a war party going out, where the warriors needed only to whip the enemy or, if whipped themselves, to run and plan revenge another day. Now all the people here and all those to be born so long as the sky stood over the earth were given into the palms of their warrior hands, to be saved or to lie scattered and lost forever on the wind.

The two leading chiefs had good warrior sons along to help them, two each. Dull Knife's older one, Bull Hump, was hidden behind the troopers watching the cannon that pointed into the camp. His knife was naked, ready to check the first cry in the throat or the finger tightening on the signal trigger. Little Wolf's son Woodenthigh was out there too, and the Wolf's favorite nephew who had been given his own name.

The chiefs had two wives each, the smallest number required by the lodges of such men, with no Cheyenne ever to be hired as his brother's pay help. There were many guests to visit a chief's lodge, guests from the village, from other bands and far tribes. They must be feasted and given lodge guest presents of moccasins and robes, as well as good young stock from the pony herds. With Dull Knife was Pawnee Woman, the one he captured as a pretty girl from a Pawnee camp and took to his lodge many years ago. It had grieved his first wife so she hanged herself, and for a short time brought a silent looking down from the women of the village as he passed. But soon he took another wife, a young woman of strong heart, short and sturdy, with soft, smiling eyes. Gradually she brought smoothness to the life of the lodge and to the village about her with the good deed, the gentle word, and the firm hand even with her man when it was a matter of the family, for this was always the first duty of a Cheyenne woman within her lodge. Tonight, while the old chief went ahead of the people, this Short One made a little song as she hurried with Pawnee Woman from shadow to shadow:

> Proudly we follow the path of Morning Star,
> The one they call Dull Knife.
> Many, many snows he has spoken for peace,
> Carrying the pipe of it in his hand
> Like others carry the bow and the shooting gun.
> Ei-e-ya!

She sang softly, so no listening soldier might hear as she passed with the chief's warbonnet and sh d and sacred lance head on her back.

So the Indians vanished from the lodges under the veiling moon, going like the fox sneaking up a gully, not like the Cheyennes of the old days, bold as the gray wolf who stalks the ridges with his tail straight up in the air. The Cheyennes were not strong in warriors now. A year ago they brought two hundred fighting men along. But now barely a hundred remained, counting all over twelve, the age not for war but to take up weapons for defense. All the others were lost—many sick and dead from the hunger and fevers and the old, old disease of homesickness that no doctor, not even Bridge the medicine healer, had the power to cure. Besides some had deserted, and that too had to be endured.

With the warriors went the people, the weak and old and infirm too, and a few lone ones, like the woman whose husband threw her away down here in the south country. It seemed better to follow those who lived in the old Indian way, where everyone would have meat for the coals if anyone did. She felt she belonged here with the strong ones, even the women here strong enough to bring courage, and envy, to any camp—those like young Buffalo Calf Road, the warrior woman who had killed in battle and had ridden against the soldiers of both Generals Crook and Custer. In this fleeing night it was good to think of this and remember that once, long ago, another warrior woman saved all the tribe when the enemy seemed hopelessly many.

But there were other courageous young women along. The Leaf, the wife of Bull Hump, was well fitted to the Beautiful People, as the Dull Knife family was called by the whites. The chief's older daughters had both dared say no to the covetous officers, even after their cannon stood on the hill looking down upon the lodges, the Sorrowing One's hair still cut short to her shoulder in the sign of mourning for her young warrior husband killed by the troops on the Powder. Then there was Wild Hog's pretty daughter, who, with her friend Singing Cloud, had saved three small children when the cannon balls were bursting right among them.

Pretty Walker, too, had saved a life in a fight, but it was never recounted at the evening fires for the man she saved was a soldier. She had dragged him away from the bullets because, in the thickest fighting, he had given his horse to an old woman who could not run. The daughter of Little Wolf was an independent, tall-walking girl, as was proper in that family of good leggers, the father still a foot racer, her brother called Woodenthigh because he never wore out. The girl had been called Pretty Walker so long that her real name seemed forgotten, but none forgot that she could go as calmly into the path of bullets as her father, the dedicated man.

The young women were going north to escape this country before the sickness shook away the roundness of their flesh. And following them were the hopeful young warriors, some from the southern people too, and some older men like Thin Elk, who had come slipping down from the Yellowstone country scarcely a moon ago—to visit his brother Bald Eagle, he announced when he came. Yet it was to Little Wolf's lodge he walked most often, and this time he could not be driven away as he was twenty years ago, when the Wolf was still only a war leader. An Old Man Chief could not warn anyone away from his wife. "Only danger that threatens the people can anger me now," Little Wolf had sworn in the tribal chief's oath. "If a dog lifts his leg to my lodge, I will not see it."

But tonight as the Wolf watched Thin Elk pass, helping the women in their flight, he thought of something else: the old Cheyenne saying that a coal once kindled is easiest set to glowing. The chief did not know that, while he walked his preoccupied way these later days, some of the women had begun to whisper behind the hand. Perhaps it was not toward one of the wives of Little Wolf that the Elk was turning his eyes in the card games and along the village path. Perhaps it was the daughter, the Pretty Walker, that he was watching.

But Thin Elk had brought important news of their relatives who surrendered to the fort on the Yellowstone last year. They were healthy, well-

treated, well-fed. The council circle made their *"Hous!"* of approval; that
was the way things were done in the north country.

Ahh-h, but all those people would be brought south too. A band of nearly
three hundred were already on the way. When Bear Rope, the violent man
among them, protested this angrily, his eyes red as the eagle's in the firelight,
Thin Elk replied that those Cheyennes could not help themselves either.
The soldiers held them in the palm, riding ahead and behind them as
Little Wolf himself had been driven south. All the Cheyennes were to live
in the south forever.

"It said forever too in the treaty that protected our north country—so
long as grass shall grow and water flow," the Wolf recalled quietly.

As he had hoped, the bad news Thin Elk brought turned no one from
the northern trail of tonight, not even after the Keeper of the Sacred Buffalo
Hat became very cautious and uncertain, perhaps because he foresaw
fighting, bad fighting with the soldiers. Yet the sacred tribal objects, the
Hat and the Medicine Arrows, had not always brought the people luck.
They were both carried along last summer, and still not a lodge was spared
the sickness and the death keening, although the Keeper and his wife had
performed a good curing ceremony with the Hat that was made of the
head skin of a mothering buffalo cow. Even strong ones died, or turned
strange, like Bear Rope, who walked so dangerously among the fleeing ones
this night of silence. He had been a good man to follow in war and in the
council. Now he might break into fighting at the flutter of a wind, striking
out at anyone with his war ax and not even the long pipe of mediation and
peace brought the light of seeing into his eyes. Afterward he would sit
shaking, so cold his wives must pile the fire high all night.

But now there must be no sound, and the Rope's son-in-law moved close
beside the sick man, sorrowful, yet with his strong fingers ready to stop
the first sound in the bony throat. There was still death among them too
this night. Just as the people started, a small girl, warm as alive, had to be
left alone in one of the dark lodges, with the buckskin fringes of childhood
on her dress, the first moccasins she was beading, and the doeskin doll with
the braids of her dead mother's hair held in her arms. Not even her grandmother dared make a sound of sorrow now, with the soldiers all around,
and the wagon gun that threw balls great as the sun, to burst with the sun's
fire among the people.

So they went, their faces turned northward under the luck of a falling star, but their hearts looking back to all those who must be left behind. Silent as field mice, the moccasins ran over the bare, horse-cropped earth, keeping to the uneven ground and hollows.

Hidden, but felt by them, Little Wolf recognized each darkening of the shadows below him, knowing each one as intimately as though of his own lodge. Without questioning or hesitation the helpless ones were following Dull Knife into the pass with the soldier guns very close on each side, for his wisdom was of the old days—of the wool-blinded buffalo feeding with his nose always into the wind, snuffling out danger, of the young grass waiting under the winter snow, and the Powers of the earth and sky and the four great directions—the old wisdom of the time when a man spoke what he believed and his word was his life. But long ago something new had come into this, the *veho,* the white man, and to Little Wolf it seemed that the whites had to be met on their own terms, for now the power of numbers and of guns and the twisted tongue was with them. Now, as for over twenty years past, it seemed that the only Indian surely never killed was the Indian never caught.

As the chief counted the passing ones, their going less than the sound of a breath, he pressed his arm against the sacred bundle, but his hand gripped the Winchester. Back behind him young men rode into the deserted camp as though returning from a hunt or a visit, shouting among the empty lodges, doing it open and natural, as on any night, for the listening soldiers to hear. They threw wet grass upon the low coals, making smudges against the mosquitoes and to send the smell of smoke over the ridge to the camp of the red-faced soldier chief, Captain Rendlebrock, who carried a smell of his own, the whisky that made men crazy. On the hillside the love flute still cried, the young man yearning for the delicate-boned Blue Fringe who must be left behind. He had asked her to come, and her relations too, for it was only right that a young man join the woman's people, as in the old, old way.

But Blue Fringe had laughed, making a little song:

> My friend, if I go north,
> I may not be able to swim across a river,
> I mean the big Platte river.

She sang it as to a small boy. It was done at a dancing, the Fringe repeating it to all the others who knew that the Platte was often sand bars in late summer, where the buffalo herds once milled around a long time before water welled up under their hoofs.

Even though the girl made small of Young Eagle, he still grieved that she would stay here among the Southern Cheyennes—the laughing, taunting girl who had stood within the folds of his blanket for a few words now and then. Perhaps he might have stayed behind, but when the agency chief struck old Dull Knife down with his quirt in the council a little while ago, it was settled. So the young man blew his plaintive eagle-wing flute, while on both sides of him lay the dark rifle pits that the warriors had dug to meet any soldier attack with down-hill cross fire. It was known that the whites could destroy the village with their cannon and ride over it in one cavalry charge, but many soldiers would be killed from the pits so long as the ammunition lasted, and perhaps some of the Indians might escape to the horses hidden in a steep canyon where even stripling boys could hold them against stampede.

And there were stripling boys, lone ones, along, some orphaned here to be taken back to their relatives, and then that other one—the light-haired Custer son born to Monahsetah. Her father was one of the southern chiefs killed in the Washita fight ten years ago, and Monahsetah had been taken with the long string of captive women and children led in triumph over a hundred miles of snow to Camp Supply. When the young girls were selected for the officer tents on that cold march, she was sent to Custer.

Later Monahsetah went along on his winter expedition that pursued her fleeing people deep into Texas. When Custer's wife was coming to him, the Cheyenne girl was sent back to the Indians, where this son was born toward the autumn moon. Years afterward the traders told her that he wrote about her in a book, praising her charm, her beauty and grace.[1] Not until she knew that Long Hair, General Custer, was dead did she take another man.

Now this Yellow Swallow was nine years old, but spindly, thin as a winter weed stalk although he was fed well by the whites. Here he was a constant reminder to the southerners of their relatives killed on the Washita, where General Hazen, the military agent, had told them was a good peaceful place to camp, not knowing that Custer could strike them at dawn. The boy had an aunt with the fleeing ones tonight, and another up near where Custer died. In that good country the sickly Swallow might live, become strong and brave as a young Cheyenne should be, as the son of Long Hair should be.

Now there were only the last soldier guns, those watching the pass, against the escape of the Cheyennes from the cannon. Then Little Wolf's people would be out on the open prairie where they could scatter for a few hours as though only walking out alone if seen. But first they had to slip by the sentinels very close together here, on both slopes, with no shadows on the narrow pass between, the ground worn smooth and bare, and the sharp eyes of Arapaho policemen looking. The people were strung far out now, each lost to those ahead and behind in the hazing moonlight as they crept along, barely seeming to move to the watching Little Wolf, his eyes straining so it seemed they were afire.

Then suddenly the haze and even the far shadows were gone in a great white light that fell over everything. It stopped the feet, the heart, but not a sound came, no earth-shaking roar of bursting cannon ball. Instead, a summer star broken loose from the sky was falling slowly, its light raining down over the people flattened to the earth—the men with their saddles for the horses, the women with the children and goods on their backs, all small unshadowed hummocks on the floor of a great hole of light.

But no shout disturbed the silence, no signal shot, and as the meteor slowly faded from the eyes, the moccasins began to move again, hurrying even more now to reach the scattering prairie because the light reminded them of other cannons whose bursting fire sought out their camps. Even the heavy-moving woman who had to drop back into a gully for her time remembered and whispered to the one who wished to wait behind with her.

"No, no!"

"You are weak, my sister. . . ."

"No—run! Let there be no more than myself and the child for the soldiers to ride down."

When the newborn son stretched for a cry, the mother grasped the wet little nose between her thumb and forefinger, the palm over the mouth, shutting off the breath until the child seemed to strangle in the darkness. Then she loosened her fingers for a little until there would be another crying, and tightened her hold again. So the small one was taught the first lesson of Cheyenne life: no child's cry must betray the people to an enemy.

Then, with the baby that was no bigger than two good fists against her starved, empty breasts, the Cheyenne woman started again, stumbling, weak, but moving faster as her strength returned, striking straight for the trail they would take up farther out, hoping to reach there before all had passed. She stopped only to pull the bull-tongue cactus from her moccasins now and then, and once when a rider came galloping through the fading light—a white man by the sound of the saddle leather but not a soldier, for the hoofs were naked on the hard, dry ground. Still he might be a scout or a messenger with word of the fleeing Cheyennes seen somewhere. He passed almost within finger reach of the woman, but he passed. When he was gone down toward the soldier camp, she ran, her skirts slapping against her hurrying legs.

Far from the hungry lodges and the soldiers, the people were met by small herds of horses. As many as possible of the women with their children and bundles were put upon them. Just a few pony drags had been made, only for the very old and the very sick. But first, as always, came the needs of the young men. They must get enough more horses for the rest if they were to outrun the soldiers. They would get these without trouble if possible, but horses they must take, any way they could—the way the white thieves had taken theirs. Then too, the young men must remain well mounted and ready to charge back to fight off the pursuers.

Finally Little Wolf and his son, the last riders of all, faded into the haze of the flat horizon, cutting across to where the scouts who went out last night should be waiting—if they had escaped capture by the soldiers. If not—ahh-h, it was known that many soldiers would be standing across their path, but they hoped it would not come until the people had been fed a little, with meat and with hope.

Drummed by the moccasin heels, the horses went too fast for those afoot, and for all those who had to stay behind entirely because there was nothing to ride, and the trail to the Yellowstone seemed very long for the worn moccasin and the sickened heart.

But many toiled along afoot, bent under the burdens of their children and their bundles. These were determined to go to their home country even though they must walk over fifteen hundred of the white-man miles. Two women called Brave One and The Enemy, both with babies on their backs, led the larger party, with a few old men and growing boys along. They hurried, but no matter how fast the line of dark figures moved over the dusky prairie, in a little while even the ear to the ground could no longer detect the hoofs of the horses gone ahead.

2 Ahh-h, Buffalo

SO THE CHEYENNES STARTED NORTH, BUT NOT AS MANY of them as they had hoped when their shadows moved from the lodges into the night. American Horse, a good man, had worked steady and hard all summer so none of the people had to be left behind. But now he came to the shadowed gathering place and said he and his eight lodges would move off a ways and let the others pass.

"Pass? You would remain here? You have the most horses, and all those our young men helped you catch!"

The man drew at his pipe, silent, and so his friend Tangle Hair went to argue with him. "My brother, it is like letting one buffalo bull with a little bunch break away from a surround. Would you split the people through the middle again, after the trouble with Standing Elk?—through the heart on this important night? You are not your own man!"

"Already ten of your people are in the red blankets," another added.

But American Horse was not to be changed. Deliberately, slowly, he spoke. "Yes, ten from my lodges are dead and more will die. It is not that I am not sick-hearted to go back to the north country. But there is too much danger, with all the soldiers and the wagon guns ready along the road, and spies surely among us even here, watching, leaving sign. The shooting may begin anywhere, in that gully ahead. . . ."

"Then you will not go?" Little Wolf demanded angrily, with his warrior blood hot as for an enemy.

"No, cousin. I cannot."

So they let him withdraw to one side, for only the whites would hold man or woman against the heart. But they let him keep only horses enough to lift the timid moccasin above the cactus. The rest they killed, all the rest of his small herd. Sorely as horses were needed, they slit the throats, making

[24]

a quiet job of it, the blood hot and sticky and sweetish in the darkness of the canyon, the choke and murmur of the horses like many people dying.

Then they moved on without him, going a little more sadly up the fork of the Canadian, although twice there were suddenly others among them, bringing excitement and a little cheer. The coming ones were mostly young men following the pretty daughters of Dull Knife, Wild Hog, Little Wolf, and the others. But three were older, men who had been prisoners in Florida.

"You cannot make us return!" Hog told them angrily when his scouts brought them in. But they wanted to join the people, to be a help, particularly in spying, for they knew something of the white man and his language. One wanted to protect his nephew, the Yellow Swallow, see him get a new start in a healthy country.

"*Hou!* We will all have a new start in the good country or we will leave our bones to bleach on the grass."

"It is good," Hog said soberly, and sent them out among the rest.

For three hours the Indians made hard travel. Scattered in little parties over the pale, moon-touched prairie, they moved like Little Wolf's name animal, the sly coyote, most of them keeping to the shadowy breaks back from the river and the soldier road, or out on the rougher tableland. Even those afoot along the bottoms sought out the dry grass that holds no tracks of soft moccasins passing. Finally the way finders of each party converged on the headwaters of a little creek where a timbered spring pocket lay in the black shadow of a canyon wall that humped itself against the Western moon.

Dull Knife and Little Wolf sat with half a dozen of their warriors at the hidden fire. Together they watched for the people coming out of the haziness, until all the headmen were past, except Plenty Bears. The Wolf was uneasy about him, now that American Horse had run back. If the Bears' lodges stayed behind too, the Keeper of the Sacred Hat would turn back, and great would be the uneasiness and the sorrow that this gift from Sweet Medicine would not be in its holy place among them, strengthening everything they did, every fight, every council and ceremonial. If they got through to the north without it, it would be that the people had indeed the courage of those Old Ones who crossed the unknown salty waters long before Sweet Medicine came to them.

The passing Indians moved silently, a horse snorting softly at the smell of water, a hoof stirring a rock, perhaps some headmen dropping out to sit beside the chiefs a while. Even Thin Elk had stopped as though he were more than a visitor, and then rode on to overtake the Little Wolf family, to help the women, the chief not daring to look after him.

Yet if they had no luck this night, and something happened so he was lost in the fighting sure to come, the Wolf knew it would be good for the women to have a strong old warrior like Thin Elk to help them get away. The Elk had fought hard beside the Roman Nose killed up at Beecher Island ten years ago, and with the best war leaders here. He was a good man at the dances and the joke making too, and perhaps this added to the heaviness under the wound-scarred ribs of Little Wolf.

There were long silences at the little fire, the men like a hunting party resting for the night, but without meat for their empty stomachs, and listening, always listening. There had been a little trouble when the two chiefs first rode in, Dull Knife with a few followers first and finally Little Wolf. Some of the warriors were gathered at the spring, waiting, impatient; mostly southern Dog soldiers, their hands ready on the guns or their bows.

The Wolf looked at them, but they held back until he settled to his pipe. Then one spoke up, his tong-scarred breast defiantly bare in the red of the coals. "We have decided to travel on the old-time north trail," he said boldly. "There are more horses to catch because there are more whites there, and more guns to take."

"Yes, and more whites with guns to shoot at us! I don't want shooting," the chief replied, and turned to ask about signals of the pursuit begun.

But these Dog warriors interrupted again, pushing in closer, guns across their arms, the barrels still pointing downward into the ground as one motioned their spokesman to begin. So Dull Knife, the old-time Dog chief, looked up from the firelight that glowed on the beaded lizard on his breast. "You know that the way has been long agreed on in council. The scouts and hunters are working up there ahead."

"Yes, and weren't some of you sent to find meat for the children?" the Wolf demanded. "What excuse do you carry in your mouth for your empty hands?"

"I say go the old way too!" Black Coyote called out from among Little Wolf's own headmen, and because this thin, sharp-faced one was of a great warrior family, and a very brave man if arrogant now, other voices shouted their *"Hous!"*—even some who doubted his wisdom. So more

Dog warriors pushed themselves against their honored man, old Dull Knife, and Tangle Hair too, the leading Dog chief of the northerners, but silent now because in the south country the society had been broken by many defeats and humiliations.

But the wrinkled Black Crane did not keep silent. "Nephews, this is not the time to avenge your old woundings down here. Wait!"

"I am of the north and I say go the other way too!" Black Coyote shouted against the old chief.

"You will go the road planned, my nephew," the Crane told him, speaking quietly, but with the power of the man selected by the council to lay out the campings all the way. Yet there were still threatening gestures from the Coyote and from the young warriors. Dull Knife shifted his tired old body. "Perhaps it will have to be as the young men wish," he said to the others around the fire. "There should be no trouble with the whites. We are not going to war, and we have the northern *veho* promise we could return."

Now Tangle Hair moved too, uneasily. "You cannot talk so, my friend— wind blow east, wind blow west. The young men who will go against the council plans will surely bring other troubles. Anyway, the west road is already warmed by the moccasins sent ahead of us."

"*Hou!*" Such plans were not to be unmade in one angry moment, old Black Crane agreed. But there was so much noise that none heard him, and so Dull Knife shook his head in the white-man way. "I am tired of trouble," he said, "and we must have the young men."

"*Piva!* It is well heard! Let us start!" Black Coyote shouted, openly, loudly, for spying ears to hear far, far off.

So Little Wolf had to lay aside his pipe and get up, his blanket carelessly about him, the light from the coals rising toward his pitted, fever-gaunted face. "You heard that our brother the Knife is tired of the trouble some of you are always making, my friends. I am tired too, worn out by your noise. Sometimes we received a little more rations at the agencies by it, but that was long ago. Now we shall live in the good Cheyenne way. We need less thunder in the mouth and more lightning in the hand if we are to escape to the north and save the helpless ones with us."

"It is the old road east of the Dodge fort we are taking . . . ," someone called from the darkness, another taking it up, and another, even a voice sounding like that of Dull Knife's younger son.

So Little Wolf saw that he must indeed work hard if the Cheyennes were not to fall apart now like a sandstone struck by a great hammer. He should not take the time for a harangue now, with the soldiers surely moving, the hungry children whimpering in their pain, but it must be done. He started with his voice low and thick with anger. It was such wild and foolish men as these here who brought the soldiers into the village on the fork of the Powder. "Your own relatives were left on the ground there, your own blood spread in a blanket from the woundings you will always carry. Your own blood, and others. . . ."

Little Wolf paused, letting his blanket fall, and his shirt and leggins too, standing a strong, scarred man in breechclout and bundle string in the light of the coals. "Your blood—" he repeated, "and mine too was left there," touching his side in the dull glow as he spoke, touching where all knew there was a wounded knotting that was like twisted red rawhide. "Here a bullet came through that night, and here and here . . . ," his hand moving swiftly over his torn body, his eyes cold as the blizzard wind on the young men standing around the edge of darkness, searching out their faces until they had to look down, shamed and foolish that their bundle-bearing chief needed to make such a self-humiliating show of his wounds, the northern men remembering how he was that frozen morning, fierce as though the grizzly had entered his heart, fighting the soldiers to make time for those fleeing over the rocks, fighting until the snow all about him was red with his blood.

"The Powers saw me that time," he said, speaking the words into the silence, "but many, many good people were left there because of such arrogant men as you. This time it will not be so. This time you will do your work, carry out the decision of those that the people selected long ago to follow. We need horses but we must have meat—buffalo, right away. For meat, and the hope of fast travel, we go the western road, the Dull Knife trail where few whites live. Many, many soldiers will surely have to be fought off, so there must be no trouble with the settlers too. If anybody dies, it must be a soldier *veho* who starts the killing."

For a moment the chief stopped, the tall breechclouted man growing taller in the dying firelight, the scars of his body deepened by the shadows, his pitted face angered as an animal's, the eyes as blazing as he snarled out the final words:

"We go the western way! This I, Little Wolf, command you!"

As the echo returned in the chilling darkness of the canyon, many there remembered seeing this gentle, soft-spoken man like this before and knew that crossing him then brought such fury that he whipped his warriors with quirt and gun butt, none able to outrun his punishment. So, not because of fear or the un-Cheyenne command, but because of the power they saw still lived in their man for all the sickness and the agency humiliations, a power growing right before their eyes, the wildest of the young warriors bowed their heads, even the southerners, who saw Little Wolf like this for the first time.

Once, after the commanding voice had died from the ear, several men did start up, but an angry snarling from the others brought them back, even Black Coyote. Gradually the young men slipped away up the shadowed gullies to their delayed tasks, or into the passing people, to help their relatives or some family with pretty girls, perhaps Dull Knife's or Hog's or the one where Pretty Walker hurried with an orphan on her back.

But it turned out that some other young men had already started up the old trail before the chiefs came, and so Black Crane sent the Shield soldiers, the society of older, steadier men, after them, the leader with the buffalo bull headdress and all carrying their red shields to show they acted for the council. They had to use up horses for this chase, when so many sick ones went with their moccasins in the cactus. And there was still anger in the faces of Black Coyote and his followers against Crane, the camp selector. "He talks with the noise of the Old Man Chiefs in the mouth," the Coyote said as he rode sullenly out for horses. "When a man takes on such ways something happens."

By this time it was plain to others, too, that Plenty Bears' few lodges were not coming. Then two riders hurried in out of the night, and dropping from their sweaty horses, they approached slowly, standing back from the fire in the shame of bad news. Yes, it was true—Plenty Bears had gone back. It seemed there might be trouble with some of the young men over the trail to take, and perhaps over other things too, and so he went back.

"The man who looks one place and plants the moccasin in another may tread on a rattlesnake," Bridge, the old medicine healer, said.

But he was only covering up the sorrow over this second desertion before there was even one whiff of soldier powder smoke. Little Wolf scraped the ashes from his pipe into his palm, carefully, to be mixed again with red willow bark, for it would be a long, long road to more tobacco. Then the chiefs rose to their horses. Now there were only eighty-seven men, counting the oldest wrinkled one and the boys of thirteen. But these were all good Cheyennes, not one the runaway kind. Eighty-seven men—two hundred and eighty-four people all together, past and coming,[1] all that was left of almost a thousand who made the sorrowful path down this way a year ago.

By now even Old Crow's two lodges and most of the walking people were safely past and into the broken country. Then, in twos and threes, the headmen slipped away into the deepening darkness without a spoken destination, for there was no telling what spies might be around, perhaps even here at the little fire left to die, the warmth of the earth under it a sign to the few still to come how long ago it had burned.

Before the whitening from the east rose over the moving people, Bear Shield, who had been away to the prison three years, too, and understood much *veho* talk, came whipping after them. The Indians stopped for an hour at a small creek, scattered far out for safety, but close enough for the runners to carry the news he brought from the fort—the news that wore out two horses.

"Our going has been discovered . . . ," he said.

Ahh-h, it was good that it had taken this long.

"The sentinels said we could not be gone, for they had been looking all the time. There were the lodges, standing, the dying fire coals still a little red."

"Ahh-h, yes, the lodges . . . ," one of the men said regretfully as he drew at his pipe. The women unsaddling about them were quiet too, thinking of the winter ahead, without meat or shelter except what they could make after they got up north, and the buffalo surely scarce up there also.

"It was American Horse and another who rode to the agency."

So? They could not wait a few hours to let the people get away. Still, one could understand this. They were hungry too, and with their horses killed—"For telling this news they will certainly get coffee and sugar again."

Bridge bent over his pipe. "It is not good that a man must choose between the honorable way and hungry children."

"In my time—" Old Bear started to say and then dropped his head.

Bear Shield told that he left a sharp-eared man who also knew the *veho* words to watch the fort. That was good, and now that the soldiers were surely started it was time to run again.

As the Cheyennes moved up the ladder of dry canyons and creek beds, they looked back from every rise, afraid to hear the far sound of hoofs coming through the lowering moonlight, a hurried column with red shooting from the middle. Many of the older ones found themselves looking another way too, throwing their hearts back over all the long time since the Cheyennes had left their corn patches near the great sweetwater lakes and moved with the sun out across the Missouri and down the ladder of east-flowing streams, each one a rung, a toe hold for a while in their climb southward until the hunting and war parties reached the Washita and the Sweetwater country of Texas. Men like Old Bear and Dull Knife looked westward, where the moon stood on the land, and remembered what had happened on each of these streams they were passing—things that would always be a part of the today here because all things that ever happened in a place were always of the today there in the Cheyenne pattern of time.

Forty years ago off westward on Wolf Creek the Sacred Arrows and the Hat were carried in a formal attack on the Kiowas to avenge the forty Cheyenne warriors wiped out the year before, not one man left to come and stand outside of the village with the shame of bad news upon him. Plainly this had happened because the Arrows had been foolishly offended by the warriors before their leaving. But in the revenge, with the good Arrow ceremony, almost an equal number of Kiowas were killed. Many men were very strong in the fight and the young warrior who now bore the old and honored name of Little Wolf got three of the enemy himself. Afterward peace was made with the Kiowas in an alliance against the whites, a peace spoken under the Sacred Arrows, one that could never be broken.

But now Dull Knife and the rest had to start on this flight north without either the Hat or the Arrows. Soldiers were coming after them and gathering ahead in clouds as thick as fall blackbirds in a strip of corn; the men and horses and guns hauled by the three fire railroads to the crossings of the Arkansas, the Smoky Hill, and the Platte; the talking wires like spider ropes all through the morning grass, to show the path of the Indians very plain. All this had to be escaped without the sacred objects along, and many were very much afraid.

But not the young men. "Let the Hat and the old Arrows stay behind," Little Finger Nail said at the dawn resting. "People have been killed in their shadows for a long time. We need a new medicine now, one to bring us wagonloads of Winchesters heavy with ammunition. We need something besides an old skin hat to grow fat beef herds among the bones of the buffalo, and make coffee with sweet lumps for the empty cups."

There was a murmur of disapproval from among the listening ones, from those who thought it disrespectful to talk so of the sacred gifts, yet everybody around drawing near, even the young Singing Cloud, daring to approach to the Little Finger Nail for this short time.

"What can the new medicine be? Tell us, Old Ones, what can we do?" the Nail demanded, half-tauntingly of Old Bear and of Bridge, the medicine man who knew the holy ways.

But Dull Knife answered the youth. "The old ways are good."

"*Hou!*" many agreed. Surely it was the power of the Arrows and the Hat there on the Little Big Horn that made Custer come charging upon the camp spread out for miles along the river, so plain in the bright sun of day. Perhaps he was made blind and foolish because he broke the promise of peace given to the chiefs in the Sacred Arrow lodge the time Monahsetah found the fleeing Cheyennes for Custer, after he killed her father and the others, the same Monahsetah whose son, young Yellow Swallow, was among them here.

Yes, surely the Long Hair Custer had been blinded to die so.

"A man has to die sometime . . . ," the younger warriors scoffed, particularly those who had been away to the prison and knew about the white man's sacred object, the Cross of Wood—not one, as with the Hat, or the sacred number of four, as the Arrows, but many, little and big, and made of many things. The white man's medicine was surely very strong, for he was the biggest tribe of the whole earth, bigger even than the Sioux. But his cross did not seem to work for all the people as the Arrows and the Hat did. The white women who came to the prison to tell the Indians about the Cross and its peace said that the northern soldiers who burned some of their biggest towns and killed very many of their people carried it but so did the southern ones, the killed and whipped ones.

Dull Knife and the rest nodded, remembering the little branched medicine trees they found on dead soldiers. But they were certain that the power of their Hat was not the same thing.

As the first sun climbed into the sky, it dried up the little clouds that had slept in the west like the quiet swans on that briny lake up along the Big

Horns. The Indians stopped a while to rest, dropping anywhere, like worn-out cattle or buffaloes after a long, long running. There was still no meat, only the wild fruits, plums, drying currants, and chokecherries and a few purpling grapes picked in the hasty passing, with maybe a snake or a sand turtle—so very little when divided that the children still murmured as they slept, and cried very softly in their hunger.

It was during this resting that the mirror signal of Bear Shield's scout came as he rode in from his watching. When the men whipped out of the agency through the night toward Fort Reno, Howling Wolf had slipped up the river, running because the moccasin was a whisper where the hoofs of a horse would have been loud as a war whoop. He followed the dark figures almost to the door of the soldier chief, but the sun stood even with the eyes before the troops started, two companies with trumpets blowing, some Arapahos, Blue Clouds, who had lost horses coming along as guides.

"So!—They are in this too, our old allies! Well, we fought off people from our own families scouting with soldiers."

There were a few Cheyennes riding today too.

"Ahh-h!" Little Wolf murmured, as he pushed away the heavy sleep that came after the shaking chills. "Then it will be better to say little of this before the women and children, and those parties who are still afoot, back there. . . ."

Soon everybody was moving again, slipping along the canyons that were the folds of the sheltering earth, trying to cross no height or tableland that could be touched by a far field glass. Then two of the meat scouts gone ahead made their far signals. It was the elder son of Little Wolf and the Black Horse who was crippled in the troubles of 1875 down here and then fled up this trail. He knew the country and had the buffalo eye, and now the two came with really good news, the best the hungry ones could know.

"Buffalo—on our chosen road," the closemouth Black Horse said.

"It is true there are not many, but with some fat young cows," the son said to Little Wolf and the rest. "They are up near the place called Buffalo Springs. The other men stayed there, watching."

"Buffalo seen!" the Crier called as he ran along the trailing people and signaled to those far out, who needed to know this very much too. "Make ready for a little butchering! Buffalo!"

"Meat!" Bridge cried, the water of his eyes running down the gullied old face as he went to make a little medicine ceremonial of thankfulness for the kill tomorrow. Only those of the later parties who had butchered the two horses that wore out had had meat since the beginning of the moon. Truly the sick and starving people could not have been taken much farther.

3 〰〰〰 Shooting, and Soldiers Going Back

AT FORT RENO COLONEL MIZNER REPORTED GOOD PROG-
ress. Rendlebrock, out 30 miles by late afternoon the
first day, sent a courier to Camp Supply for more cavalry because the Cheyennes were traveling very fast. He had found the trail that gathered plainer
as he followed; the Indians pressed too hard to hide it. Their horses were
tiring; the scouts discovered where a couple had played out, the bones
stripped bare of meat by the Indians to carry along. Off under a little
bank was a place where a woman had given birth and hurried on. There
was something more, something the Indian scouts did not tell Rendlebrock
—the woman's hurrying tracks joined a little party apparently far behind
the rest of the Cheyennes, all small moccasins, the tracks far apart and very
fresh, women and children running fast just ahead of the troops.

Nor did any of the scouts seem to see the little scattering of people huddled in a washed-out gully as the blue column passed. When they could
run no more, the women and children had flattened themselves in the holes
and the sparse gray sage, so afraid of the soldiers close upon them that only
the stern commands of Brave One held them down, kept them from flush-
ing like frightened young quail before the pounding of the iron hoofs. Not
even the sharp eyes of the Blue Clouds seemed to see them as the soldiers
lengthened the string of red dust left behind.

A few days later Mizner reported that the Indians were well mounted.
The best he hoped now was that they could be overhauled at the Arkansas
River, high in flood this wet summer. Although these Cheyennes had complained repeatedly about the meat rations, abandoning their standing lodges
and their few goods showed a greater desperation than he had realized.

From Kansas General Pope wired his plans. Lewis of Fort Dodge would
take command when the southern troops neared there, and the two com-

[35]

panies of infantry from Hays, to be joined by over a hundred civilians, mostly Texas trail drivers, cowmen, and old buffalo hunters gathering at Dodge. A special train would take mounted infantry to west Kansas, while troops from Lyon were to scout the rail line east and west. Washington ordered that, unless the intercepted Indians surrendered at once for dismounting and disarming, they were to be attacked. Four companies of infantry and some cavalry were headed out along the line of the Platte to take the Cheyennes at the probable crossing.

But that was in Nebraska, far, far ahead. Now, still in the Territory, the scouts found the remains of a buffalo hunt on a branch of the Cimarron and a scattered but slowing trail beyond. It seemed the Cheyennes were waiting.

It was true that the Indians were preparing for the soldiers. The day after the hunt, when the sun was over the head and the panting grouse had nothing except her own shadow to stand in, Little Wolf signaled two gun seekers in. They were bringing three, a few cartridges, and a little gunpowder and caps, badly needed but very costly because they were sold to the Indians against the law by a trader hidden in the jack oaks. Little Wolf had hoped for seven, eight guns and some horses for almost all the beadwork saved from the north and what the women could make here. There were two fine quilled otter skins from the old, old grandmothers too, and the medicine headdress of a famous man far back in the corn days of the lake country and coveted by all the old-time traders. The seekers had to give up even the saddle trappings of their wives, and so if there were ever horses again and a peaceful life, they must ride poor as any agency woman in the ceremonials.

But the soldiers were coming hard, and now the people tried to hurry through the low canyons, going like cattle from a runout stampede along this draw and that one, all still headed in the same direction but wearily, the moving a slow desperation. The party of lone women and children was far back, too late for the hunt but fed by meat left for them, and keeping well hidden and close to good fleeing places. Brave One still led them, the woman who got her name because she and her sister ran for an entire winter month from the shooting at Sand Creek. The two women had carried a six-year-old girl in their arms all that time, with only one blanket and a knife for the long flight. But it was said that a wolf took pity on them and led the hungry women to meat under the snow. This time the soldiers were almost upon them, but it was well known that the Great Powers are very strong for people of such heart as these walking ones.

In the main party Little Wolf sent most of the women with Old Bear and the Crier, to hide ahead in some canyons cut deep into the red earth. Dull Knife was still hopeful. "The soldiers know we have the right to go back north," he said. "They could have caught us earlier—yesterday while we hunted, or the two days before—"

"Maybe they were waiting for the others to get here from the north forts and the fire road along the river," Black Crane said cautiously.

Although Dull Knife was convinced the soldiers would not shoot, Little Wolf and the others selected a good place to meet them, the men going back a ways on the trail into some steep red hills where the many guns and the strong, well-fed horses of the troops would not be worth so much, and where they could not get to water. The Indians had the little timber with springs where great flocks of wild turkeys once roosted, and with many red draws and gullies that led off northward. "Better not all be caught together," Old Bear had said out of remembrance. So they scattered, some of the young men still away looking for horses, as important now as standing off the troops.

When the scouts signaled with their swift circlings that many enemies were coming close, the women and children back in the canyons ran together and then apart, starting to scatter in the fear of guns. But Old Crier called gently to them. "Do not be afraid, my sisters. There are those among you who have stood against the soldiers many times. Your men are brave. You are Cheyennes. . . ."

But the women kept going with their children, even Buffalo Calf Road, the warrior woman, for now there was a small one on her back. So the old man let them go, knowing that in a little while they would be slipping back, looking over the hill to see their men fight, singing strong-heart songs, making the trills for the brave ones. It was the way with women and he was too old to wish it otherwise.

As the dust spot on the horizon lengthened out, Little Wolf rose from his watching on the red slope. "Do not shoot first," he charged the warriors, "but get the arms and horses ready and I will go to meet the soldiers and try to talk to them. If they want to kill somebody, I will be the first man. Then you can fight."

So the Indians spread over the steep red hillside, looking dusty and unwarlike, with only a few guns and some bows, waiting. But Little Wolf knew how excitable these young men were, even the leaders like Bull Hump and Black Coyote, and so he sent his most trusted Elk warriors out among them to see that no one fired a hasty and foolish shot. He had very good men for this, old-timers like Great Eyes and the fine shot, Left Hand, all steady, with sons or grandsons on the hillside—young men hot to kill, to count coups right away, as though they had the ammunition and good war horses for an attack, a war.

When the long string of troops with the little pack train behind broke into a trot, dust rising faster, the Cheyennes began to ride back and forth before their position, some whipping their horses to get the second wind that is the preparation for a good fight. Out in front of them stood Little Wolf, the President's silver medal of peace shining on his breast. Beside him were Dull Knife, Hog, and several others, the little row of dusty men in plain leggins and old cotton shirts, their braids unadorned, the blankets folded formally over their arms, the hands all empty except Dull Knife's, carrying the pipe.

Rendlebrock stopped his troops out of rifle shot and sent a Blue Cloud forward to talk. But the man did not come closer than his roaring Arapaho voice could carry against the light wind. From there he called out the names of the chiefs standing together. "The whites want you to turn around," he shouted. "They sent us to overtake you and bring you in. If you give up now, you will receive your rations and be treated well. If not, you will be whipped back."

One after another the chiefs spoke, short words that could be guessed if not heard. They did not want to fight, but they would not go back. "We have no quarrel with anyone," Little Wolf said. "I hold up my right hand in the white man's way that I do not wish to fight him, but we are going to our old home and stay there."

Again the Blue Cloud called his demand for surrender, looking uneasily up the broken red slopes where only a few Cheyennes could be seen now, the sun glinting along the gun barrel at a rock or a weed or brush patch.

So once more Little Wolf said what he had been saying for a year. They were going back north as they had been promised they could. "We will go peacefully if we can, not hurting anybody or destroying anything of the whites on the way. We will attack no one if we are not first molested. If the soldiers come shooting, we will shoot back, and if the white men who are not soldiers fight us, we will fight them too."

So the Blue Cloud returned to Rendlebrock, and the chiefs to their men, all except Little Wolf. Holding his folded blanket up above the brushy clumps, he walked down toward the soldiers, hoping to talk a little. He would tell them how the dysentery was already better among his sick ones from a little fresh buffalo meat, and the shaking disease better too. Even the babies in the cradleboards were stronger. Couldn't the white men find it in their hearts to let sick women and children go to be well again?

As he walked, Little Wolf heard Bear Shield and even Thin Elk shouting their "No! No! Do not go closer!" down to him on the shifting wind. "They will capture you," the southerners warned, "lock you up in the ironhouse as they did us! They will kill you like they did Crazy Horse up in your own country!"

But the dusty Rendlebrock, his blond face burnt raw by sun and whisky, seemed to notice the Indians moving away through the ravines as though to escape. While the Blue Cloud was shouting for surrender a third time, and before Little Wolf was close enough to be heard, the trumpet made its call to war.

In the echoes the soldier guns roared out and spurts of dust flew up all around the chief. Above, the Cheyennes were suddenly like many colored bushes and tree tips in their warbonnets and feathered lances along the crest of the hills. Their guns boomed into blue smoke as Little Wolf turned and started back, walking through the fighting—bullets thudding into the soft red earth and rock around him, whining in ricochet through the smoke and the roaring and dust, the man going through them as calmly as to his evening lodge that seemed up a very steep slope now, with too many guns shooting.

On a hill off to the west his daughter Pretty Walker watched with Singing Cloud, Bull Hump's wife, and a few other young women who stayed with the fighters, all making their trills for the Wolf's great power. And when he reached the Cheyenne line, the whooping warriors charged from the front and the side upon the soldiers, holding the bullets, using mostly the bow and war ax, fierce and angered by this attack on their chief while he tried to make the talk of a friend.

Before the arrows and the driving charge of such reckless young men as Little Finger Nail, Woodenthigh, and the others, the soldier horses shied, reared, and plunged away or went down, the men up and running fast, except one who was left, a blue bundle on the ground, and another who was crawling away not far from the motionless Blue Cloud talk-maker. Somebody had picked off the Arapaho after the first firing, perhaps Left Hand, the slow-angered, straight-eyed hunter.

On the rise the women trilled again, for the soldiers were falling back and digging hurried rifle pits. Now there was a little time to look after some hurt Cheyennes. One had fallen down near the pits, under the smoke. A warrior with only a bow at his back charged out on his good horse to carry him away through the rows of spurting fire. It turned out She Bear was only stunned by a bullet that walked its little path around his head. The medicine he made before he went in must have been very strong.

But Little Wolf was getting uneasy. "Careful!" he warned his warriors. "I don't want any more people hurt. Don't shoot foolishly; there is very little in your guns!"

But then he saw that Dull Knife, who had been so certain the soldiers would not shoot, was now making a fighting harangue to the Dog soldiers, his gaunt, holy-man face impassioned, angry as when his village was attacked on the Powder. Only that day he was helpless. Now he was challenging the young men, whipping them with his words to make another charge, this time clear down and over the smoking rifle pits. He and others had done it several times when they were young: real old-time Cheyenne war charges.

"Ahh-h! my brother, truly you have done many brave things," Little Wolf interrupted heartily. "And thank you, Dog men! You kept the soldiers so busy shooting at you that they let me get back from down there. Now we must smoke a little and rest. We don't want anybody to die today, and perhaps it is not good to shame this yellow-haired soldier chief by riding over him. If we let him seem a little strong too, he may go back when he gets tired and very thirsty."

But some of the Dog soldiers were quick to taunt this head of the Old Man Chiefs who was still a leading chief of the rival society, the Elks. "It seems," they shouted, "that our warrior friends need a new leader! The one they have has softened very fast in the coffee and molasses talks of the agencies!"

"*Hou! Hou!*" many others shouted. "*Piva!* That is good."

"Ahh-h, we remember also that our Brave Man did not come to us from the agency until the soldiers with the Long-haired Custer were scattered like skinned buffalo over the ridge!" Bear Rope added. "Then, when the stink of the powder was gone on the wind, he came looking over the hills!" The Rope shouted this, joining the noise of the wild young warriors against those of his own time and age.

Dull Knife shook out his pipe bag and reached inside for the cleaner. He had nothing left to say now. He was away too during the Custer fight, at the agency. Besides, Bear Rope was still a sick man from the poisoning *veho* disease, and that must be remembered.

And Little Wolf found other work to do. He helped to set a row of little fires to run together in the dry weeds and grass and move down over the rifle pits, the horses plunging and afraid in the little draw of the holders when the wind rolled the smoke that way. A pack mule broke loose and was run down by Young Hog, who found a big bundle of green money on him. Finally the troops took their stock back into a deep rocky ravine to escape the fire and the arrows too, but in another place without water. When their guns quieted in the shadowed evening depths there, Little Wolf called his warriors in, except the watchers.

"You have made a good stand, without angering the whites too much. Now I think enough ammunition has been used up. The women are all safe."

But the rebellion among the younger men was hotter than ever now, for coups and killing. "Let us go clean out these soldiers down there—leave them scattered over the ground like they have our people! It will teach the others who come following us. . . ."

"*Hou, hou!* Good men have been hurt here! Let us pay the soldiers for that!"

But Little Wolf and Hog and now even the young Dog leader Bull Hump were firm. This was not like the old times, the Wolf said, when they were free to avenge the injuries. In these new times even the fighting against the whites had to be with the *veho* weapons, which could be kept from the Indians entirely if they were made angry enough. All the people could then be killed, every Cheyenne living between the earth and the sky. "See how little for defense there is in your hands, my friends," he reminded them earnestly. "We will need it all to protect the helpless ones later. Let us run as soon as we can."

But once more the young men got support from Dull Knife. Sitting at the dusk-time fire, he had the comfort of old friends of the buffalo days, Crier, Old Bear, and the others, the stale powder smoke firing the blood of these old warriors. It seemed that they were back in the good days of the buffalo and the wars with the Crows, the Pawnees, and the Snakes.

"The soldiers should be killed," Dull Knife said. "Cheyennes cannot let such shooting at them go unavenged. The whites here are not the same as those in the north, but like different tribes among the Indians. Those in the north said one thing, these another."

"The north ones sent us down here; they are the same . . . ," Little Wolf replied.

"I do not think so," Dull Knife insisted quietly, with the old stubbornness that helped bring him great honor in the battles. "Do you not remember two kinds of whites making war?"

"Ahh-h, but the north men won, and they are again the same," Howling Wolf, a prison man, interrupted from behind the chiefs.

"Perhaps, but the Great Father's picture in the agency house down here is not the man we saw in Washington."

"They have changed them. Do we not change? Dull Knife here was the one our fathers followed when they were warriors," Young Eagle dared remind them, and many who saw the strong medicine of Little Wolf in the shooting today called their *"Hous!"* to the youth's bold words.

"They are all the same whites," the Wolf repeated, "and angering them here will bring trouble up ahead, make the soldiers in our own country hot to fight us." He spoke easily, not needing to point out that the dew time of night softened the moccasin soles and stretched the bowstring so the arrow could not be sent beyond the arm's reach. Everybody knew night fighting brought bad luck.

The Knife did not reply or look up from his pipe, but he gave the sign of agreement when the council selected the Dog society to watch the soldiers for the night.

"Make no attack but let nobody get away. Hold them close like the *veho* herds his cows. Ride around them, and even sing them a few songs if it pleases you. . . ." Little Wolf said, his face lighted with a thin smile, one of the first since the agent offered him his own granddaughter for a wife.

Tangle Hair and his Dog warriors accepted the honor of this responsibility, but that did not keep those riding with Bull Hump from sending some arrows and a few bullets down into the draw as they kept up their intermittent whoops and howlings to scare the eastern recruits down there. They made a little dancing around the watch fires too, drumming for the three dead soldiers, men whose guns and other things they had, and whose scalps they could have taken if they had wished.

All this noise was an annoyance to Rendlebrock, who hated Indian fighting. Prussian born and trained, he liked orderly battles and the Civil War had already been a disorderly conflict in his eyes. "Is this then work for a soldier, skirmish with whooping red savages?" he growled a dozen times during the night, so even Howling Wolf, who crept up close, heard him. But those whooping red savages managed to keep him from getting men out for water or for reinforcements.

There was other work for the Cheyennes this night too. Some went for more horses, and a few to help bring in the Brave One's party of women and children. There was laughing and crying and a song of thankfulness when they came plodding wearily through the firelit warrior camp, many barefoot, the children, even those seven and eight years old, too worn to walk. The few women at the fighting ran to see the newborn son. The little one was shown for a moment at the red coals of the council fire and named Comes Behind by Old Bear, his great uncle. The Bear made the motions of the pipe to the Great Powers as he said the words. It was a good omen, Bridge agreed, that their journey was begun with a new life the first night, and now the naming when they had just won the first little battle. So far none had died with them, although the father of Singing Cloud had thrown himself from the travois into the grass once, but his dutiful daughter had lifted him back and whipped her old mare onward.

Tomorrow?—Tomorrow one would see, old Bridge said, as a shot boomed out down where the soldiers were surrounded.

Many of the warriors had gone to the women's camps to watch that no soldiers came upon them from the other side. A few of the young men managed a moment of talking with the soft-voiced girls, perhaps held one a moment within the folds of the blanket. Some shy ones were bolder now, with the watchful old lodge women in a weary and frightened little huddle at a few coals. Young Hog was there tonight, and Little Finger Nail and

Little Hump, the younger son of Dull Knife. All of them walked taller from the poor whipping they gave the white soldiers, the first such fight some had seen in a long time; some never before.

Back at the warrior fires there were the hurt ones to be cared for. One was Thin Elk. Little Wolf went to examine his wound too, the chief hoping that his women would not hear of the injury. Even the most carefully reared Cheyenne woman became foolish over an injured warrior. But the Elk was up and sitting at a fire eating soup cooked for him by the younger wife of Dull Knife, so his wounding was plainly a little thing.

"You are old enough to have your son fighting in your place," Little Wolf said.

"Then my son would get the good soup of comfort . . . ," Thin Elk replied. It was a bold speech to make to Short One, and boldly spoken, but it cheered the evening like the last sun touching the eastern crests to a brighter redness. This was one elk who would never be thin from hunger.

Laughing a little in spite of himself, the Wolf returned to his fire. As he approached, he saw it was tended by Feather on Head, who had left the care of their few goods in the farther camp to the other wife and slipped back. She glanced up at the man's moccasined approach and then stooped silently to the cooking, as was proper for a warring chieftain's woman.

"You know you are not to get near the fighting," Little Wolf said in his soft tongue, as though speaking to no one. Feather did not look up again but filled her great spoon, the only spoon of the horn of the big horn sheep left to the Cheyennes here. She gave it into the hands of her husband in the good way. Gravely, with his knife point, he offered a bit of the meat to the sky and the earth and the four directions. Then he ate. "It is good," he said once, and Feather sang her little song of happiness, very softly, so not to be an embarrassment:

> I have a good man.
> In the village circle
> The women have called out his name many, many times,
> And the children follow his tracks.

After he ate, Little Wolf went through the rising moonlight to look over the slopes of the fighting and to listen to the occasional shot from down around the soldiers as he walked. On the hillsides of the fight, still in deep shadow, boys and youths were carrying torches and with their knives digging for bullet lead in the soft red rock. He saw the flaring light on the smooth brown faces as they ran here and there, or stooped to pry eagerly and seriously for the mushroomed bullets they needed so much. Among the boys was the light-skinned one called Yellow Swallow. He had not brought bad luck today, as some had feared, no matter who his father was.

All night the Indians held the soldiers in the ravine, shut in with their wounded men and their horses, alive and dead. Now and then there was an exchange of shots as some Indian slipped up too close or a courier tried to get away. Early in the morning, when the fog began to creep out of the red canyons, redder from the wetness in the sun, the fighting started again. But the soldiers were surrounded and their ammunition about gone. By the time the sun poured down straight upon the thirsting horses, the dry canteens, and the wounded men, the Indians saw the troopers mount and start back toward Camp Supply on the fork of the Canadian. Astride their horses the Cheyenne warriors watched from the bluffs on each side, standing out boldly against the windy sky, in easy rifle shot, letting the dusty blue column pass in peace below, since they were going back. But the warriors whooped along those who had no horses when they saw that some were of the Cheyenne scouts and the Indian police.

"It is a longer way, going back!" one shouted.

"I have the extra moccasins your mother gave me for you . . . ," another offered.

Afterward, while the women stripped the skins from the dead horses, Little Wolf and Hog went over the fighting ground together. They picked up a field glass covered by the earth stirred up in the charges and saw where three soldiers had died. One of them, from the coat, was a sergeant, as Little Wolf had been when he was a scout for Braided Beard Crook at Fort Robinson. The dead Blue Cloud lay there too, with flies on his eyelids, and from the horse litter and the white bandages in the retreating column, it seemed three more soldiers were wounded.

But five good Cheyennes were bad hurt defending themselves at this place called Turkey Springs, where once the clouds of wild turkeys came to sleep. One was a small girl, six, an orphan, the mother shot in the Powder River fight, the father crippled and then killed by the spotted disease down south here. Now the shy little girl had been hit in the foot, and crawled away under a bush some time during the fighting. It was Bullet Proof of the searchers who found her. She lifted her arms to him, and he took up the child, light as a doll made of rushes or willow sticks. He carried her to Bridge and together they drew the bullet from the shattered ankle. More and more of the people came to stand silent while this was done, their faces unmoving as they heard the soft little whimperings. She was a brave Cheyenne, this little girl who would be known as Lame One from this day.

After a while she slept, but the hurting of this child who belonged to them all made the people angrier than anything of this day. It had been done in the place called Indian Territory, the Indians' own land, and no whites anywhere had been molested. Now three of the soldiers who came shooting had been killed. That and not the five Cheyennes hurt, one a small child, would start the talking wires, spread the story all the way to the north country.

4   The First Man Killed

NOW THEY MUST TRAVEL VERY FAST AND HIDE THEIR trail as well as possible. So the Indians scattered into little parties but close enough to gather quickly for protection. The young men went out for more horses, and guns too, if any could be obtained now after the news of the fight.

"Nobody is to be killed, only the soldiers that come shooting at you," the warriors were still told.

But it was difficult to hold some of the young men, those who had grown up around the agencies and had never struck an enemy with the hand or bow or quirt; never counted this coup that was always the measure for manhood, for warrior society membership, and for taking a wife. Dull Knife and the other old ones were angry too because injured Cheyennes went unavenged. But most of them saw that it would be difficult enough to get through to the north now, with the talking wires telling of the fight and the whites angered that their soldiers had been driven back like prairie dogs running for their holes at the sound of thunder. So the Indians moved out as soon as they could, with two more drags needed now, one with Lame Girl and the other with Old Grandmother, who was worn out. Not wanting to detain the flight, she tried to be left along the trail like the ailing father of Singing Cloud. Twice the old woman rolled herself off the drag, but the short tawny grass refused to hide her poor calico and someone came back scolding, "Grandmother! You went to sleep and fell off! We must tie you in," or "We must make a cradleboard for you like the new child with us, young Comes Behind."

But two days later the sixteen-year-old Spotted Deer came riding from the south, his horse white-frosted with lather. They had heard about the good little fight and so he was sent to look after Old Grandmother, help her get north, his mother said. The two other young men who rode in with him came because even a little fight seemed better than sitting on an agency.

"Many back there are singing the brave songs for you, throwing their hearts over the grass country between," the newcomers said. It was a strengthening thing to hear.

Brave One and about twenty others were still walking along behind, carrying their children or those of others, but with new moccasins and a few pieces of new meat in their packs now. It was good that they had found the buffaloes. Stripped into flakes thin as the finger edge, the meat had dried quickly for carrying. There would be little hunting now, with the buffalo bones everywhere, the old chips bleaching and crumbled. But it seemed the Powers were not entirely against the Cheyennes, for the summer had been wet. There was good grass for the short stops, and the water holes usually dry in September were lakes, even many of the wallows where buffaloes no longer rolled to cake themselves with mud against the gnats. But the gnats were still waiting, fine as whirling dust in the air, and there was no bear grease to keep them from the children now, from the eyelids and the ears, not even the white man's stinking coal oil.

The wildest of the young men knew now that it was better to take the trail Dull Knife laid out long ago west of the Kansas forts. They whipped their tired horses over the high ground, the foot-going ones slipping from hollow to weed clump, and yet even here it was hard to keep hidden from the eyes of the whites with their little dugouts, their houses cut from sod, their traveling cattle everywhere.

Perhaps too many people did see them, for soon more soldiers came. The Indians were going up one of the Bear creeks, the Cimarron not far behind, when suddenly another double row of soldiers approached from ahead, men on gray horses. There were fewer than the other time and the troops fired from far off, making a line and charging so there was no time for parley. The warriors met them and it was shooting and retreating and more shooting for the whites, until they were driven back in the direction of the Dodge fort on the Arkansas. Only one soldier was killed, the Indian camp moving right ahead all the time because now there was no place to run. Little Wolf wondered if there ever would be, with the big bunches of soldiers surely marching against them, walking soldiers who could not run away either, and carrying the good far-shooting guns.

The ammunition lost in the little fight here was more than in the saddlebags Young Hog had picked up at Turkey Springs or the bullets molded from the lead dug along the red slopes. Little Wolf talked for the pleasantness of big fires, so they stopped near wood. They could not hide anyway, and the people would have to live a long time on the road. There was even a little singing tonight. Girls and older boys like the young Spotted Deer, who must stay near his grandmother, went along the scattered fires, a Contrary Society youth with them, making the people laugh in his turned-around way, his front-behind clothes. With the white-man hat over his face he walked backward, showing only the black Indian hair where a nose and eyes should be. Flexible as a mink, he could stoop down behind, seeming to peer over his hand for the enemy, his bow drawn against himself. He crawled through fire and mud, jumped over shadows, and escaped from pursuit running backward to it, on his hands. It seemed very funny in this anxious time, and Spotted Deer found himself laughing with a shy, pretty girl called Yellow Bead, one who had an aunt she must help to the north country, and whose eyes strayed to Little Hump, the son of a chief.

But suddenly the laughing was done. Little Finger Nail and his horse hunters came in with a few and with bad news. Black Beaver who had led them was left back there on the ground. They had seen some horses down near a ranch. Not wanting to scare the whites, Beaver took only one man down to buy some horses with the paper money from the pack mule. But the white men came shooting and hit the Beaver's worn-out horse. The other one escaped over the hill, and when the cowboys saw all the Indians, they spurred back. Afterward Little Finger Nail tried to get the body of his friend, but a lot of gray-horse troops came riding and about eighty went to stand around the Indian, poking him with their gun barrels, taking the green money and leaving him naked like an uprooted brown tree fallen beside the trail. So the Nail took all the ranch stock they could get, shooting the colts too young to live alone or to follow north. They left Woodenthigh and a man with medicine eyes behind to watch and to carry the Beaver's body to the rocks.

So now a good man had been killed by *vehos* who were not soldiers and the hearts of the Indians were very bad. Little Wolf talked against revenge, for coolness with so many in danger here. "Hold yourselves," he urged. "Black Beaver was a very good leader who always looked straight along the path of the people. That was why he was selected to go buy the horses. He would work for peace even now, from his place in the grass. . . ."

"Nobody had hurt anything of the settler whites!" Little Finger Nail protested hotly.

"Ahh-h, already the whites are afraid and shooting at everyone. So it will be all the way now," some of the older men said morosely, and Black Crane too, as the keening started among the women. It ran back along the narrow canyon, rising like a sorrowful dust. The Beaver's wife and two young daughters slashed their arms and legs so blood ran, and Little Wolf and several others let their hair stream loose with earth and grass in it. That was all they could do. There were no presents to make a giveaway for Beaver's good friends, and little time for the mourning, so little time now for the decencies of death, or birth or life.

That night Tangle Hair and three of the Dog soldiers who guarded the rear divided the camp into smaller parties, to travel all they could in this darkening moon time, keeping out of sight in the day. Even so there was trouble, the scouts signaling danger from the night. Then everybody had to turn aside because white men lived where there should be only grass and buffalo—the *veho* sign perhaps a settler's light like a star pinned to the ground, or several together, and many of the rough places where a plow had traveled the earth. The people became more and more fearful, with these unexpected enemies everywhere, and once Medicine Wolf had to hurry back to Bear Rope in the darkness of the moving line.

"Come, oh come! Our man is very strange," one of the wives pleaded. "He carries the voice of the enemy in his mouth, and enemy words. . . ."

Because the son-in-law and the other men of that family were away, a wife had to run for the medicine man herself, afraid and so very much ashamed at this admission of fault in her husband that Medicine Wolf could barely hear her words. And when he came to Bear Rope and saw how it was, he signaled the leaders to stop the moving people, and for a while the Indians rested in the darkness or slipped away to their needs—but not far, with none knowing when night-charging soldiers might come. The men smoked their red willow bark, women fed their babies, and some of the young men went for a whispered word with the girls, perhaps even a little laughing away from the bereaved ones, the softly keening ones who had lost the good man Beaver.

Medicine Wolf worked to quiet the Rope with his sleep chants, his gesture singing. But the man had been very sick in the fall, the medicine

men helpless and the agency doctor not coming, so when her father seemed
dead, the daughter vowed to cut off her little finger if he lived. Almost at
once he was breathing, and when he managed to crawl out into the daylight, he found that his strong son and thirty others had died that week.
The vow of the finger brought on a furious anger. "It is the whites who
should be bleeding for my sickness!" he cried. "I command you not to
fulfill the vow!" From that day he had the twisted times when he reached
where his gun should be because those of the lodge were enemies, or when
he spoke to his wives and his daughter as loose women come so familiarly
to his lodge.

The sleep Medicine Wolf brought him helped, but Bear Rope needed
more; he needed a long time of good village life, the easy cycle of eating,
hunting, and sleeping, and then eating and sleeping again, not this running,
running, with danger behind every hill, riding through every gully, and
never a lodge over his head or even a willow shelter that need not fall before
the sun returned.

Toward morning the meat men came in under the pale horned moon
with fresh beef. If there were no need to fight the soldiers, travel would be
easy now, with so many cattle moving north or just scattered out alone
around the new living places of the whites.

"The cowboys will not like this butchering; they will shoot. . . ."

Perhaps it could be done as with the Sioux, Crow, an old agency man,
said. Sometimes when there were no buffaloes, the Indians killed cattle to
get back to the agency. It was taken out of their beef appropriation from the
Great Father, from the pay for their lands.

Yes, that was true, but some whites liked the opportunity to shoot very
well, and shooting Indians best of all.

Then when the wind clouds of noon veiled the sun, the soldiers were
suddenly there again. The medicine-eyed watcher had come in to say the
whole country was full of them. He and Woodenthigh had followed the
whites from Black Beaver's body for horses, and saw more and more of them
gathering like ants running before the winter, coming with pack horses of
guns and ammunition, and all moving toward Bear Creek here.

Little Wolf and Hog were taking their turn leading the people, going
up the narrow canyon when the soldiers were signaled just ahead, many
more this time, with many other whites. The frightened people turned

back upon themselves, crowding together, the warriors hurrying up the
sides. There was no place to run, to hide, so the Cheyennes waited, packed
in like antelope in a drive trap, the whitish windy sky standing over them,
two eagles circling high, and the soldiers charging. Howling Wolf of the
powerful voice rode out to meet them, calling the *veho* words: "We will
fight the soldiers! You other whites go away or we will have to kill some
of you too!"

But the answer was a lot of revolver shots from the cowboys who kept
well behind. Howling Wolf raced back to get his medicine protection ready
against these many guns. He looked off over the frightened people reaching
down the canyon out of sight, the horses with their heads down, too worn
to shy from the bullets that hit among them, the people bowed too, the
walkers dropped like resting bundles. Above them the eagles floated like
two bits of black hair. Somehow it seemed that all his life Howling Wolf,
the southerner, had known nothing but this.

> It is a good day to die!
> All the things of our life are here,
> All that are left of our people.
> It is a good day to die!

So Howling Wolf sang his song of death. He was not a crying man, but
he could hardly see anything before him now for the water of his face.
Others had given up in the years back there in the Florida prison, some
dying, one or two becoming strange until none could understand their
words or their torment. Howling Wolf had held himself together, worked
hard. He discovered that the whites were very many and so he learned to
build tables and benches and cupboards with the saw and the hammer—
and then asked to have his wife sent to him. He would make a new life with
these things called tools.

But he was brought back to the agency and still he talked for the white
man's road. Then his small daughter died in his arms, feeling like loose
bones in a thin flour sack. So he had returned to the breechclout and the
growing braid and joined the medicine ceremonials with the people from
the north. It was not done in hope but because the Cheyennes all seemed to
be living in a canyon now, with men always pointing guns into their faces,
men hired only for the killing, and no road around for the Indians, or to
turn back.

"It is a good day to die," he sang again and went down into the fight where the Indians were returning the fire, but carefully, intending to hit the horses at first, then more if it must be done. Even Left Hand had settled himself for very deliberate aim. But when the horses in front went down like falling over a caving bank, those behind began to plunge and were jerked back with the iron in their mouths. Several soldiers seemed hurt and one died. Then the trumpet blew, the echo sweet and clear in the canyon, and suddenly the troops turned and galloped away with the swallowtail flag going up and down, the other whites running too, many already far ahead, but some behind and looking back,[1] half-minded to stay.

"Truly it seems as Dull Knife has said all the time. Perhaps the soldiers do not intend to fight us," Left Hand admitted, for a moment almost disappointed, now that he had worked himself to a fighting pitch, not easy for this man who followed the hunt as the wolf follows the scent of a new-born yellow calf. Commonly he liked to spend his time feasting on roasted hump ribs and talking about the great hunts that had been made.

But there was bad damage today. Sitting Man had his leg broken. Seeing this, everybody was hot to fight more, but the horses were too poor to chase the running whites. So the warriors caught the loose horses and skinned the dead ones, while Feather on Head and Short One helped the women gather up their goods and the leaders smoked and hoped for Sitting Man's life. The bullet went through the thigh, the bone sticking out, with blood gushing around it like a welling spring. Bridge had been hurried up from his singing for help in the fight. His special medicine, the last ear of sacred corn of the Cheyennes, had empowered him to stop dangerous bleeding, but it was lost in the Dull Knife village fight, and perhaps his power with it.

Fearfully the wife of Sitting Man brought the needed water and wood. With Young Eagle blowing his medicine flute, Bridge gave the wounded man a red drink and by rattle and song put him to sleep almost at once. Then he passed the painted gourd over the naked breast, always slower, until the heart under the brown skin seemed to slow with it and the pouring blood became only a thin red thread. Making his medicine gestures to the flute's song, he wiped the wound with silver sage weed, sprinkled it with dust from a puffball, and bound it. Then he pulled the leg out long and covered it from body to foot with the green hide of a soldier horse

sewed on very tight so, when it shrank in the hardening, the broken bones
would be held straight and strong, with only a little hole for the stink of
the healing wound. It was a fine thing to hear the wife singing her song
of thankfulness as she led their only horse to the side of the medicine man
and his helper, as was their due.

But others pushed up to offer horses instead. "You will need yours very
much now, sister, if you and your hurt man are to get away," Black Crane
said.

"Hou," it was good. And good to know that old Bridge still had his great
power. In the curing, Young Eagle had forgotten the pretty girl back in
the south for a while. When this hard road home was finished, Bridge
would make a son of him, teach him what he must know of healing, for
the old-time power seemed to live in the youth.

Up to now Little Wolf had controlled his young men well. He had made
them wait until the troops fired, even in the face of charging cavalry, and
kept them from attacking the other whites or committing any depredations
except killing a few cattle and taking some horses, both fairly military
necessity. But now many men had been hurt and Black Beaver lost, and it
was as Little Wolf had warned. If people shot at them, they would shoot
back. Then the next day the scouts found that two of the young Cheyennes left to watch the soldiers had been killed and scalped in a little draw
near the position of the cowboys yesterday. One was the nephew of Left
Hand and now this moderate man would gladly have brought down a
dozen soldiers instead of just their horses.

From the first day the foragers had been led by reliable peace men, but
now the wildest young warriors sneaked out with none to know what was
done unless they told it. Near a place the southerners called Protection, they
found two more horses that were stolen from their herd last year, one
from Black Coyote, whose warrior wife was afoot now too, with the child
on her back. The Cheyennes shot the rider when he fired, but not yet ready
to kill everybody, they let the other man get away wounded and brought
in the stolen horses with four other good ones. The new stock was afraid
of Indians and very hard for the women to handle with their children and
bundles, even for Bull Hump's Leaf, who used to rope any horse she wanted
from the family herd and ride it, no matter if the earth was frozen to stone
for the falling.

But now the Indians must get away fast, for soon there would be too many soldiers to shame themselves by running. The scouts who followed those of today came back through the blackness of a raining night, with three horses worn out. All the whites had gone to the Arkansas, but certainly they would be out up ahead and many more.

"Ahh-h, yes, at the river, with the wide flat valley that must be crossed . . . ," Little Wolf murmured. His Feather on Head looked anxiously toward her man as she leaned her blanket protectively over the wet, sputtering coals, then to the twinkling little fires scattered along the sheltering canyon. But the rain fell straight down, and none had a lodge, not even the sick and old or the crippled Sitting Man or the child now called Lame Girl, with her bullet-shattered ankle very swollen.

Once more the Army was protesting the treatment of the Cheyennes by the Indian Bureau. Amos Chapman, Cheyenne interpreter at Camp Supply, had been to the agency recently and found the northerners so hungry that they were eating dead horses, dead from disease. "Unless the rest of the Indians are fed, he anticipated a larger outbreak in the spring," Colonel Lewis of Fort Dodge reported.

There were recollections now that, when it was first proposed to settle the Northern Cheyennes in the Territory, both the Indians and the whites there protested to Washington, and that the ratification of the Sioux treaty of 1876 forbade bringing any of the troublesome Sioux there. These Cheyennes, allies of the hostile Crazy Horse, were no more welcome. Besides, the Commissioner of Indian Affairs had protested sending northern Indians south. In two years over 800 of the 2,376 Pawnees taken there had died. But the funds appropriated could be used only if the Indians were moved away from Red Cloud, either to the Missouri or Indian Territory.

By now stories of a great Indian uprising flooded the newspapers, the office of the governor of Kansas, and the army posts through the state, with many hundreds of telegrams and letters from everywhere demanding arms, guns in hundred lots, ammunition by the 20,000 rounds. The governor thought at least the bad-man town of Dodge should have the arms and the men for its own defense, but he sent the two hundred stands they requested. Many men were reported killed, children injured, and women raped.

To the query, "Where is Sherman, our General of the Army?" political enemies answered that he was probably in a sulk somewhere because, not a Catholic himself, his only son had become a priest. It turned out the general was about his regular business making an extended inspection tour of the very frontier posts that must subdue all the Indians that Congress had made hungry. He was in Arizona by the time that Hemphill reported his retreat from the Bear Creek region [2] and was not due back in Washington until the middle of October.

The general had an Indian war on his hands, the Western papers warned, with at least a hundred people killed on the south Kansas border alone, and the Cheyennes just reaching the settlements. Now even Mizner was disturbed; when caught, fully one-third of the Cheyenne men should be banished to the Florida prison or some other safe place. "Dull Knife, Crow Indian, Wild Hog and Little Bear should be made special examples of."

Around the Dodge City saloons it was said that Captain Hemphill's gray-horse troops were too weak against 250 or 300 Indians. He had retreated to get the reinforcements he knew were due. That night a train of stock-cars was ready to haul everybody up to the Dull Knife crossing of the Arkansas: five companies of cavalry, two of infantry, about fifty cowboys and ranchers, and wagons to haul the infantry and the supplies. But they found no sign of Indians there, and so the next morning the long ragged column started across the bare table to Crooked Creek and made night camp in a hard rain. It rained so hard that Bear Shield, in his blue soldier coat from the Florida prison, was able to take his listening ears right into the camp.

To find meat for almost three hundred hiding people was hard for the hunters, and even Little Wolf asked few questions when they drove a herd of thirty beeves right into the camp and brought them down with arrows there, the bawling longhorns running wild, the dust rising to meet their thudding bodies.

The women worked fast, their children under the hand if the bullets started to come. By evening the knives were at the women's belts again, glistening clean. The beef paunches filled with the good inner parts steamed like kettles from the tripods of sticks, cooking with the hot stones the boys carried from the fires to drop inside. Stripped meat hung in dark rags along the drying ropes. The hides were staked, flesh up, to the Kansas wind, some stretched over pits of embers to harden for moccasin soles. Even a few rough skin wickiups would now protect the wounded like Sitting Man and some with the ague.

For a few hours it seemed almost like long ago, with even the good smell of coffee. The southerners got a little from a store they raided along the Dodge trail. Browned on a thin slab of heated stone and pounded in the little skin bags, it went into the one kettle that someone had managed to carry all this way.

Fresh coffee—with sugar in the bottom of a cup as it passed, the first since the wintertime! Soon now they would be across the Arkansas, their moccasins firm on another rung of the Cheyenne ladder to the north. While they ate, three more young men came in, deserters from Standing Elk's band.

"It is said somebody here has very strong medicine, to make the soldiers all run back," one explained. "It seems they fly back like a bullet hitting a stone."

Already Feather on Head and Short Woman had their blankets tucked about their waists to free their hands and were bringing the welcoming meat, their faces broad in happiness. Perhaps all the others would soon be following north. Later a big fire was built up against the night, with a new-made skin drum and some singing, Little Finger Nail's sweet voice joining the others until Singing Cloud came shyly from among the maidens to draw him into the weaving dance circle about the fire. But Yellow Bead hid her face and dared not approach Little Hump.

For a while the fun was like that of the small boys running and shouting among the watchers, the strengthened Yellow Swallow with the rest. Later he was lifted to the top of Little Hawk's head while two other boys balanced on the wrestler's shoulders as he made his ponderous dance that always ended with them all in the dust, the people laughing hard. Truly this was the best time since the Cheyennes had to leave the north country, since before Custer came riding up there. And tonight none seemed to look with darkness in the hidden glance against Long Hair's son among them.

But in the middle of the evening there was a sudden shout and running, with thick, angry bellows, like a buffalo bull fighting, and cries of terror. People ran toward it, the women too. At Bear Rope's little fire they found the whole family crying, one wife with blood flowing over her face from the war club of her husband, the other hurt too, the younger children knocked aside, and the son-in-law rushing in.

But he came too late. After Bear Rope had chased all the others away, he grabbed his daughter, Comes in Sight, and threw her down to make a wife of her right there in the light of his own fire, although the family was always watching now. But the daughter managed to draw the butcher knife from her belt and slashed the father so his bowels hung out, laying across his arm now as he sat hunched over in the firelight, trying to hold himself together, the grayness already in his eyes. Then, before all the people, he started to settle downward, his face unrecognizing, the violence draining from it as he went over sideways to the earth, his arms relaxing, their bloody load spreading out and moving a little, like a live thing.

Afterward the pipe was passed around the council and Little Wolf spoke. A Cheyenne had been killed by another, who must now be driven out, ostracized for perhaps four years, and never sit where the medicine pipe would pass again. But this was done by a woman. Never in all the lifetime of even Old Crier here had one of their women killed a tribesman. And her own father—

Yet a woman was in honor bound to defend herself, Dull Knife pointed out. Besides, none here could say how much of this happened because of the vow of a finger for the father's recovery, and never fulfilled. And how much because of the chasing whites who brought their sickness upon Bear Rope, and all his loss and humiliation? It was enough to make a good man go down the violent road.

There were grave *"Hous!"* "—Yet we must try to keep the darkness of this bad day from following the people," Bridge said, and Medicine Wolf and the others who knew the holy ways agreed.

"Tomorrow it will be light again . . . ," Bullet Proof predicted, always one to believe, and now Little Wolf and the others nodded tentatively.

But the goodness of this night was gone, and from many nights, from all the nights of one young woman. Before morning the scouts signaled more soldiers close, and once more everybody got ready to run, harder than ever now for there was blood upon the people.

5   Soldiers, Soldiers, and the Flooding Arkansas

AS THE SOLDIERS CAME CLOSE AGAIN, THE RAIDERS OUT for guns and horses were signaled in. One party had found a wagon train and brought in what they could carry, the drivers taking a paper with Howling Wolf's name in *veho* words. Others found many of the sheep that no one wanted. At one place a long-bearded herder ran out shaking his fist. A wild young warrior put a bullet through the beard and laughed to see the man run, the long face hair streaming out behind him, his frightened sheep sweeping together like a whirlwind lifting dead gray leaves. One place a herder shot at them and so they whooped his flock in a bleating dirty blanket over the prairie and into a lake, the Indians along the bank watching them crowd together, trying to walk on each other. It was strange how silly the tame creatures of the *veho* were, all the things that made themselves tame for the white man.

That day Little Finger Nail saw two buzzards circling in an odd way, low as the feather in his hair. His horse side-jumped and before him lay a dead man, face down, a bullet in his neck. He was swollen high, dead for days, and scalped in a foolish way, a patch big as two palms cut off from the side and down into the face hair. Surely no Indian had done this, and no Cheyenne was taking scalps.

But the buzzards kept flying over Little Finger Nail. At a lone tent with cattle around, two cowboys started shooting. The others whipped away, but the Nail lifted his hand, palm out for peace. His horse was brought down and he hit the ground so he seemed dead. The others charged in to carry him to a medicine man. But soon the Nail was alive again, with only the memory of a dream that he must talk over with Bridge—a dream of himself walking ahead in a strange white land and all his people following.

Farther on they saw a dusty trailing of longhorns up a small creek. The cowboys fled with most of the loose horses, and the Indians looked down on the scattering cattle and wished the beef could be moved along with the people. But cows walked slower even than Old Grandmother and a great herd could not scatter like Indians. Besides, buffalo tasted better, so they took only the five horses left behind, one of them the black and white spotted one stolen from Little Wolf last year.

But the young men killed some more people, one a black man that they regretted shooting because the gun he pointed at them turned out to be a long stick blackened with axle grease to look like a rifle. Another man was shot by the southerners at a place of five, six houses with everybody else gone. The Indians looked for powder and ammunition; they took some hoop iron for arrows, bedspreads for blankets for the Dull Knife daughters, and some dresses and pretty pictures for the small children. A singing bell like on army mules in a gully turned out to be on worn-out *wo-haws,* the work oxen of the whites. They got a little powder and a gun, but they had to kill a man for them.

"Two years ago there were only buffaloes here," they told Little Wolf, to break his angry silence over the killings. "Now there are only cattle and the sheep who make the lakes so no horse can drink."

Ahh-h, it was well to leave the poisoned southern country, the Wolf admitted. But now there were these dead men to be counted against the Cheyennes too.

This time the soldiers came in a great column that circled to a camping on a part of Sand Creek, cowboys and soldiers mixed together. Roman Nose of the medicine eyes stayed behind and saw the red-faced Rendle-brock come again, the man whose cannon had looked down into their village back there, and then was driven back at Turkey Springs. The soldiers unsaddled and scattered over the evening ground, but five, six cowboys went scouting and ran into Black Coyote's men guarding the canyon of the women and children where they would not see the great swarm of whites.

At the first shot the Coyote started to clean out these foolish cowboys, but suddenly Little Wolf stood in the canyon before him, his spotted horse blocking the way. "My friend, these soldiers here have always gone away. Perhaps it was because so few whites have been hurt," he said. "If they stay to fight us we may all die."

More whites kept coming, and in a little skirmishing Black Coyote and his helpers were driven back because they shot mostly arrows, with only a few bullets weak in powder. At sunset everybody went back to camp, but the chiefs sent their sons Bull Hump and Woodenthigh ahead to the Arkansas crossing to make ready if anybody got away. The rest of the camp slipped away about three miles west, to another sandy little creek. There was an alarm in the night, but the shooting was soldiers mistaking a lot more cowboys riding out of the darkness for Indians.

In the morning the troops moved up with at least forty wagons and many, many men. The women started to run, but Dull Knife walked among them with Old Bear and Crier beside him, and just seeing the calm of these men they had trusted so long quieted them.

While the warriors held off the walking soldiers with their dangerous long guns, the cowboys were free to charge in and out as they liked, making the air thick with dust and smoke and noise, but all running away every time that a horse went down. Yet this freed the cavalry to go around below the Indian position, to surround them, corral them. Little Wolf and Hog decided there were too many enemies for this place. They must move back into the broken hills.

So the people moved behind Old Crier, going swiftly, heavily, knowing that in this place the fight must be made. No warrior rode out in taunts now, showing off, charging foolishly. Everybody made his best defense for the frightened ones behind him.

"Remember your guns are almost empty!" Little Wolf cautioned the young men as he walked among them, standing out plain for everyone to see, with the bullets making dust jumps around him, but only until he had the young men calmed. The sons must not need to outdo the fathers in daring today.

While the soldiers moved in below them, rifle pits were dug around the ridge, two of them back to protect the little spring of water, and all big enough for six men. Everybody knew that, if the whites fought with all their guns and ammunition, this would be like the ridge where Custer died —the last stand by the Cheyennes. So few here had ever faced hard-shooting men, and these old warriors were scattered among the others, to hold them, see that somebody grabbed up any weapon that fell. Even Sitting Man, with a forked stick under his arm for a hobble leg, had been helped into a pit. He was a strong man, one to teach the young warriors how to die.

While some dug, others hurried to paint themselves and put on the little war regalia left and to sing their songs of death. Old Great Eyes made the medicine for the shield of his grandfather—a feather-tailed shield from long, long ago in the far lake country and never lost to an enemy in all the battles since. He sang his death song with his nephew beside him, the youngest Red Bird, only thirteen, but ready to shoot if a gun fell free, and finally to run with the medicine shield.

Little Finger Nail was getting ready too, repeating what he said back at the agency for his small cousin, who might never live for another day. "If the young men die fighting here, their names will be remembered forever." He showed the boy how to aim the rifle a little high for those keeping back. "The bullet gets tired going so far. . . ."

The dark eyes watched the young warrior's lean face soberly, understanding that, and many other things unsaid between them, even something of the Nail's repeated search of the sky. But nothing flew overhead, only the spreading wind clouds like the tails of white horses running.

The women were all singing too, for strength as they prepared for attack. Holes were dug, the first to protect the children. The wife of the crippled Black Horse and others who had been in the Sappa fight tried not to remember how the buffalo hunters there had pulled the babies out of the holes, clubbed them, and then threw them into the fires of the piled lodges. It was mostly the other whites with the soldiers that did these things there, and many such men were very close now.

The women worked fast, with no sound except their singing and the cut and thrust of the butcher knives against gravel and stone, Moccasin, who had power in this, leading them. Afterward Buffalo Calf Road and Yellow Woman gave their small ones to the others with babies at their breasts, the eyes of the women meeting over the little heads a moment in naked sisterhood. Then the two went gravely to the rifle pits, where Bull Hump's Leaf and several other women who could shoot the guns or bows were already waiting. They were dressed in the poor best that was left, like warriors going out to die. Pretty Walker and the two elder daughters of Dull Knife wore the new fringed white bedspreads brought in yesterday; those with husbands here were combed and painted in the way of a beloved wife by her man.

Many noticed that the boy Yellow Swallow was kept out of the way, and were grateful that Comes in Sight had slipped out right after her dead father was hauled to the rocks, her husband and her mother and the other wife of the Bear Rope going along. It had to be done so the medicine men could hope for power to help the people, Bridge already in his third day of fasting for a guiding vision that did not come, and now the whites were down there moving closer and closer. The forty wagons were drawn up side by side in a row, the tail gates toward the Cheyennes so the mules would be harder to hit. The walking soldiers came from there in a skirmish line beside the dismounted cavalry, blue men rising, running, dropping to fire, and then running again, closer and closer, with some of the other whites coming behind them on their horses. It was like a solid wall pushing in until the people became very excited, afraid because this time they could not run.

Little Wolf walked from one rifle pit to the next, through the spurting bullets. "No one is to fire a shot!" he commanded. "They have wagons of ammunition to our handful. Keep down and wait until something happens."

But the soldiers seemed so very close, the smoke blowing thick and blue over the pits, the bullets striking along the tops, spraying those inside with sand and whistling on over the people behind. Finally Little Wolf let a few warriors fire. One soldier grabbed at himself in the middle, turned half around, and fell dead. The rest were on their bellies now, staying there, firing at the Indians along the slope above, keeping it up a long, long time, the noise like a rolling hailstorm, like thunder shaking the earth, the whole ridge lost in smoke and dust, with only now and then a shot coming from it, just enough to hold the enemy off so the bullets would go over the Indians.

Finally another white man seemed hit, for he stood up straight and then fell backward. About twenty more men jumped up, but they ran back to their horses at the wagons. From there they rode around the hill of the Cheyennes, some of the other whites following, so Little Wolf had to charge out to meet them with his best Elks and some Dog soldiers, whooping and firing from behind their running horses until the soldiers were driven back to the wagons, leaving another man dead. At the same time Dull Knife, Hog, and Black Crane sent a mounted charge down the slope upon the whites. Before its force the cowboys started away, the women calling insults after them, shaming the manhood of the whites who were not soldiers but had come out to shoot women and children like game on a hunt. "Run! Run for your mothers' houses crying that the bad Indians chased you and now you have to be washed in the pants!"

Then everybody else left too, running on long-shadowed legs through the evening sun, on horses or the full wagons that bounced as the mules galloped. A great cry of thankfulness rose from the women. Some of the young Cheyennes tried to overtake the soldiers, but Little Wolf signaled a stop. They were too few, without ammunition, and their horses must be strong to save the helpless ones another day. So the young men returned, except those to scout the soldiers, perhaps to cut off the couriers sure to go to Fort Dodge for cannons to shell the Indians out of their good position the way General Miles had done up on the Tongue River.

Perhaps the medicine of the Cheyennes was still powerful, even after the Bear Rope killing, for while couriers got away on their fast horses, there was no guard over the Indians. Hurriedly the women cooked a little meat after the hungry day, while the young men searched the fighting ground with their burning twists of grass. They found a wooden box of cartridges that the soldiers did not have time to load into the wagons and a half box scattered out. There was a broken rifle too, that Howling Wolf could per-haps repair.

The headmen made their evening smoke, quiet as any time. But they looked different in the red fire of this dark night than they did half a moon ago when they started north. Dull Knife's lean face carried many harrowed lines and Little Wolf's gentle words seemed gone forever. His face was gaunt too, and fierce under the pockmarks of the white man's disease— more and more like the angry bear's.

After a pipe the Wolf spoke. "My friends," he said in his flowing Chey-enne words, "there are too many troops here for us to fight. We must move out before the stars turn even a hand's distance in their path. We must try to get away north before somebody comes who is not playing, somebody hot to kill. We might have been with our faces to the sky right here. . . ."

Ahh-h, it was true, the others admitted, guttering their pipes.

The next morning it was discovered that the Cheyennes were gone, slipped away in the night. And in a few days most of the men who had been reported killed in the raids began to show up, one after another, some surprised to hear that there had been an Indian scare at all. Finally instead of a hundred, there seemed six civilians actually dead, and some claimed this was no more than the normal killings for ten days in that region of outlaws and horse thieves, of cattle and sheepman fights. Surely the man found with his six-shooter still beside him was not shot by Indians.

But by then troops were moving as far off as Utah, coming from the far east and the south too—wherever any could be found. Then there were those from the upper Missouri River—the Seventh Cavalry, Custer's regiment. Now the death of Long Hair would be avenged.

Toward the river the main body of Cheyennes came upon some buffalo hunters: those hide men who had destroyed the meat, the shelter, and clothing—all the wealth of the Indian—and left only bleaching bones on the prairie. Such men had killed many Cheyennes on the Sappa and other places, left many carrying lead to itch and pain before the winter's storm, and with the weight of bereavement upon them like a stone in the breast.

"Let us charge them! They are going against the white man's laws here, hunting south of the Arkansas!" Bear Shield said when the scouts brought the news. "We will avenge the Beaver!"

But Little Wolf would not permit it. "Black Beaver has been avenged," he reminded them quietly, "—as much as can be done now. And the white men will not let you punish their hunters who break their laws. You should know this from the years some of you spent in the stone prison for trying it."

So Little Finger Nail and the other warriors held their whip-plunging horses back; sullenly, but they did it, while Bear Shield was sent ahead to use his *veho* words. "Say nobody will be hurt if they give up their guns to us."

"They will shoot him," the Shield's wife mourned softly beside the wife of the crippled Black Horse, always afraid too, both with children on their backs, the cluster of anxious women around them.

But those hunters must have been strong, for they did not start shooting when the wild young Cheyennes charged in close behind the Shield, whooping like a war party as they surrounded the hunters and took the eighteen cows that were killed. Little Wolf hurried in to control his young men. But the hunters were standing off, letting the Indians take the guns laid out on the curly buffalo grass, the ammunition too—long cartridges for the buffalo guns and little kegs of powder, lead, bullet molds, and caps. Then the white men shook hands with the chiefs and drove their wagons out through the circle of dark faces. Little Wolf looked after them, sorry that there was no gift of beaded robes or anything at all to give them.

As the warriors pulled the hides from the buffaloes, the women came running with the sun on their knives. Quickly young hump ribs were leaned to roast over the coals for a little feast while the others stripped the dark meat into drying flakes. Far out, all around, scouts watched for the soldiers, the old people against this stop, complaining that they would all be butchered like the buffalo. All except Old Grandmother. With dust and grass in her straggly braids she was making meat with the young women, showing them old ways forgotten because they had the good kettles and other things of the whites so long. Although she had rolled off her drag to die in the grass a few days ago, she rode as well as anybody since, whipping her old mare into a spraddled trot in her haste. "Am I to shame myself as an old woman before my handsome young grandson?" she demanded when the Dog soldier police saw her burn her travois poles to cook meat the morning after Spotted Deer came to help her.

In her gossipy way Old Bear's wife reminded the others that Grandmother was a wicked old woman. Twenty years ago, at sixty, she stole the husband from a young woman's lodge. She could not have been a member of the Only-One-Man society anyway, not since her fourteenth winter. But what really had shamed Old Grandmother's daughters was that she had sent a grandnephew with a fine white-faced horse and a roll of red dress cloth to the man's young wife. "Say I will return her husband when he no longer pleases me. . . ."

But when that happened, the man took his humiliation to the Sioux and never returned. Now, twenty years later, the woman was busy with knife and knowledge, and when the camp started again, she climbed in between rolls of half-dried hide hanging across her horse, the evening sun on her gnarled old face. Sitting Man was riding too, his hide-splinted leg hanging straight down, so there need not be a travois to slow them when the soldiers came again, or to show their scattering path on the fall prairie.

The gathering place was in a big draw back from the flooded Arkansas, with Bull Hump and Woodenthigh signaling the dark way. Silently the Indians came out of the moonless night, the wind cool with the smell of sweetwater, the far sound of a shitepoke making a foolish thumping call in the late summer marshes. Nothing had been seen, but there must be soldier ears down there, waiting for the sound of horses breasting the high water and quicksand. And just beyond lay the iron tracks of the railroad, a watching snake, the one great eye surely ready to break from the night upon them, bringing troops and guns into their helpless illumination.

At a gunshot from down toward Fort Dodge the horses of Bull Hump and Woodenthigh were spurred forward, the rest following toward the dark stream, where so many things had happened to the Cheyennes. All the things that ever happened here were as of today, because what has been done in a place is always there.

Just up the river was the spot sacred to the Great Mother of the Cheyennes, the woman who brought them their plan of government from the far north, carrying it over the wide prairies in the palm of her hand: forty-four chiefs, four each from the ten bands, and four Old Man Chiefs. With this plan she brought also a small son, Tobacco, named for the gift from the Powers. Tobacco grew to be a great old chief and in the white man's 1846 he was shot crossing here. Some soldiers were camped close by and a sentry challenged Tobacco, who understood no *veho* words and kept going through the river that belonged to anyone using it. That one bullet seemed certain to bring death to all on the little islands of whites scattered through the great sea of Indians in the buffalo country.

Dull Knife remembered his night of talking there beside the dead Tobacco, against the Cheyennes suddenly painted for war. He was as angry as the very powerful and very angry Dog soldiers, but to a band chief the people must always come first. So with the hot blood burning in his tong-scarred breast he closed his ears to the throb of the avenging drums and against attacking the few soldiers here. Their bodies would sprout into dark clouds of troops riding. He talked as strongly against carrying the pipe to the Kiowas, Comanches, and Sioux for a great concerted war on the whites, to wipe their tracks from the whole country between the Red River and the villages of the Assiniboin. He could not look on so much bloodshed, and knew too that many Indians would die—his own warrior sons and the small boy who was now Bull Hump, and perhaps his beloved first wife. But those warrior sons were lost anyway, with many, many other Cheyennes, most of them to the soldier bullets, and the wife had died on a tree, because he took the Pawnee woman to his lodge.

Somehow unlimited killing never turned the *veho* officers from their path. Was it because the white man's fighter was not from a home, not returning to his house to eat and sleep and to live as the Indian warrior did, but was a pay man who did nothing but kill? Was it because the stink of all the blood could be kept away from the living, off in the distant forts?

The Sweet Medicine who brought the great gifts to the Cheyennes had warned them what would happen if they let the white-faced ones come among them. If Little Wolf and the other warriors had driven out the whites when Tobacco was killed, it would have prevented the Big Sickness from the forty-niners who ran thick across the Indian country for gold. At a big intertribal dancing here at the Arkansas that summer an Osage fell and died of the cramping cholera. The brother of Old Grandmother here saw this and kicked his horse into a run out around the great Cheyenne camp, crying, "The Dying Sickness has come!" The painted lodges fell as from a great wind on his passing, but soon the women could not wait to pack, running straight for the handiest horses, even wild ones that shied and bucked at the flying skirts and the children sacks that pounded their bellies. Sticking on any way they could, the women whipped to both sides, fleeing.

"Leave the river! The sickness of the whites follows the water!" Old Little Wolf, uncle to the one here now, called out, and the people fanned away toward the hills, escaping even from each other. And all around it was the same, all the tribes scattering, people running north and south and east and west.

But it was too late. Before the Indians were out of the broad cottonwooded valley of the Arkansas, they began to go down. Here one doubled into the cramp and slid from his galloping horse, there another, and for the first time barely a Cheyenne dared help another in trouble. People died all the way to the Cimarron, dropping like worthless bundles or like the buffaloes left behind by the hunters. Even the Keeper of the Sacred Arrows was struck. Calmly he told his wife what must be done. "If everybody is blown away by the wind of this sickness, the Arrows must be taken to a high hill by the last woman among you and laid down there for the time when the Cheyennes shall return to the earth, as Sweet Medicine has promised when he foretold these trials. . . ."

Afterward the Keeper sat there, looking away to the hills until the flies crawled over his eyes unprotested. So the people fled again, his wife running ahead, the Arrow case on her back. When it seemed they must all kill themselves in this flight, even if the sickness could be left behind, a very brave man turned his horse into the moving path.

"Now it is time to meet this enemy who kills the people," he called out, riding back and forth in scalp shirt and paint, his warbonnet blowing.

Gravely he pointed his plumed lance toward the sky and to the earth and all the directions, crying to the Powers to see their helplessness here, and challenging this enemy that struck down everybody. But even then the cholera sickness was in him. Suddenly he bent forward in the saddle, his face dark, and then slid from his horse to die in his wife's arms.

Now the Indians broke again, turning back northward to the river, where they met Cheyennes from the Smoky Hill and beyond, whipping south in little bands too, all frantic as elk herds caught in a surround. So it went until the leaves began to turn and the pooled beds of the streams flowed clear again. Then it was found that about half of the tribe lay dead, their places marked only by the talling grass of the next spring. Since then the Cheyennes were a small people in number.

Now Dull Knife started his horse in the darkness, his grandson riding at his side. They passed the watching Little Wolf and headed for the Arkansas at the wide place, where low, bright stars trailed a vague path of mica dust over the flooding waters. Fearfully the people listened to the first splash, expecting an attack in their helplessness, perhaps bursting balls from the cannon that had been seen at Fort Dodge. But the young men had marked a path through the shifting quicksand with tall willow poles and helped whip the plunging, swimming horses across. Sitting Man was carried over, held high between Little Hawk and another powerful wrestler to keep the flint hide around his broken leg dry, while from the ridges far to each side of the river came the wolf signals and the soft hoots to say there were no soldiers yet, and no strong yellow eye roaring on the iron road. But the people must hurry.

Finally all were across except Old Crow's party and the Bear Rope family. At a little creek beyond the river, fires were already built up by young women who rode with the first of the warriors: Buffalo Calf Road, Bull Hump's Leaf, Pretty Walker, and Hog's Daughter and Singing Cloud, the two friends who were sometimes called They-Talk-with-Nail because they were always laughing with the young warrior. But Little Finger Nail was off west with a party of wild-horse catchers working to get the moccasins out of the cactus without making trouble with the whites up here.

There were a few buffaloes just a little ways off, all they could butcher before the troops came. Little Wolf had men under the old hunter Left Hand guarding the little herd carefully, turning them from far off with some man smell for their snuffling noses, but not enough for a stampede—herding them like the *veho* did his cattle. Scouts watched at the river for soldiers, and to help Comes in Sight and the others across.

It was the older Indians who made the meat, with Thin Elk and his brother helping the women, the younger boys like Yellow Swallow and Red Bird gathering chips for the fires. One fat cow was driven off to a gully and shot there for Comes in Sight's ostracized little party to butcher.

But already they must think of defense. Early in the morning the younger women had gone along Punished Woman Creek to some low breaks around a dry branch. With their butcher knives and the waist axes they dug breastworks overlooking the canyon of Punished Woman and then built the camp in the creek bottoms, the circle of fires pleasant against the shadowing canyon walls, beavers splashing in the glassy ponds, and late blackbirds whirling in clouds against the evening sky as the meat makers came in, a long laden file.

The next day the women roasted meat and pounded it with chokecherries, plums, and sandcherries, easy to carry in half and quarter bladders dipped in hot tallow, and easy to divide when they must scatter. The arrow makers were busy with the kettle of glue that Medicine Woman made. Her hoof glue would hold the feathers solid, but it would take strong medicine if they were to go against guns with nothing but arrows.

But many talked of other things at a secret fire up a dark draw, those related to Black Beaver and the two young southerners killed and those who lost people up ahead there on the Sappa three years ago, the nearness of it heating the blood. And around the camp some began to look with guarded anger at the darkening face of the son of Custer. Yellow Swallow saw it as he had all his boy's life, and slipped away into the shadows, sitting hidden so none would be reminded to cry out against him as bad medicine.

On the streets of Dodge City there was anger too, even though many men showed up who had been counted as dead, and trail herds that were considered lost. But the raiding Indians must be stopped. Colonel Lewis, it was said, considered the campaign shamefully mismanaged. He was taking up the trail on the first train west, and he would wipe out those murdering redskins or leave his body dead on the ground.

6

A Soldier Chief Dead

THE TRAVEL-WORN COUNCIL MET IN THE YELLOW EVE-
ning and considered what must be done. With the
fire roads of the Smoky Hill country and the Platte River to carry the
soldiers, here in the canyons of Punished Woman Creek was the last good
place to stand off an attack until they hit the breaks of the Pine Ridge
standing toward the Black Hills.

The council sat in the midst of village life, for even now the Cheyennes
could not be like the white man's soldiers—so much like their bullet molds
that serve one purpose and then are folded away until another time. Even
such a warrior as Little Finger Nail worked with his soldier society, re-
paired his weapons and regalia, made games for the small boys, sang,
courted the girls, and helped the old women with the horses. Often he sat
alone drawing the picture stories of his exploits in a paper book taken at
a place down south of the Arkansas, his little box of colored pencils from one
of the raids. With yellow and blue and red he made the flying horse herds,
the fights with the bluecoats, himself identified with all the regalia he once
owned, spread in delicate detail and color.

The two days before the soldiers came upon them were much like the
time before the *veho,* with feasting from fire to fire, and gambling, too,
but with the white man's playing cards because the race horses were worn
out and the runners gone on ahead. There was visiting and love-making and
jealousy, yet even the old envies and hatreds were suddenly managed better,
more in the old way. For these two days the Cheyennes seemed almost
whole again, all except Comes in Sight, somewhere alone with her grieving
relatives.

Young Eagle still blew his love flute up on a hillside but with a more
hopeful cadence now because the second daughter of Dull Knife was soft-

eyed and had walked fearlessly through all this time. Other young men went to wait at the water path for the few girls along, to get a teasing word or an earnest one, the girl perhaps laughing, but low, as becomes a Cheyenne maiden, suddenly with the old-time reserve. And there was drumming and a little dancing as the early new moon settled toward the west, thin-horned as a startled young antelope and promising the warm, dry weather of fall.

The second night they built great fires in the center of the camp for there was no use to hide, with their wide trail so plain over the high flat country. No one would have guessed from the way Bear Shield rode in and threw the reins to his young wife that he brought bad news. The soldiers were camped only a few miles back. "Many cavalrymen, and very many walking soldiers in wagons, and other wagons of ammunition. A great angry snake of whites comes against us in the morning, so long that it cannot be seen at one time," the Shield said. "With them rides the officer Lewis who said at Dodge that he would capture the Cheyennes or leave his body on the ground. I listened to the soldiers tell it at the fires."

"There has already been too much shooting . . . ," Old Crier said, speaking into himself, ashamed. Yet it was not decent for man to live so, in flight, always in flight.

After Bear Shield went from Little Wolf, the women stooped over the fine smell of roasting ribs, coffee cooking, and then mixed up all the flour taken below the river for fried bread, the dough twisted around sticks to cook over the coals because there were no frying pans. It was the first good bread in over a year, and as they ate it, slowly, now and then one looked southward into the darkness that was without even the heat lightning that played far off in the west.

Later most of the young men went to the dance fire, an older warrior called Limpy and Thin Elk following along. Perhaps some pretty girl would ask them to join in the dance, the youths said, making an over-boisterous play of it tonight, pushing, laughing.

"Dance? You? So clumsy and awkward! What girl would ask to dance with one who is like the *veho* wagon . . . ?"

"Ahh-h, but I might be very good protection for the marriage lodge," the powerful young Charging Bear boasted.

"There too you would be awkward as the wagon!" another retorted, and was tripped and thrown and ran, shaking the dust from his braids.

Thin Elk was silent in this, pretending he was just looking on, but seeming as hopeful as Limpy, who was drawn to Big Foot's eighteen-year-old daughter as though there had never been the beloved young wife who died in the south. "The Broad-faced One, the laughing one will surely approach you this time in the dancing," the Elk said.

But she was not at the fire and few had the joy for dancing tonight. Yet the camp was barely quiet when there was a cry of excitement near Big Foot's fire. There, where the lodge should have been, were two new horses tied in the dark, two extra ones, a great fortune in these times. People came from all around to see, but no one knew the new horses except young Charging Bear, the son of Big Foot who had seen Limpy catch them today and now offered them toward the family herd as the husband of the Broad-faced One, for the privileges and protection as son and brother.

Before them all the mother took the ropes in acceptance, without the coy waiting for a second offer, a third in a week or a month or a year, the girl pretending that all was as before. No old woman ran to carry good words of the suitor's bravery, particularly in the fight against Crook on the Rosebud, and of his honored family, his own honorable path. No others spoke on this side or that, for across all things of life lay the shadow of a long column of approaching dust.

The Indians had little time or substance for a Cheyenne wedding, but Limpy's friends set the Broad-faced One on a ragged old blanket and carried her to a bare fire in a canyon instead of a decorated, festive lodge. Limpy's mother made the feast for her son's wife, just more young buffalo and nothing else of the old-time feastings that sometimes lasted until the people were fat as prairie dogs in the sun.

Afterward Limpy and his laughing one went to a hillside with a robe. The chastity rope was not untied this night, for they had had little time to become acquainted and a maiden cannot be hurried into good wifehood. Besides, tomorrow would bring fighting, and continence made the warrior's medicine strong.

Some scarcely knew of the little marrying among them. They sat dark and alone at their fires, men like old Spotted Wolf and Bull Hump and Black Horse who was crippled when he fled north from the ironing for Florida, his leg painful tonight. They sent their hearts back to the killing up on the Sappa, three years ago but almost today now, just one long day's travel ahead. And out in the draw the young Dog soldiers made their plans. Whatever happened tomorrow, some must get away to avenge those killings, the death of old Medicine Arrow, the famous chief and Arrow Keeper.

The smoke rose straight and blue from the morning cooking fires in the canyon, with no other sign visible on the prairie above, nothing of the fresh earth where the women dug new rifle pits, a few more pits farther back too, to protect the last little draw of their people's retreat.

Finally Old Crier went slowly through the camp. "The soldiers are seen coming! Everybody make ready to go back behind the breastworks! The helpless ones should gather in the narrow canyons behind them. Nobody need be afraid. Your men are brave!"

Already the pack horses were thundering in, and then the warriors went to make their medicine as well as they could for this stand, with the strong help of Bridge and Medicine Wolf. More horses came in, captured ones, whooped along with waving blankets, those with saddle and collar marks turned over to the women, the horsebreakers taking charge of half a dozen wild ones, manes long and shaggy, the noses round and snorting. It seemed a bad time to break such stubborn stock, but the horses would be needed before another sun, for plainly this would be war.

The helpless ones were taken away, Singing Cloud moving her father there too, sorrowfully, because it seemed his body was strengthening, and now the peace medal was gone from the breast of Little Wolf. Did that mean that she would have to leave her father behind? She saw the young men making the first warrior parade through the camp below her, those with guns holding them up high, even the old flintlock and some for which there were no shells. The women gave their trilling cries and sang strong-heart songs, the Broad-faced One too now, knowing that the soldiers were very many and only seven cartridges stood in the belt of her Limpy for this day.

"One could wish we might run now . . . ," old Moccasin Woman muttered, seeing these few plain, paint-breasted warriors in their ragged leggins, on horses thin and worn. But there was the strength of stone in their faces, and the woman dropped her head in shame that her young grandson in the cradleboard might know her complaint, for sometimes the early things are well known, perhaps even the things heard before the birth.

Swiftly she led her old horse to the deep ravine where they must wait, ready and out of the way of the bullets. She knew a better today here beside Punished Woman Creek, when a young man returned with much glory from a fight with the Kiowas and a girl was chosen as one of the four virgins of his warrior society ceremonials. But he was dead a long time now, and here was their grandson, his mother in the rifle pits, ready to take up a gun or a knife against another kind of enemy, and there seemed no road of any honor at all for this new man-child.

Little Wolf had most of his able men in their places before the mirror signals told the Crier to get the people away into a little half-dry creek. The sun was past the standing feather when the first soldiers came down a gully to Punished Woman Creek, where the stream cut 75 to 100 feet into the sandstone, with narrow willow-clumped bottoms between the beaver ponds and the almost perpendicular walls. Up a dry creek in from the west the canyon branched to several smaller, shallower ones and reached in a long snakehead draw northwestward far out on the prairie. The women and children were hidden in this, the steep slope full of fallen rocks, the narrow bottoms spring-fed and well grassed until the thread of water was lost in the sand.

Just above the junction with Punished Woman one of several steep bluff points pushed in very close to the dry creek bed, narrowing the Indian trail to stony single file, the opposite canyon wall only 100 yards away. Here, on this jutting point, the Indians had a few advance rifle pits overlooking their fresh and inviting trail—the jaw of their ambush, the steel jaw of the trap that would catch the soldiers.

The Dog soldiers had been selected for the ambush pits because they included some southerners, men Little Wolf must keep from running back home. But he was not too easy in his mind. "The time for peace talk with the whites sniffing on our trail is past," he told them. "You should keep hidden up there, let them get past you through this narrow place, and the wagons too, if they climb down into the canyon—let all get past you. When we charge them from the front, you start picking them off from behind, shooting down, stampeding the horses with arrows. Three or four good men who have no arms will hide in the willows close there, to take the guns as the soldiers fall, and set fires in the narrow place to close it. Bear Shield will listen to the *veho* words there and lead."

"*Hou! Hou!*" the warriors shouted. "Let us go!"

But Little Wolf was not done. "My friends, you must remember to wait.

You are brave, but there are excitable young men here who have seen little fighting. Even warriors with many coups have spoiled a surround by getting overanxious, shooting too soon. We have lost great men because a decoying was spoiled by foolish boys. But this time we are not just a war party that can run away. Our helpless ones are back in that far canyon. Hold yourself!"

The wagons kept up on the prairie, trying to get around the canyons, or down, the string of them creeping like a long gray worm, some spilling, the mules whipped, but moving all the time, heading around behind where the Indians waited. In the canyon the soldiers must have known that they were getting close, for the trail was broad and plain, the horse droppings very fresh. One of the scouts stopped at the deserted Cheyenne camp and knelt to scrape at a fire hole and waved the officers up. Then, with the flag flying before them they came fast down the west side of Punished Woman, the scouts 300 yards ahead, with Amos Chapman, the one-legged man the Indians all knew, up in front.

At the head of the dusty blue column rode the soldier chief Lewis. He sent no flankers out,[1] so little did he value the power of the Cheyennes, although the main body of Indians was already plain for everybody to see up ahead, standing around their farther rifle pits. Little Wolf, Tangle Hair, and Hog passed the far-seeing glass among themselves. And between them and the soldiers was the ambush place that looked like any other empty bluff but was a lance head pointed against the trail the soldiers were following so fast now.

But even before the scouts got near to the ambush, one of the young agency Cheyennes suddenly became very hot to fight, and before he could be stopped, he fired. The excited shot missed, but the report echoed through the canyons, and a cry of sorrow and fear went up from the watching women as the little blue puff of smoke rose from the ambush pits and spread into the clean afternoon air.

There was shouting and pointing along the bottoms below, the horses plunging, the scouts falling back. The troops, although still out of range, broke back too, scattering as they sought a place to climb out of the canyon. When it was done, they charged along the top of the bluff toward the ambushing warriors and caught them in a cross fire with the scouts down in the bottoms, the smoke blowing thick over the point.

The Indians tried to fight there a while, but finally they had to run. Little Wolf sent a fast, whooping charge out past the soldiers to cover the flight, a careful charge, the warriors hanging to the far side of their horses with the moccasin toe over the back, and by a knee under the belly rope or an arm through the neck loop, shooting a little with the gun barrels leveled through the flying manes. The ambushers had to be saved, but Little Wolf was so angry at the decoying spoiled that he had his saddle whip ready for the foolish one. The young man took the sharp cut across the face and then stumbled off to sit on the ground alone, his arm up to hide the raw welt and the shame.

Little Wolf was angry with himself too. It was not all the fault of the young man. Many here had done very little fighting—some grown ones knew less of it than a boy at his first fasting did in the old buffalo days.

The little Cheyenne charge was turned back very easily by the flying blizzard of bullets, most of the warriors luckily hidden by the smoke that rolled over toward them. But just as they got out of range, the man ahead of Limpy let his wrist slip from the loop of mane and went down, dead, the horses behind jumping his crumpled body. Three soldiers went down too, one of their frightened horses running in among the Indians, the troopers retreating to reorganize and then coming again, charging along the middle bluff, the one that jutted out between the ambush point and the horseshoe of rifle pits around the canyons where the people were hidden. The Indians fought their best to prevent this advance to within two hundred of the *veho* yards of their position, where bullets could hit all around the pits now, even Little Wolf keeping down. There was no ammunition for another charge against what had happened so quickly because one foolish shot spoiled a very good plan.

By this time the long wagon train had moved up around the canyons pointing westward and circled to a corral out on the open prairie, and men thick as a buffalo herd spread out from the wagons. Now the watching Indians had to see the cavalry on the ridge before them dismount, the horses taken away to safety, and so they knew that this time the soldiers did not plan to run. Colonel Lewis really would catch the Cheyennes, as he had promised at the Arkansas.

Already the soldiers were moving again, firing under their smoke while a company of infantry with their long, far-shooting guns was sent out around the Indians and across the dry creek, to close in on the bluffs along the other side, seeking what had seemed well hidden—the women and the pony herd. One of the scouts there shouted and waved his hat toward a little pocket full of horses loaded with packs, ready. Sharpshooters began to drop bullets among them, the dust spurts creeping closer until the horses began to jump, breaking loose, going down, the Indians knowing it was happening, having to see it and helpless, the women crying from their watching place, the goods of many lost, their whole way of flight.

As the afternoon lengthened, the wind died and the soldiers began to close in, coming on foot from both sides against the last little canyon and the pits above it until they had the Indians almost encircled, the women and children in the trap too, with the smoke standing high on both sides of them until it became two creeping walls with shooting underneath. Now and then Colonel Lewis could be seen riding among his dismounted troops. His horse, a strong bay gelding, let the bullets of Left Hand and Little Hawk strike all around, not even jumping much when he was hit to lameness. The men close to the soldier chief motioned him down too, but he just kept pointing them toward the Indian position. It was a strong thing to do, and very hard for the Cheyennes to watch with their children there ahead of his guns.

In the pits the men were being struck as the soldiers got up higher and Little Wolf knew they must move or be killed right there. Slowly, under the smoke and roaring of the guns, returned only now and then by a shot or two, the fighting women crept back and then the men, back under the lengthening shadows of the standing smoke. So they were driven to their last half circle of rifle pits, the ones that protected the huddle of frightened women and children and the few horses down behind the shadowing canyon, with the walking soldiers on the other side, close. It was all Brave One and Feather on Head could do to hold the helpless people from running, haranguing them as Cheyenne women had in other desperate times.

"Will you shame your brave men?—Make the place they are dying to defend only a foolish empty sack, the treasure dropped out?"

Truly it was time for every Cheyenne to make a stand to the end, but Black Coyote, Whetstone, and Black Horse with some others were not willing to wait so. They prepared to charge out afoot, into the guns. "We will not sit here and let them come to shoot us like rabbits in their holes!"

"No!—nor live to see them burn our families in the fires of our goods like on the Sappa! Better to die fighting!"

And when they were done with their paint and preparation, the women came to stand beside them, his wife with Black Horse, Whetstone's sister beside him, and Buffalo Calf Road with Black Coyote, a gun in her hands, ready, the baby tied securely to her back, to fall with her.

But old Black Crane came running in protest. "No, no!" he shouted. "You must not throw yourself away like that!" And when they did not hear him, he stepped solidly into their path, his bow strung, Hog, the big broad man, beside him, the two putting themselves against the scarred breasts of these determined men.

So Black Coyote and the others fell back, sullenly, the crippled Black Horse finally too. Others talked of sending a few people out, young men and women, but back, to slip up the long snakehead draw that reached for miles out to the northwest. "We must help a few strong ones save themselves, to preserve the seed of our people, so we need not end here."

That, too, Little Wolf would not permit. He was making a round of the last few holes, steadying the men. "Do not shoot now, my friends," he said. "Wait, keep down. Something may happen," repeating it like a medicine chant, over and over, a little like a drumming. "Wait—wait—"

But it was hard to hold the warriors now, with the soldiers on three sides, running in, falling, firing, sending dirt into the faces of the Indians, who could only cower in the pits. For a while Little Wolf sat looking over the patch of ground left to the Cheyennes, and Tangle Hair beside him saw that he was like a bear again, as he had been the day of the attack on Dull Knife's winter village on the Powder. He was a cornered bear now, waiting; not like a man at all but like a grizzly bear, fierce, fearless, ready to lunge, to slash and claw. Then some of the soldiers got very close and started to come up the side of their bluff, with Colonel Lewis not far behind, still on the lamed horse, driving his men on. So Little Wolf spoke, not snarling as Tangle Hair had expected from his pale twisted face, but gently.

"Now fire, my friends," he said softly, making the explosive downward sign with his hand, the Indian sign for *kill*. "Now fire, and let every shot bring down a man."

The guns exploded, the big ones from the buffalo hunters roaring like a thousand bulls in the canyons. Some of the white men fell; it looked like the soldier chief was among them, but none could know for sure in the smoke and dust and confused running back, the Indians whooping, wishing they could chase the fleeing now. But there were all those fresh soldiers over around the wagons waiting their turn, ready, cartridge belts heavy at waist and shoulder. And soon the troopers reformed and came again, always again, their shadows lengthening ahead of them on the prairie.

In the pits there was no talking now, not even from the garrulous Little Hawk and Thin Elk. They brushed the spurting sand from their eyes and kept down. "Always we must keep down!" the furious Black Coyote snarled while others sang their death songs, quietly, with more and more wounded among them, one suddenly hit in the forehead so he stopped with his mouth half open in the chant and then fell.

Now some of the older men came to Little Wolf. "Friend, we ask that you let us give up," they said earnestly. "We will all be killed. We cannot fight or run any more. Give up."

"Give up—!" the chief roared against them, the hoarseness of the grizzly in his voice now.

But he was silent when he saw some of the council members coming with the white bedspreads fastened to the two long medicine lances, the white fringed spreads that Bull Hump's Leaf and Dull Knife's eldest daughter had worn for the dances two days ago.

"We are ready to hold up the white signal," the men said. "We wish to make a talk with the soldier chief. Perhaps he will take pity on us."

"Pity!—They gave us pity on the Sappa!" Black Horse shouted angrily against them, running up in his limping. "Our Good Man who carried the white flag that day was shot down like a mad wolf, the women and children dug out of their hiding holes and thrown on the fires of their lodges. . . ."

"We say give up. . . ."

"The stench of the people burnt that day will never be lost from the nose of the Cheyennes! Will you add another such time?"

"We say give up—"

But Little Wolf was silent, pressing his arm to the Chief's Bundle against his ribs, wondering how he could go against them all, all except Dull Knife. At least the one he called brother was not in this.

But before he must make a reply, Bear Shield came slipping out of the rocky, shadowed canyon close to the soldiers, the late sunlight touching his hair as he climbed over the rim.

"You hit the soldier chief!" he called to them from far off. "The big officer Colonel Lewis!" having to repeat it, although the gunfire had almost died.

Everyone lifted the ear now, knowing the Shield's power with the *veho* words.

"Yes, it seems Lewis is very bad wounded."

It must be true, for the troops were falling back. Stretcher-bearers came to carry several men out to the ambulances that moved up close through their shadows spreading far along the ground, Lewis surely among them. Others walked as with wounding, or were helped. By the time the dusk from the canyons had reached out over the rifle pits and all the flat prairie, most of the soldiers were gone to the wagons. The white bedspreads for the truce were gone too, their shadow lost in the sheltering gloom, their story to be forgotten so long as one man of those who would raise the white signal lived.

In the light of the thin westering moon Little Wolf went down to walk among his people, scattered in the rocks of the canyon slope. Some had crawled away into holes, or were covered with leaves and dead brush and afraid to come out even to his soft call. At last he had everybody collected as well as could be done without making too much movement for the listening scouts.

"My friends," he said, "we must try to get away from here, reach home without more fighting or else we will all be killed. We must go fast now."

But it would be hard, with all those horses down there lost and about sixty more, many with the women's packs in a canyon too close to the soldiers. Some of the young men would stay back to see if these could be taken, but one must not hope. Many would have to walk now, very many. Yet if they were silent as the night that they slipped past the soldiers back at the place of the Standing Lodges, they could escape once more.

This time the early setting of the little moon helped hide the people creeping up the snakehead draw. But many had been wounded, and two good men were left dead, covered with a few rocks, none of the people keening for their warriors, so necessary was it that they be not heard. At least one woman and her son were lost in the darkness of getting away— no one knew where—and the father of Singing Cloud, too. When the girl went to his hiding place, there was only the mark of his thin old body left for her searching hand and finally for the twist of lighted grass she risked. So he had returned to the earth. Crying a little, softly, the girl followed the others. One young man was gone too, seen to slip around toward the south alone. They let him go. It was the one who fired the foolish shot and spoiled the decoy.

By the next morning the weary, footsore Cheyennes were far away, turned from a white-man place by sign left for them where Comes in Sight had passed. The band was hidden in a narrow draw cut deep through the flat country, so cleanly cut that it could barely be seen until its steep walls dropped away before the foot. They were butchering a few beeves there from a ranch herd to help replace some of the freshly dried buffalo, the bladders of pounded meat, the hides, the moccasin leathers prepared so carefully and still in the packs on Punished Woman Creek. Some scouts crept in during the morning. The people lost back there in the night could not be found, not even a fresh moccasin track. Perhaps they were hidden, afraid. The soldiers made a lot of shooting this morning. The sixty horses the Indians left behind were killed with a great echoing in the canyons, the smoke cloud rising like a thunderhead into the air, much of it from the packs that were piled and burned. Then the scouts had taken the Indian trail, leading the soldiers fast upon it.

Ahh-h—

Toward noon two more men were suddenly there among them. It was Howling Wolf and the Roman Nose with the medicine eyes, bringing news. When the long pipe had gone around, Howling Wolf spoke. The ambulance of Lewis had been followed to the crossing of the Smoky Hill on the way to Fort Wallace. They had slipped up to hear that Colonel Lewis was very bad hurt, bleeding from the leg, it seemed—such a wound as only a medicine man like Bridge could cure.

Old Bridge made a grave murmuring to hear this. He would gladly have traded his powers to the soldier chief for the safety of his people. But such things cannot be between enemies, although he did not feel like an enemy to anybody now.

Roman Nose had followed the sick wagon a little farther. "The man who said he would catch the Cheyennes or leave his body on the ground is dead," he added.

There was not a *"Hou!"* from anyone to this, only a slow getting up and going among the people to prepare them for more running.

7

Sappa—Meaning Black

AFTER THE ESCAPE FROM THE SOLDIERS ON THE PUNISHED Woman, some things were done that would not be brought to the tongue so long as a Cheyenne lived. Even among themselves the names would not be spoken, as the names of those killed near there in the Sappa fight three years before were not used except when adopted by a grieving one, in honor.

The 1875 trouble had started from a bad year too. The winter of 1873–1874 was like frozen rain upon a whole nation of naked people. Even the whites, with all their goods, their guns, fire trains, plows, and great herds of beef, were dying in the roads of their great cities. Dull Knife and Little Wolf heard the bone hunter tell this to the chiefs at Red Cloud Agency. He said the banks, the places of the white man's money, were slamming their iron doors against the owners of it. Those with work for the people had locked it away, and those with food shut their doors too, against the hungry.

"It seems strange that a man would think the Powers made the good things of the earth for just him and maybe a few, only a few, of his own people," Little Wolf had said thoughtfully, trying to understand these whites with whom the Cheyennes must learn to live.

It seemed the whites were making no such effort. True, the Secretary of War complained the Indians were given insufficient provisions, and General Miles, who whipped the southern Indians to their hungry agencies, said, "The strong, industrious but degenerating tribe of Cheyennes proves the folly of the fruitless experiments and vacillating policy that has governed them for the past twenty years."

But the general policy was for extermination. The Indian and his treaties stood in the way of progress. Custer headed into the Black Hills where by treaty no white man was to go, looking for gold to help raise money for another railroad, a fire road to thunder up the Yellowstone, the last of the great buffalo grounds. In the south the Medicine Lodge treaty had promised to keep the buffalo hunters out. The Arkansas River was patrolled by a few men, but the hide hunters shot their way across it and on to the Cimarron and the Canadian. It was the same with the Kansas law against the buffalo hunters, the Indians thought, not knowing that the act was never signed or that Grant had vetoed the same bill for the territories. So everywhere the hide hunters crept up the wind to the great herds, their heavy guns set on forked sticks, the boom and the smell of the blue smoke carried away as they worked, the plain darkened with dead animals that dropped suddenly, perhaps kicking a little, sometimes the buffalo nearby turning their shaggy heads to peer curiously through the little, hair-blinded eyes, and then eating again, snuffling, grunting their way into the wind. Finally a shift in the wind direction or a crippled one turning into the herd brought the smell of danger, of man or blood and sent thousands of thin, rope-ended tails up as the buffalo broke into a run, the earth thundering under their hoofs, the herd one dark, swift-flowing robe before the blackbirds could rise from their backs.

So the southern warriors undertook the agreeable fight against the hide hunters. But it was called raiding and soldiers came thick as grasshoppers that bad year of 1874. Little Robe, the southern chief who struck Dull Knife down with his quirt back there at the agency, was promised that the hunters and horse thieves would be kept out of Indian Territory, while at home his horses were stolen and his son, who went after them, was badly wounded by the soldiers. The angry warriors charged the agency, the agent fled, the soldiers came and stayed, setting up Fort Reno where no soldiers should ever walk.

Some of the angry Cheyennes went with a Comanche bulletproofing man in an attack on the buffalo hunters at Adobe Walls. Six of these were killed, and the rest rode silently away. For revenge they shot a surveyor and his helpers measuring the Indian country for the whites and then attacked an emigrant train up on the Smoky Hill trail where Colonel Lewis died. They took four captives, the captives that make trouble, as the northerners down there for a visit predicted. "We were a small people and good captives made us more, so now there is scarcely one among us who is not enemy by blood," Little Hawk, the joker, once said.

But the whites did not laugh. Soldiers came and the two smaller, weaker of the Germaine sisters were left behind for them. Still the troops gave chase, so not even the northern visitors could get past them to go home. Finally the Southern Cheyennes surrendered, the two white girls dressed in blankets and moccasins like the rest. The Indians were disarmed and dismounted and put into a prison camp near the new Fort Reno. Everybody who ever felt the power of a Cheyenne war charge could see them look whipped now. Spring ran in a pale greening along the sunny slopes, but there was no joy among them. One day soldiers lined up all the men, from youth to blind old age, in a double row through the camp. Then the two older Germaine girls, fifteen and seventeen, came. Dressed like visiting white ladies, with plumed hats and dark red cloaks bought by General Miles, they walked stiffly down the line pointing this way and that, and with them went a Mexican who had been around the Cheyenne camps too.

Back a ways, where the Indian women watched, a moaning and crying started up, a keening as for the dead. The northern Brave One saw men great in war and in peace taken from the line to be ironed and hauled away to a far stone prison. It was done on just the finger pointing by the two that the Indians considered foolish children, not women as Cheyennes would be at that age. Surely no soldier chief, no men among the whites would be judged guilty of any wrong because two such children walked along a row and pointed here and there while General Neill sat red-faced and unsteady on his horse overseeing the picking.

The double row of ragged Cheyennes, gaunt and poor, stood unmoving, the braids barely stirring on their breasts as the girls whispered coyly together, their sharp eyes running along the men and beyond, to the watching women. So honored men like Medicine Water were selected— some of them the Old Man Chiefs of the southerners, some who had worked hard for peace even when there was only the stink of the buffaloes left. Finally one of the girls pointed beyond to the watchers, to Mochsi, the warrior woman.

"She helped!" they both cried. "She helped kill our family!"

So Mochsi was put with the group of men held by the bayoneted long guns. Brave One was very angry that nobody told how Mochsi became a warrior woman—because at Sand Creek all the men of her lodge were wiped out, and later her cousins and her new husband too, so there was only Mochsi to carry the gun of her grandfather, a present from two gold seekers he had saved from starvation on the Smoky Hill trail. Now Mochsi was standing there for the irons.

By evening fifteen Indians were selected, and with anger and impatience Neill cut off eighteen more men from the right end of the line to make the thirty-three Cheyenne prisoners General Sherman had ordered. Neill would proceed with the identification some other day and release any found innocent, substituting proved offenders.[1]

Then the Germaine girls were hurried away in the carriage, for it was seen that some women had their long butcher knives out of their belts.

Three days later the whites brought chains fastened to cannon balls, a roaring forge, and an anvil to pound the chains to the legs of the prisoners. Soldiers ordered all the people back to their shelters. They stood there, watching, angry, sullen, some furious that the prisoners let the ironing be done easier than horses accept the fire-heated shoes. When they got to the younger men, the women lifted their voices in scorning, particularly against Black Horse, who had counted more coups than any other warrior there.

"Where will we get fathers worth giving sons to?" the women taunted. "We see there are no men among you worth taking to our beds!"

This was bold talk, bold Sioux and Comanche woman talk, and heating to the blood. When the hammer slipped and hit his ankle, Black Horse could endure no more. Powerfully he struck the blacksmith aside and ran toward the Cheyenne camp. Half a dozen infantrymen pursued him and fired several volleys after him, hitting his leg, most of the bullets striking into the camp, women and children falling, crying, scattering like leaves in a whirlwind. A woman and her three children were left like bundles on the ground, but the hurt ones were helped as the arrows came back thick. Some of the soldiers were hit, and while they retreated, Black Horse was dragged away by the many friends he had saved in battle. Then the cavalry came galloping out of Reno and the Cheyennes fled to a little sandhill in the bend of the river, the older Dog soldiers helping the women and weak ones, while the younger men ran ahead to dig up some guns hidden before the disarming. There were only a few, and little ammunition, but not everyone need die with empty hands.

While they scooped out holes in the sand, Black Horse dragged his bleeding leg from one to another. "Hold fast! Fight hard!" he said, and sang:

> The women will see they still have men
> To father their sons!
> We will not sit in chains!
> It is better to die fighting.

Two hundred and fifty men, women, and children cowered on the choppy little hill under cavalry fire, three companies by now, with two Gatling guns dragged up fast.[2] The Indians dug like badgers to get below the blanket of driving bullets that came from all around, very close, and kept coming, the ear deafened by them, their wind lifting the hair, the smoke shutting off all that the soldiers did, even on the north where the flooded Canadian cut into the sandy hill. For the first time Cheyennes had let themselves and their families be completely surrounded, and in a place smaller than a village ground where the soldiers could come charging over them any beat of the heart. Some of the women were so afraid they had to be held or tied down. It seemed they must stand up into the thundering fire, try to run, if only to go down quickly.

Then there was a trumpet's thin call and the three companies of cavalry attacked from all around, charging up the steep, smoke-drifted slopes. But the footing was too loose and the horses too easily hit with the arrows and the few guns of the Indians. They retreated and came again, afoot through the smoke, sneaking from bush to weed or up a little brush-filled gully. The bullets drove the sand upon the Indians like frozen sleet whipped by a blizzard; the thunder of the Gatling guns hammered the shaking earth, women screaming as they were hit. One Indian was killed trying to see down to shoot, then another, and a third, and many more wounded until there was a terror and crying in the sandy hilltop such as no Cheyenne had ever heard from his people. One strong warrior could not stand it. He would not have his children live this life, even if they could be spared by surrender now. With the little one in his arms he started up into the bullets, but his wife flung herself against him. In the struggle the baby was shot, and while the woman moaned over it, the man arose, arms folded across his naked breast, and was knocked straight backward, almost cut in two, so suddenly red.

The spring clouds thickened. At early dark the shooting stopped and the troops withdrew to the foot of the hill, settling to a ring of little fires, watching. While some Indians crept out to strip the meat from the dead soldier horses, a couple of scouts who knew some *veho* words got close to the soldiers. There were nineteen whites wounded, they heard, and entrenching tools and food and ammunition were being brought over from the fort. The Indians would be starved out.

"It will not take long, with no water for the wounded . . . ," Bad Heart, the holy man, said.

No, and daylight would bring a strong charge.

When the women dared move again, they made little lights of twisted grass. With these the men went around the holes in the sand to see what had been lost: those left dead in the camp down there and six men here, with two people missing, one an old woman who had been very much afraid—twelve good people without even as much as a stone to keep the wolf away.

While the horse meat was roasting, the medicine man and his wife made their curings, with Black Horse the worst, perhaps hurt too bad. But there was something good. Black Hairy Dog slipped in from north of the river, from his father, Medicine Arrow, who had not surrendered because he carried the Sacred Arrows. Now the Keeper was hidden in the blackjacks and broken country only two travois days northwest, up the river. He was waiting to see what happened to the people who came in, to Medicine Water and Grey Beard and the other old chiefs who were not coffee coolers.

"They are used up—with irons on their legs, as they tried to put on Black Horse here. . . ."

Irons on Medicine Water and the others? Ahh-h! It was good they stayed out. They had only about forty men, but their women and children were strong so they had managed to escape the soldiers and live during the winter. Now they had enough meat and horses to carry themselves and these here to their relatives north, if it was carefully done.

No one asked if they would go. Black Horse had spoken for them all in his song that afternoon, even though it was two travois days away and they were afoot, bad hurt, and the soldiers would ride fast. Here they were already caught. So they started—the fourth flight of the Cheyennes to the north.

Silently, under the light patter of spring rain, the Indians crept through the sentinels, waded the hip-deep river, and scattered. They were cold and wet, poorer than even after Sand Creek, with not one horse and only the little fresh horse meat. But traveling so light they could go fast, and the rain that chilled them washed their passing from the places of their moccasins' touch.

The next morning, the seventh of April, General Neill reported that 167 warriors with their families had escaped and were joined by some still out, perhaps 250 warriors all together, and their families. They were being pursued.

Once more the Cheyennes climbed the ladder of the east-flowing streams, going in small parties, keeping away from the whites. They were peaceful, and the Sacred Arrows must never be exposed to trouble except in a regular war party after the carrying ceremonials of the pipe. Medicine Arrow had given the crippled Black Horse a handsome golden pinto marked in the Keeper's own medicine way with four straight tattoo lines like arrows on the jaw. No horse so marked had ever been shot.

Soon after the escape the soldiers had come close enough to be seen, but the Indians scattered and got away, remembering the time six years ago when they let Custer's Monahsetah come to the camp and make the good promises of peace. Medicine Arrow had been cautious even then, and called the council with the Long Hair in the sacred lodge. There, while Custer promised them his peace forever, the Keeper smoked the pipe under the Arrows and, in the ceremonial of truthtelling, emptied the ashes on Custer's boots, to bring death to the one who breaks the promise of peace spoken here.[3] After the Indians started to the agency behind Custer, the general called a council with a trap. Medicine Arrow escaped, but three men sent to look were taken, to be hung unless the Indians gave up their white captives right away. These were with another band, but Medicine Arrow got them freed, and then Custer kept his three prisoners, took them up to Kansas where two were killed and the other wounded. Now six years later there was this ironing and killing again, after the Cheyennes came in on another promise of peace and safety. Truly it was better never to be caught.

The newspapers reported that eight hundred Cheyennes and Arapahos used the old Dull Knife crossing of the Arkansas on April 18, 1875, going north. Troops from Dodge chased them, but the Indians scattered. "Bloody work may be expected."

When the Indians got up toward the Republican River, they found signs of big camps, surely the hungry Sioux and Cheyennes from Red Cloud, trying to get a little meat. The buffalo were very wild, only a scattering alive among the carcasses left by the white hunters, who seemed gone now, with the robes thin and shedding with spring. The Cheyennes found one of their drying camps still used, with nobody around. They carried away the ammunition and some flour and coffee to the people that were scattered along the forks of the Sappa, the creeks brushy and black with beaver dams. They had scouts out on the trail south. Any soldiers from the north would know that this was Cheyenne hunting ground by treaty. With the weather suddenly rainy it was a good time to stop a while, old Medicine Arrow said, a time to heal the wounded, a good time for them all to rest and warm the knees and grow quiet and good in the old way.

"Ahh-h, it is a fine thing to live peacefully . . . ," Bad Heart said as he rubbed the dried willow bark for his pipe, sniffed it before he mulled the bits with a little tobacco in his palm, and then set the fire stick to the bowl.

But the next morning, the twenty-third of April, a lot of white men charged out of the fog upon Medicine Arrow's camp, shooting into the few lodges with the heavy buffalo guns, some bluecoat soldiers riding among them. The warriors ran out of their shelters and sleeping holes, many half naked, grabbing up guns and bows, some heading toward the nearest horses. But there was already shooting up around the herd.

Then Medicine Arrow came from the sleeping robes, his gnarled old legs still bare below his shirt, but he had slapped on his buffalo-horned feather headdress that trailed back to the ground, to show who he was, the representative of Sweet Medicine, the Keeper of the Sacred Arrows. He ran out with Bad Heart just behind, shouting back to the women, "Do not be afraid, my sisters," as he waved the white cloth. "Nothing bad has been done by us. We will make a talk with the soldier chief."

Then, walking in dignity, even as he was, he called his greeting to the white men: *"Hou! Hou,* my friends!" his right hand raised with the cloth of parley, his left one up also, palm out in the sign of peace and friendship of the Plains Indians. So Medicine Arrow went through the fog and smoke and bullets that did not stop coming, on toward the soldier chief * watching from a higher place. Many Indians watched too, but the buffalo guns kept roaring, echoing like cannon over the little snake bend of the Middle Sappa and against the low bluffs beyond. Men went down behind him, but for a while it seemed the medicine of the Arrows was indeed strong

* Lt. Austin Henely, April 23, 1875.

that the Keeper could walk so, but finally he seemed hit, and then he fell, going forward on his face, the white cloth blowing back against a fallen lodge in the smoke.[4]

The women saw this and started running every way, grabbing their children, fleeing down to the brush of the creek, where they were met by shooting too, then up over the little ridge behind the camp, but there a row of men lay with their big buffalo guns kicking out fire and smoke.

By now some of the Indians had got away toward the pony herds. The rest made a charge afoot, led by Bad Heart, the man who had ridden through the whites on the island in the Beecher fight seven years ago. They drove the hunters back a ways before the Heart and the warriors in the front fell and the rest had to retreat behind a little bank in the weeds. But now some soldiers were beginning to shoot. The Indians got two of these as they held them off so the wounded Black Horse could gather the women and lead them into a washout, where the young men had their sleeping holes. There they dug very fast, cutting the holes deeper under the bank to get the children away from the bullets. Before long Medicine Arrow's wife came crawling through the smoke from her hiding, with the Arrows safe on her back.

"I am putting the sacred duty upon you, my children," she said to Black Hairy Dog and his wife as she divided the Arrows between them. "Now you must get away, both of you, even if you are the only ones of the people saved. Do not stop to help anyone. You must go different ways and run very hard to the faraway safety of the north country."

With the Arrows tied stoutly to their backs, and without a look to where the feathers of the dead Keeper's headdress were blowing on the fighting ground, or toward each other, Black Hairy Dog and his wife crept out into the weeds and smoke. First one went, and then the other, so the Sacred Arrows might not all be destroyed, for these men would not preserve them as the time they were lost to the Pawnees. The whites would burn them, in the white-man way.

When the Keeper's old wife saw they were gone, she slipped back to the fighting, and not even Brave One tried to hold her from this death. Several times now the Indians tried to reach Medicine Arrow and the others who fell in their first fighting, but the Indians were shot down as fast as they came out over the bank. It was not only that they wished to save the Keeper and the others, wounded and dead, but those first men had carried their only good guns and most of the ammunition. Without guns they could not even avenge the fallen, already over thirty people.

"We have to get away!" the crippled Black Horse said. "Keep them shooting, so as many as possible can slip out into the smoke."

There were almost no shells left now, and no arrows, so all the men could do was jump up and be shot at, hoping to get down too fast for the bullets. Some good people were lost that way, including three young women who jumped too. One made a song for it:

> Earth have pity, Sky, see your daughters!
> It is a good day to die!

So she fell too, and was laid to the side, her blood mixing with the rest in the muddy bottom of the washout.

Several times small parties with flags of truce came out but were shot as soon as their heads rose into sight below the fluttering white cloth. Once a lot of women, most of those left now, came out with the last piece of white they had, all rising together. There were so many, about the number of three times the fingers, that for a moment no bullets came. The women separated two ways, running for the soldiers and the others, as though to surround them, capture them in the old-time woman's capturing, but the guns started again and they were brought down, one man yelling, "Hell! They's women!" as Sorrel Deer's dress was cut open by the bullets in the falling, her brown breasts laid bare to the smoke and stench.

Then for a long time there was almost nothing, not a moving from the washout, and finally one of the hunters began to shout, "Hell, them damned Indians's just playin' dead waitin' till night. I had me a brother killed by them lousy bastards around here only couple weeks ago. I don't aim to let one damn nit get away!"

With a revolver in each hand he took a running jump into the hole, firing right and left. The few women left alive got him, hacking him with their butcher knives until he was a part of the blood and mud soaking their moccasins. Now there was the order to charge the washout and the soldiers came from below, their guns going fast, and the hunters from above, jumping into the hole. Almost at once there was not even a woman with a butcher knife left. And when the white men climbed out of the place, only one had a wound.

Afterward some threshed the brush and weeds for any children who might have crept away, while others gathered willows and built great fires. The lodges were thrown on these, the robes from the shelters, the saddles—all the goods, and the bodies of the Indians too, except the head-men, stripped bare on the prairie. Then there was suddenly one more Cheyenne to kill, an old man in a warbonnet, coming on horseback. He had got away, but all his family lay back there on the ground, and when he saw from a ridge what the whites were doing to them, he charged back down, riding hard into the buffalo guns that suddenly roared out together. He fell, seeming to be tossed a little by the bullets, as if he were light enough for the wind.

His body went upon the fire too, swung in by two hunters who shouted, "Houp! Houp! Houp!" and let go. Then while the smoke and smell of burning flesh spread along the Sappa Fork, the hunters dug out more women and children, clubbed them, and threw them into the fire.[5]

Scattered behind a little cut bank away along the creek, Black Horse and some others watched, silent, with no words for this that was done down there.

"It has happened that now a man must let them put irons on his feet!" Black Horse cried at last. "Iron balls!—or he will bring such destruction upon all his people!"

And as he spoke, his face was like a dark bluff washed by rain.

That night the snow swept over the smoldering camp, but the wounded and the broken had to keep running. By the middle of May the scattered ones and the other camps from the Sappa were reaching their northern relatives, even those who went back with Medicine Arrow's headdress and spear that had been rescued in the fight. They found his body, unburnt, and put it into a bluff across the creek, dressed properly, with blanket and horned bonnet. They took Bad Heart to another place and then did what they could for the burnt ones too.

It was reported that fifty men and their families were seen on the Cheyenne trail going toward White River in western Nebraska, and a week later the agent at Red Cloud wired that all the Cheyennes who escaped their agency in Indian Territory had reached the north. Black Hairy Dog and his wife came there too, neither knowing if the other lived until they met in the camp of Little Wolf and Dull Knife on the Powder.

There was little in Lieutenant Henely's report of the Sappa fight to reveal the victory of his troops with the buffalo hunters: The Indians had refused to surrender; two soldiers were killed and twenty-seven Indians—nineteen men, eight women and children; the lodges burned and one hundred thirty-four ponies taken. "It is believed that the punishment inflicted upon this band of Cheyennes will go far to deter the tribe from the commission of such atrocities in the future as have characterized it in the past," General Pope wrote that spring.

But there was other talk around the frontier posts. The hunters and the civilian ambulance driver laughed when they heard the official figures, some a little angrily, because it was really a fight of the buffalo hunters, twenty-five of them, but they were ordered to silence by Henely.[6] Still the story of the butchery got out, with varying figures, several of the hunters putting the Indian dead between seventy and a hundred and twenty, mostly women and children, and some not proud of the fact that not one was taken captive, not even an infant or a wounded woman.

One knew something of what had been done: the Cheyenne wife of John Powers, army contractor. Among the trophies of the returning troopers she saw the little bundle that her uncle Medicine Arrow, the great holy man of the Cheyennes, always wore tied in his hair, and his medicine headdress for the Arrow ceremonials, with the little buffalo horns too. She made the mourning ceremonial, keening and crying for three days, knowing that he must have tried to surrender, for his vow demanded that he avoid fighting near the Arrows. She predicted that the officer who refused his flag of truce would be dead within a year. She was wrong; Lieutenant Henely was drowned three years later, July 11, 1878.

By midsummer there was much protest over the ironing and imprisonment of the Cheyennes. Not half of them were proved guilty of any crime, and to the Commissioner of Indian Affairs it seemed only just that the eighteen arbitrarily cut from the end of the line by General Neill be given a trial and, if not guilty, be returned to their friends. But one of the men had already killed himself, another went insane, a venerated old peace chief had been shot while his legs were in irons, and another sang his song every day for three years from the stone prison in Florida:

> Sun, with the great seeing eye,
> When you move westward today, over my wife and baby,
> Speak softly of seeing me
> And my sickness for them and for home.

Now it was three years later and the Black Horse who had cried to see his people thrown into the fires on the Sappa was fleeing through this way again, where it was once more all of today. Spotted Wolf, Brave One, and many others along had been in the Sappa fight, and all were relatives of those who did not get away from the place now called Cheyenne Hole.

Although Medicine Arrow was dead, perhaps it had been the ashes he dropped from the peace pipe over Custer's boots that made them carry him to his foolish end on the Little Big Horn. And some thought that the death of the Arrow Keeper, too, came from that ceremonial. He made war afterward, although not until Custer had killed his men gone to a trapping council. Yet can a bad man's lie ever release a good one from his word?

Now as they neared the Cheyenne Hole country, there was a rising anger and sullenness on the faces of the people, a dark silence upon the southerners and many of the others too. Little Wolf, Hog, Bridge, and even Dull Knife made strong talks for peace. Perhaps they harangued the stronger because they saw the same darkness in their own breasts. All the helpless ones along, all their need for the good heart of the white men of the north spoke for the wisdom of peace, but the ears were closed here.

8   To Make the Bad Heart Good

LITTLE WOLF STOPPED HIS SPOTTED HORSE ON A RISE TO look back over his hurried, worn-out people straggling behind, moving in little parties, many afoot, trying to keep near rough country where they could scatter like mice under leaves. He recalled what the men who came to buy the Black Hills had said: "The Indian is left without protection of law in person, property or life. He has no personal rights. He may see his crops destroyed, his wife and children killed. His only redress is personal revenge."

He thought about this and hoped that something would get them through this country very fast, before some bad things were done. Besides, they must hurry. The troops knew just where the Cheyennes were; even pulling down the telegraph wires told that, and whites lived all over now, whipping their cattle out of the way or standing horseback on some hill to look as the Indians appeared, and then be gone as though fallen off the far side. And close on the trail rode the soldiers of Lewis, led by Mauck, angry as a gut-shot panther.

Other troops that they had not seen were coming from every direction, striking like lances at the trail up ahead. General Dodge was marching toward the Sappa and then down it, two companies of infantry and some cavalry would come down the Little Beaver, while another force would strike the Beaver itself below the junction and then turn on to the Republican to meet Mauck and catch the Cheyennes as in a surround. "The Indians are very tired, push them as vigorously as possible," were their orders.

With all the young men out for horses and scouting, the women were very silent, the Broad-faced One riding as much alone as a thrown-away wife. Little Wolf, too, seemed gone, shut away in a cave, his eyes not moving toward the things around him or toward his wives and the Thin Elk with them. Even the eating from his big horn spoon was like putting one weary foot ahead of the other in the troubled walk of sleep.

As they neared the Cheyenne Hole, Bull Hump and some helpers whooped a small herd of horses out of the chilly sunrise. Among them was a fine spotted yellow with silver mane and tail that made all the southerners, the women too, stop to look under their shading palms. Spotted Wolf went to see. "Yes, this is the one with the jaw marks of the Medicine Arrow, the one he gave to Black Horse, and got lost in the Sappa fight," he said angrily, as the horse let the crippled man take his mane.

The other horses with work marks were given to the women, the strongest to those who must not be overtaken—the families of the headmen who would surely be sent away if caught, perhaps hanged or shot. A fine black with a white patch like a mountain goat skin over his back and white eyes went to Dull Knife's family. The new horse seemed well-broken, even offering his head for the rope halter in Bull Hump's hand, after he had time to examine the smell of the Indian.

But as Short One took the rope, there was signaling from the hills that soldiers were seen coming from several directions to cut the Cheyennes off, and other whites were seen riding very near.

So the women, the old men, and the children worked fast with the packs. Short One got the new horse loaded quietly enough, but his white eyes rolled and there was no time to get him accustomed to her calico skirts blowing in the rising wind, or to a rider mounting from the right, the Indian side. With a hold on the halter rope and the curly black mane she tried to clamber up between the packs. But the horse shied away, jumping. The long hide sacks hit his spotted ribs and he began to buck, the black head down between his knees, his back humping into it. The woman tried to hang to the mane, but she was flung to the side and battered against the packs, back and forth, until her hold was broken, and before her daughters or Leaf or anyone could get to the horse, she went under the bucking hoofs. Almost at once her hand let go of the rope and the horse broke for the hills, bucking the packs to pieces, scattering the goods to blow over the prairie, as Bull Hump and some others came whipping back to help.

The people in the camp ran to the woman, but Dull Knife was already back and off his horse, his face lined and gray as he raised her carefully, for the Short One seemed so caved in, and a string of bright red blood ran from her mouth over his arm.

Bridge came running with his bleeding rattle, making a chanting as he ran, but there was no time now for the long ceremonial, with the signals of chasing soldiers close, and the woman not breathing. So she was put on a makeshift drag of cowskin behind an old mare and then whipped along, the poles bouncing over the rough ground, the people afoot breaking up into smaller groups again, each with a man or a boy carrying a revolver or a bow. But a little string of people followed behind Short One's travois, a file of grief and honor—all those who called her mother, whether their first or their second, and many others too, for now she belonged to them all even more than before.

Now Little Wolf could no longer place caution upon the warriors going out for horses. They must get them today, in daylight, and there would be shooting; besides, with the hearts so bad, foolish things would be done, and with the oath of an Old Man Chief upon him, the wearer of the Chief's Bundle, all the foolish things done would also be his.

When it was plainly too dangerous to carry Short One farther, to hold the people back with a travois, she was taken off to a slope where a shallow hole could be dug in the stubborn ground. Then most of them went on to overtake the band, the urgent signals of the scouts hurrying them. But Brave One and three others stayed behind, dragging a few stones there in the travois, stones red from the pool of blood in the bottom of the hide on which Short One had been carried. With their arms and legs gashed as for a warrior killed in a fight, and with dust and grass in their hair, the four women followed behind the moving people, Dull Knife far back too now. He had not needed to put on the rags of mourning, for rags were all he had, his blanket mended, the holes stitched up by Short One's needle just the night before.

As the old chief rode along, kicking his horse into a little half trot, his moccasin heels drumming on the tired ribs, he thought of all the lost ones of the last three years. "The Beautiful People" Lieutenant White Hat Clark, the friend they hoped to find up north, had called the children of Dull Knife, and Short One had borne some of them. The Beautiful People! And now many of them lay on the earth, scattered from the foothills of the Big Horns to the far south country, in less than two years.

The old man slumped forward a little, so tired he could scarcely sit the Indian saddle, but by habit his hurried heels kept up their drumming as his hands urged the horse on northward, always northward, knowing without turning his head that his sons had put the fleeing aside for a while.

Now the Cheyennes were taking up a new thing, a new way. Never had they attacked a scattered people before, not unless it was in the forgotten time before they crossed the salt sea in the boats made from the long-haired bulls, so long ago. Always within memory it had been an enemy bunched in villages of bark or grass or earth, or the skin lodges of the Plains. Even the war against the whites in 1864 had been made on the trail stations, more like little forts than isolated homes, on the emigrant trains that killed the game and brought the sicknesses, and on the troops that came chasing on Indian lands. This attacking homes with families in them, scattered out alone, this seemed a poor, unheroic kind of war.

But Black Horse would not let the warriors hesitate. "We must not forget our Holy One dead over there on the Sappa! His blood calls to us from the rocks!" he told the excited young men, in reverence still not using the name of Medicine Arrow, nor adding anything of the newly bereaved ones, of Comes in Sight and her people moving only in the darkness, far away from the rest now, of the mourning Dog soldier Bull Hump and his brother Little Hump, and of their father sitting off alone, not smoking, the old chief's eyes turned toward the ground.

"These scattered settlers of the earth houses here, with no fighters, no warriors—" Old Crier said sadly, "they are not fit enemies for a Cheyenne. Do not go near them."

"The soldiers are coming very fast, Uncle, and we must get our horses where we can," Little Wolf replied quietly, but without conviction, even now. He spoke quietly to the others too, the noisy ones. "I cannot find it in my heart to say you Dog soldiers must not avenge your dead, nor any of you who would wipe out the offense to the Arrows. . . ." For a long time the Wolf was silent, looking to the earth before him. "But I will not have any *veho* women and children hurt, and as the bearer of your Chief's Bundle I must advise you to pass these whites all by, harm no one, and take only their horses. Many good people will suffer for every piece of bloody work you do."

But some of the young men were already gone, fanning out in little groups of two and three and coming together in a larger party. Black Horse went too, with only his twelve-year-old son. From the bluff where Medicine Arrow lay in the rocks Black Horse looked down upon the place called Cheyenne Hole. He was on the golden pinto with the tattoo marks of the Arrow Keeper on the jaw. There was still blood down one bright spotted side, the dark dried blood of the white man who had been shot from the saddle last night.

Suddenly the crippled Cheyenne whirled his horse and started down the Sappa, his rifle out of the scabbard, balanced before him, ready, his son following close behind.

The main band was still spread out, the walking ones never stopping because they must catch up while those with horses made the scattering camps, cut wood, and built up the little fires for all. But this hurrying was very hard, and when young Stick Foot came shouting that he had seen a horse loose in a draw, Buffalo Chips and his wife, the parents of Limpy, followed him, hoping they could get their bundles off their backs. As they came out into the bottoms, they ran into some horsebackers with guns. They tried to slip back to the main band, but they had been seen.

"Save yourselves if you can! Get away!" Buffalo Chips shouted.

They dropped the bundles and ran for the brush along the creek, but the cowboys separated into three parts, two cut them off, and the middle ones charged their hiding place. The woman fled up over a bank, bullets whistling past, one hitting a little as she got out of sight. Buffalo Chips had dropped back into the willows to hold the men off a while, and as they spurred up, he rose before them and shot. The cowboy closest slid behind his horse and fired a revolver over the mane. Chips had only an old long pistol with four weak shells. He used them and then ran across a beaver dam, his moccasins squeeging full of blood. For a moment he had to rest, flat on the ground, his breath tearing where the bullets had gone through, but then he pulled himself up. His wife and the young Stick Foot were out of sight, and so he settled himself against the brush and sang his death song. Before he was done, the cowboy came galloping back with a rifle. Buffalo Chips smiled a little and started to lift his hand to show he was not hurting anybody now, but he fell over and was dead.

Afterward the woman and the boy, together, watched the whites ride back in the direction of the coming soldiers. They knew Buffalo Chips must be done, for the men waved something on a rifle that was like a scalp. They wanted to go down to do something for him, but they had to overtake the moving band, the woman limping, hurrying, the boy running ahead at every rise to look over and then signal to her to come.

When Limpy heard what had been done to his father, he left the horse catchers, exchanged his rope and revolver for a rifle and a handful of cartridges, and then rode out with two cousins. The Broad-faced One looked after him, afraid now as no maiden could fear. Little Wolf saw him go too and knew that whites would die. He knew too that the Custer son, Yellow Swallow, must be kept out of the way of the anger and avenging of this time, and so he sent the boy and his aunt ahead with two members of the Shield society who had managed to save the red shields that showed their authority. He tried to send Thin Elk, but his accoutrements were still up north on the Yellowstone. Sitting Man who needed to rest his broken leg would not go. "I will die in my place. . . ."

Gradually little parties from up and down the Sappa country began to bring in horses, not many, and mostly old and worn from the plow. They brought a little meat too, and coffee, sugar, and a few blankets and dresses for the girls. It was said that this last day of September they shot nineteen whites, the number of Cheyenne men that Lieutenant Henely reported he killed on the Sappa three years before, with nobody for Buffalo Chips today or all the others who died on this way north. Nothing for all the Indian women and children; for these there is no power of avenging. Only men had been killed today and in this at least they had followed Little Wolf's command: "I will not have women and children hurt. . . ."

But a little party of southerners captured two girls back there and did not tell anybody, certainly not the chief, who was not their man anyway. They sent in some horses, including the spotted one, yellow too, that Crazy Horse had given Dull Knife when the Cheyennes fled to him after their village on the Powder was burned. The horse was found where they took the girls, the man in the saddle sliding into the dust after he had wounded one of the Indians a little. At the camp the rope was offered to Pawnee Woman. She accepted it in gratitude, Dull Knife standing dark beside her. If this fine horse had not been stolen from him on the hunt last year, his Short One would be alive.

At night the Cheyenne headmen took the women and children across the moonlit Sappa divide and down a long, deep-canyoned draw that opened to the valley of the Beaver. Later scouts came in to the hidden camp to say that a herd of cattle was bedded down several miles up, near the head of the draw, with a night herder watching, and that soldiers had reached the Sappa where the settlers were dead on the ground.

Ahh-h, now was the time to run for the next stream of their ladder, the Republican, over another bare, far-seeing tableland. But as Little Wolf walked among the shadowed sleepers, he knew how many would drop in such a flight. They must have rest; horses too, but at least one day of rest. By the frost time of morning he knew they would get it unless they went on without the warriors. Even his own sons were gone, Pawnee and Woodenthigh both.

Pawnee was with those trying to run the cattle off when the day herder came out. The white man was shot and his saddle cut up for the leather they wanted, while others got to the horse herd with a waving blanket and turned the bunch, over thirty head, toward the draw. By now more cowboys spurred in to get between the horses and the Cheyennes. There was a lot of whooping, shooting, and breakneck riding through the dust until the Indians managed to sweep the herd away into the draw, sending back one last wave of the blanket to the cowboys. Pawnee and two others stayed back to delay the two cowboys who started toward the Sappa trail and the soldiers, Pawnee dropping from one place to another, shooting like many men.

There was a shot down near the mouth of the draw too, one shot, where the Indians found a little bunch of cattle herded by a lone youth on a big black star-faced horse. They killed him, and while the young women butchered some of the cattle, others dug a few rifle pits. They did it angrily because the warriors were out killing people who had harmed no one, instead of helping them get away, and three commands of soldiers were so very close.

Little Wolf was above the camp watching and molding a few bullets, the hot lead a fine young smell in his nose. But every few moments he rose to look under his palm around the fall-hazed horizon. There were far shots, and twice small herds of horses came dusting down the draw, Thin Elk with the first. He loafed around the camp the rest of the day, helping Little Wolf's shier wife, Quiet One, and the girl Pretty Walker comfort the children and the old ones. It was a good thing to do and yet somehow it angered Little Wolf.

The young men had gone scouting along the breaks both ways on the

Beaver before the sun had warmed the shoulders, beginning a sweep that covered the valley for ten of the white man's miles. Some of those from the cattle herd found a settler at his plowing, called a friendly *"Hou!"* and rode on toward his dugout. The man left the team with his son and came running so they shot him but let the boy slip away to the creek brush and a woman too, who ran for a gully, her sunbonnet flying off. One of the warriors scooped it up from his horse, put it on his head, simpering and laughing in the white-woman way for the others. Inside the dugout they found bread and a wooden bucket of sorghum. With their hunting knives they dug out the thick brown sirup, letting it drip from the blades into their mouths, spreading it on torn loaves, wolfing the sweet stuff they had missed so long. Another white man came from somewhere and they shot him and then went away with the horses, adding two more from men who came riding, but letting the men run away.

A larger party shot a little at a man well hidden in a buffalo wallow and then went to pick up a few more horses, not many, for the whites along here seemed very poor. Soon the settlers became wild as buffaloes after a long hunting, running away from far off, hiding very well. One raiding party met the horse catchers with Big Foot, the father of the Broad-faced One. He was very angry at this killing and sent Bullet Proof to ride the breaks with the far-seeing glass and keep the count. Once Proof came near some whites who had a woman along. "Keep going! Keep going!" he called in badly spoken *veho* words. But he made them understand his pointing down the creek, and was glad they went because he wanted nobody killed.

In the bottoms one of the parties still found some settlers, these men speaking a thick unknown tongue. The Indians motioned them to leave their guns and get away from their house. They went without protest, seeming to think these were small thieves. When the Cheyennes had the guns, they shot the men, a bullet grazing the baby one of them carried.

"You are a fool!" the leader shouted to the young warrior. "We do not shoot at children!"

But the youth soon forgot this blaming as he helped slit the feather beds and toss them from one to another, laughing at the blizzard of feathers on the wind. Another party found a man and a boy whipping away in a wagon. An Indian who had the new black horse with the white star roped the galloping team in one big loop. The wagon was cut loose and the horses led away, the man left on the ground, the boy running for the house, crying. The young Indians raced after him, riding around him as he fled, shouting *"Hou! Hou!"* and laughing.

Another place four men were digging potatoes as though it were any other September day and suddenly a party of Cheyennes was upon them, shooting. Several Indian women and boys had come to hurry everybody in, with the soldiers near. Some were relatives of Buffalo Chips and so angry they finished the killing and then went to the house, carrying away blankets and goods and clothing.

But now there was an angry signal from Bullet Proof. It was enough. He had counted up the dead whites here and back on the Sappa and found them equal to the men left on the ground at Cheyenne Hole and those killed this time north. None here were as big men as Medicine Arrow and Bad Heart, the healer, but the great ones of the *veho* did not live in this country. As for the Cheyenne women and children left dead on the Sappa, and Short One back there—for these there could be no thing to make the heart glad.

Late that afternoon there were healing chants over the wounded in the narrow, walled-in camp. Then suddenly the soldiers were there, firing, but Mauck pulled back easy because the Cheyennes were in such a strong position, a stronger one than the Indians could find for 300 miles north, and many troops were coming along the streams to help him.

The Indians got away very fast, leaving one man still out and a boy who got his leg crippled in the soldier shooting. Somebody went to find these later, but the country was full of soldiers by then, men digging graves everywhere, even for people killed where no Indians had been. Very many whites were around, mostly just riding and looking, until a great prairie fire began to roll its pale yellow smoke into the sky and spread over all the ground too, so nothing could be seen.

The girl captives of the southerners had been turned loose as soon as Little Wolf discovered about them. First the smaller one and then the older too, after some of the Cheyenne women had taken her clothes and struck her hard over the shoulder when she fought.

"Let her go," one said. "She is foolish. Tell her the whites shot all the Cheyenne women and children back there on the Sappa, clubbed their heads in, and threw everybody into the fire, like big trees and little trees. . . ."

Bear Shield told the girl what was said, but she could only cower her whiteness into the grass, bending over her nakedness, and so she was left near the path of the soldiers, their dust already like a little whirlwind standing on the horizon. The southern young men still turned their heads toward her as they rode on. She would have made a very good captive, they said to each other, and at the next stopping place it was noticed that these warriors were gone.

"They have started back south, I think—" young Little Bear told his father, Tangle Hair, who interrupted him angrily. "They must not go back to the white girl!"

"No!" Little Wolf roared. "We make no war on women! I should have killed those men for it—"

But the bundle-bearing chief had to stop his tongue, suddenly like a man caved in, a man who had looked into a great hole within himself. Those beside him noticed that even in this anger he had named no one. The avengers were never to be named, even though many of them were of Medicine Arrow's southerners and gone back now, leaving the fury of the two bloody days to fall upon others.[1]

9 The Parting

SEVERAL TIMES NOW EVEN LITTLE WOLF, WHO MUST
be everywhere, see everything, and lead them all,
found himself falling far behind in this flight from the Beaver. He was
taking his turn afoot with the young men whose horses were led back to
bring up the other walking ones. But in this way the few horses they had
were kept running from the soldiers until they fell on the trail, going
down among the scattering of goods dropped off, everything dropped off,
now that almost every hill showed the pursuing dust.

When he was afoot, Little Wolf fell into his old Indian runner's trot
that he could hold mile after mile, waving his horse away to the others, still
managing to keep in sight of his people. Even in their fear many looked
back to him with swelling breast. He was fifty-seven, their head chief with
the Sweet Medicine bundle tied next to his ribs, and yet he ran between them
and the soldiers, a lean, hard, straight figure, his braids dusty, the silver
medal of friendship from the Great Father out again, swaying a little on
its black tong, his moccasins a whisper on the dry buffalo grass as he
passed.

There was much for Little Wolf to think about this day, things as tough
for the mind as the chunk of sinew that hung from the cradleboard for the
infant to try his coming teeth. The chief had lived through the entire bridge
of time from the old days when no whites had yet come running through
their country to the now—when only the Indians ran.

Once the Indians ahead of the Wolf stopped for a little, barely longer
than an arrow's flight, at a strip of ripe sod corn to grab up three, four small
ears for everyone and every horse. The chief drove them on, but this long
field, stretched where there had still been a few fresh buffalo tracks last
year, made him very certain that the old ways had to be forgotten, the

moccasin set on a new path. The Cheyennes could escape the *veho* only by the *veho* road. The white man had the power and the Indian must learn to smile too when his heart was bad, say *"Hou!"* when he meant a roaring against it, say the "Yes, yes, this will be done," when it is only for so long as the eye was there to see.

The Indian had always lived by knowing the ways of the things about him. Now, far too late, he must study these whites and their Great Father who could talk soberly of peace while big bunches of their young men did nothing but practice charging up and down, shooting at a target that was like a man, stabbing with the bayonet, crushing with gunstock. Then when what they wanted was already clutched in the palm, they said, "Sell us this for peace. . . ."

So the whites had talked for selling the Holy Roads of the Platte and the Smoky Hill, the countries of the south, the Powder River and the Black Hills, each time for peace, while their soldiers destroyed the camps of White Antelope, Yellow Wolf, Black Kettle, Little Rock, Tall Bull, and Medicine Arrow. The names of these dead men were like a song, a song of the sun dance bloodletting, a great red blanket spread upon the ground to plead for a vision to save the people. But nothing came of all their dying, only more blood. Even one moon ago Little Wolf had hoped to get his people away because a long chase after so few would seem very easy, very foolish and worthless. Now it could never seem foolish to chase and kill Cheyennes after so many lay back there, their faces open to the sky.

He tore at himself, as though he were both the rabbit and the eagle who fed on the quivering entrails, and ran behind the people like a youth who could be spared. Yet Little Wolf was still the confident commander. By the time they neared the breaks of the Republican Valley, so golden down there in the fall sun of midafternoon, his young men were once more the peaceful horse catchers.

"No one has hurt our people in this country ahead," he told them at the last council, when he drew the silver peace medal out upon his breast again. "We are now going into the country of our friends and nobody is to be hurt there except soldiers who shoot first. Not one other white. . . ."

Although much darkness sat between the people over the white men just killed, in this all the leaders were behind the Wolf, even those of the wilder young warriors like Little Finger Nail. But they must have horses, and those sent out from the Beaver should meet them at the Republican with word of what was ahead and surely with a little stock, taken without making trouble, it was hoped. The chief could not tell how many would be there, how many southerners would have run back now, after their avenging. Or perhaps gone on alone, with those taking Yellow Swallow, afraid of the grieving ones in the fleeing band, and the soldiers hot for killing.

For a while Little Wolf hurried beside his brother-in-law, Left Hand. The Hand was traveling with Great Eyes, the two men taking turns riding a broncho-nosed, tough-hided, and tough-spirited gray that kicked at every tumbleweed. It was curious what troubles between people could be melted in the fire of emergency, like bullets of enemies heated in the same lead kettle. These two men had been good friends in their youth, both Elk soldiers, Great Eyes often at the lodge of the good hunter Left Hand where a quiet, friendly young woman liked to cook for her husband's many friends. When Left Hand went on a war party to avenge a southern uncle, Great Eyes offered to see that there would still be a little more than the regular sharing of the game brought in.

But the war party went far; there were injuries to heal, several revenge fights, and then a formal pipe offered by some Sioux friends who had been helping the Cheyennes. It was many moons before the Hand returned to see his wife lower her shamed face because there was a growing fatness under her buckskin dress.

The husband was angry. Who dared violate a Cheyenne chastity rope? —and what had her relatives done to avenge the wrong? Scarcely able to speak loud enough for the hearing, she admitted that she was a guilty, worthless woman.

"Guilty!" As he said this, Left Hand, the bold war leader, had to sit down. After smoking a while, he spoke quietly, in a friendly way, asking his wife to name the man.

"It is your friend, Great Eyes," she said, her face dropped to her fingers.

Although Left Hand was only a little soldier chief then, he was already a man of steady heart. The Elks should decide what must be done. Great Eyes' father, hurrying to avoid bloodshed, had already sent an old chief with a horse for Left Hand, saying, "I have driven my son out to live at the soldier lodge. . . ."

The Eyes admitted the greatness of his wrong and would help care for the child. This the Elks approved, provided that Left Hand remained a strong man and did not throw his wife away. Now here, many years later, they were hurrying together, Left Hand pulling the gray horse along when it was too played-out to carry anyone, Great Eyes with the beating stick behind. Both were grandfathers now and between them they tied these people together like beads of two colors, one from each side, woven into an intricate, beautiful Cheyenne pattern. Great Eyes, an Elk chief, was the descendant of a fine line of warriors and shield makers wise in council. His daughter was Leaf, the reckless young wife of Bull Hump, the prominent Dog soldier, the son of Dull Knife. Left Hand's son, Young Chief Little Wolf, the favorite nephew of Little Wolf and his name bearer, was an outstanding Elk soldier. Married into a Dog soldier family, he was a little chief in that society too.

So tightly were the two men, and with them the people, tied together. It was well, for now there were the soldiers of Crook waiting ahead there on the Platte, and beyond them the guns of General Miles. These northern troops would not ride in, shoot a little, and then pull back. Besides, the soldiers coming behind them were very angry now.

They crossed the fall-golden valley of the Republican and camped at the mouth of Cheyenne canyon, good in water and wood and grass, and with a place higher up, between steep narrowing walls, to hold the horses, even the new ones Woodenthigh just brought in, and naturally very anxious to get back to their home pastures. There was a good place to fight up there too, to dig in away from the bullets for a while.

But mostly the people wanted to sleep tonight, to sleep all the days left of the growing moon, particularly those who had been out on raids along the Sappa and the Beaver or had been with the raiders in anxious heart. Yet next morning Little Wolf had the people moving before the sun darkened the thin white frost of the bottoms and glistened in dew on the golden boxelders and cottonwoods. Some deer had been brought in for meat during the night and a few more horses, but not enough. Many young men were still out, yet when the scouts signaled the soldiers near, the people had to start.

At Frenchman Creek the troops were suddenly plain for everyone to see, charging down into the hot, noon-yellowed valley from the south as the Indians climbed out upon the wide north tableland. The Cheyennes had made better than 25 miles since morning, but there was still half a day of short-grass country ahead before darkness would robe their escape. As the dust of the soldiers neared, a soft monotony of crying and lament started among the people, a woman here, another there, then old men singing too, their voices joggled cries for help from the Powers, the people as hopeless, as worn out as the horses that fell and were left.

Now the few warriors there shook out the regalia left to them, smeared their paint on hastily without plan, and fell behind, between the troops and the fleeing ones. They could make no stand, for there was no ammunition for a fight, but now and then one charged back a little, to be angrily recalled by Black Crane, Hog, or even Black Coyote. They showed their daring, but it did not stop the soldiers or the other whites riding fast ahead of them, so anxious now to kill Indians, but it gave the people the courage to make this last run.

The courage was needed. Just ahead of the thin scattering of rear guards were the drags of the people, straggling women and the weak and sick on poor horses, the boys and old men whipping them along until the animals fell, swiftly changing the saddles or packs to others, or just doubling the people up on the horses that were left. They lifted the old, the worn, and those very heavy with the child soon to come, and then they ran along behind again, whipping, all the singing stopped now, the breath and the hope for it gone.

Then suddenly the soldiers stopped. Maybe it was to rest the horses and men, worn out by the many days of hard riding. It saved the Indians there north of the Frenchman, although the other whites, out only for a day or two, kept coming. Left Hand dropped behind to shoot from the bunchgrass on the top of a little knoll. He brought down two horses and lamed a third, moving between shots so it seemed like more from the smoke. These white men began to lag a little now, those afoot doubling up as the Indians had. Finally they returned to the soldiers at the creek. The Hand could have hit more, even killed most of the men, but he had only those three shells for his good, long-carrying gun and his steady eye. Unless he got some ammunition, he would have to use the gun butt or rocks—very strong in his hand against a buffalo but poor against bullets.

By midafternoon the soldiers were close on the dust of the Indians again, an occasional bullet striking the earth among them, but mostly falling short. The young men had brought in more fresh horses, wild stock without saddle mark or rope burn anywhere. There were good horse tamers here but no time for that now. So they roped one after the other, held their fighting heads by twist of neck or ears for the saddling. Then, with ropes stretched out both ways they held the bucking, running bronchos between gentler, wearier animals, the women hanging on any way they could, the small children in the skin sacks hammered against the bellowing ribs until the horses were played out and dropped their broken, lathered heads. Always leading these younger women with the wild horses rode the self-reliant Leaf, wife of Bull Hump, for now they were in the country of her childhood where she knew the rise and fall of every prairie. Always she whipped her horse on, faster and faster, Buffalo Calf Road with her revolver close behind, to help, yet angry that she did not have the fastest horse, as was due the warrior woman. But there was danger ahead and the soldiers always just behind, a dark twisting snake in the dust, with the flag flying.

This time they had to run until dark. When the scouts came to say that the soldiers had camped, the people fell like dead ones anywhere. Now it was discovered that, although over two hundred horses had been captured the last three days, more than half as many had been left, worn out. People were lost too. Three of the old and the sick were gone, fallen off or hit in the hard runs before the bullets. Two of the smaller, weaker children were dead from the pounding in the hide sacks, their mothers quietly carrying them to a little bluff to be left there between the stones. But the youngest, little Comes Behind, was still on his walking mother's back, the woman far behind again, and off to the side, once more missed by the soldiers. She still followed the moccasins of Brave One and the others who had walked almost all the way from the Place of the Silent Lodges in the south country. Burden on back, stick in hand for staff and for small game, a sand turtle or a foolish rabbit, or to pin down a rattlesnake's head while the body was cut off for roasting over the evening fire, they slipped along from gully to washout, on and on, taking turns carrying Lame Girl too, so thin now from the bullet-torn ankle that she was like a child on the back. These were the strong women, women of the old Cheyenne kind, and, beyond asking for news of them from the scouts, Little Wolf would not shame their courage.

Many things were of the today in this country that they had to cross, a country that was as fat as fall buffaloes with memories. Ahead was the Platte, called Geese River because the Cheyennes found it dark with migrating flocks when the old, old ones planted their moccasins solid there on the way down from the Missouri. It was a country warmer than any these Indians had ever known, with so many moons of grass for the horses that they grew smooth and shining as a maiden's hair, more summer for the dogs too, and the growing children. With the grass very thick it was called the Country of Resting Buffalo, but now even the bones were gone.

Although the Cheyennes were always running through here on the way north, this was the country of their greatest glory as a people—back before the white man's diseases made them few, and before Bent, with his trading place on the Arkansas River, married a Cheyenne and drew her relatives away. But it had become a country of sorrow in the time since. Just over west there, on the Ree Fork in 1868 the Cheyennes found a soldier chief without soldiers but with scouts and other whites, out looking for Indians to kill. There was some good fighting around the island, but the war leader Roman Nose died there, his greatness remembered in the naming of three men with them here now, helping the people.

But the soldiers had become hunters of women and children in sleeping villages long before this, and so often that the ground here seemed worn by moccasins fleeing north—not of hostiles but peaceful people running. First Yellow Wolf in 1857, then after the massacre at Sand Creek in 1864, where the peace chiefs, Black Kettle and the rest, had been told to take their young men out of trouble. Through the traders' sons, Little Wolf heard that the soldiers had been called to help in the big war, the *veho* one, with food and guns and ammunition all hauled up so there need be no stopping to hunt, to make ceremonials, to live. Many die in such fighting and a little Indian war at home would be safer, particularly against those feeling safe under Black Kettle's flag of red, white, and blue. Dead people were left there in piles, and in reply to the avenging pipe sent around Little Wolf went down with a party from Powder River, Crazy Horse and his Sioux along—a combined force of young warriors who would fight side by side against Connor, Fetterman, Crook, Custer, and Miles, until the buffalo was dead.

But the warriors gathered to avenge Sand Creek did not have to run through here like Little Wolf's people now, and chased by soldiers. They went in a powerful march of allies, a great war camp with the women and children along and thousands of horses, all sweeping through the country, climbing the ladder of streams toward the Powder, raiding and burning a path a hundred miles wide, the whites deserting even the little forts along the trail and no soldiers daring to come very far after anybody.

More Cheyenne villages were burned. In 1867 Hancock struck the rich Dog soldier camp of Bull Bear and Tall Bull down in Kansas, where the chiefs had gone to make a talk with him. It was good that the Cheyenne women run easily and fast, for although Hancock destroyed 251 lodges, the homes of over 1,700 people, he caught no one except a visiting Sioux with a broken leg and his wife and little girl. He was peaceful and would not be carried away. But the little girl died, from mistreatment by very many soldiers, it was said. Little Wolf was glad that the captive girls he released yesterday had not been treated like the Sioux girl, like some evil women put on the prairie by the council, meaning given to the warrior, as he had seen done once.

And still Black Kettle had hoped for peace. After Sand Creek he took his band south, out of the way, and there Custer struck him on the Washita and left the last of the peace chiefs dead on the ground among the people who followed him.

Little Wolf talked of all this as he led the fleeing Cheyennes toward the soldier-guarded Platte. "But that killing all happened back behind us, not in this good country," Dull Knife argued.

The Wolf did not reply. He knew Dull Knife must be thinking of what happened to some who fled north in 1869 after Custer grabbed the three men as prisoners from Medicine Arrow's village. Some were with Tall Bull heading for the Platte too when he was attacked by soldiers and a lot of Pawnee scouts over west at Summit Springs. Once more women and children fell, this time to the whooping of enemy Indians. Tall Bull got away, but he rode back because his wife was caught. He knew what was done to the little Sioux girl in his village when Hancock captured her. He died at the mouth of a ravine where his wife and child were hidden.

Then there were those who fled from the Sappa three years ago, and now Cheyennes were running again. It seemed that the earth must be worn hard as a sun-dance ground this way.

"Soon we will be with our friends beyond the Running Water," Dull Knife said, still seeming confident. "Only a few more days and we will be among our friends and relatives with Red Cloud."

But Little Wolf was not so easy in his mind, with all the soldiers just

behind, on every side too, and Crook's army on the Platte, and the railroad waiting to hurry them to any crossing. Against these the Wolf had
drawn in every man except the advance scouts and those with Comes in
Sight's little party. Now he had to see how very few young men were
left to him. Many had gone back south, or seemed lost, and some who had
ridden all this way as young men, skirmishing, fighting, hunting horses,
had only seemed young in the need but were really tired old men with
the years for the council, for wisdom and storytelling and playing with the
small ones.

Although the newspapers said there were 13,000 soldiers out against the
Cheyennes, almost 1,000 ready to move within an hour against any crossing,
there was not one in sight when the Indians reached the South Platte and its
railroad. They crossed below the cattle town of Ogallala on October fourth,
with the bright sun not yet high as the eagle flying overhead, all anxious
that it must be done so openly, but the great flocks of ducks rising along
the sandy banks showed that no one was around.

The Cheyennes crossed in a long dark string, the warriors watching, the
shallow water splashing high in the hurrying, and then the North Platte
too. Even the walking women had been brought up, and it was a joyous
time for the many who still believed that the soldiers would not follow them
into what they called their own country here, although it was taken away
long ago. They knew that Comes in Sight and the others were over too,
gone ahead as she had since Punished Woman Creek, without the stops at
the Sappa or the Beaver. They had no avenging to do; no blood could
pay for what had come upon them and upon the dead Bear Rope's memory.

North of the Platte the Indians went along the bottoms to White Tail
Creek and stopped inside the mouth of the steep, shadowed canyon, with a
good grassy place farther up to hold the horses, even to stand off attack
if necessary, at least to let the people rest a few hours. She Bear and Little
Finger Nail had a few cattle hidden there, ready for the silent arrow and
knife. Later wolf signals came out of the dusk, reporting that the soldiers
were close, some already crossing the river in the pale moon of evening,
many wagons following. Then Thin Elk and another came in from around
Fort Sidney with two men of Little Chief's band, the Cheyennes being
taken from the Yellowstone to the south, men who had been allowed out

to hunt and had not returned. They said their troop escort was of Custer's Seventh Cavalry, some who crossed the river with Reno and attacked Sitting Bull's Hunkpapa circle and lost five of their company there.

"Ahh-h!" Old Bear, who saw that fighting, exclaimed in concern. They would kill the helpless ones.

They seemed friendly. Ben Clark, who had the Cheyenne wife down at Camp Supply, was the interpreter along. "He tried to say that nobody wants to go south, that your families are broken like stones under the hammer by hunger and sickness."

Piva! It was true.

"And White Hat Clark, he too."

"Then he is with you here?" Little Wolf exclaimed. "Our friend?"

"No. He was with Bear Coat Miles on the Yellowstone when we had to come south. He couldn't help us. Little Chief and the two hundred had to come and we will be taken south from here as soon as you are caught, so none of you can get to us and make trouble. All the Cheyennes are to live in the south. Two Moons and the rest too."

To this there were no words, only the guttering of a pipe at the low, hidden fire. Finally Little Wolf spoke. "Is it true that the soldiers are thick as blackbirds up beyond the Running Water?"

"Yes, soldiers are camped all over the White River country and at Red Cloud's new agency, with Spotted Tail too, we hear."

"Ahh-h! Soldiers surrounding all my Sioux relatives!" Tangle Hair murmured in concern. "We are shut out. . . ."

The visitors made no reply; they told what they had seen.

The little circle of headmen was silent a long time now, the small glow of the coals reaching up to their gaunt, worn faces, the blackness of the canyon walls bending over them. All the people in the dark close around were silent too, with only a fall cricket somewhere, and the howl of a coyote out on the prairie where the rounding moon stood. And still not even Black Coyote spoke.

After a while Dull Knife rose from beside the dying fire. He was no longer as straight as when Little Robe struck him down with the saddle whip a little over one moon ago. His old blanket was in tatters, his grief-loosed hair ragged, a touch of red from the coals sitting along the broad naked bones of his cheeks.

"We are almost in our own country, my friends," he said slowly, as in an unused tongue. "The soldiers up there with our friends the Sioux have always been good men."

"The soldiers are up there to catch us and kill us," Little Wolf answered quietly. "We can trust no one except White Hat and that man only after we are in our own country of the north."

"We have a right with Red Cloud!" the old chief retorted, angry at the interruption. "We were on his agency before we left to look at the south."

"With the whites you have a right to nothing that you do not already hold in the palm."

But Dull Knife, who had spoken almost no word since the death of Short Woman and the Sappa killings, now broke into a sudden snarling of impatience, of exasperation, of fury too long contained. "I am the one who is speaking now, my brother! Too long your tongue has been the thorn in my moccasin!" he said, making a harsh, angry thing of the soft-flowing Cheyenne. "You know we cannot last as far as the Yellowstone now, running, running. Look around you, my iron-legged brother. See the dead bones in the faces of the people! You say we go on; I say you are a fool!"

"So now I am foolish . . . ," Little Wolf said softly.

"No, not foolish! I repeat, my brother, you are a fool!" the old chief shouted. "At least four died in the chasing yesterday, and not from bullets. There will be many more, and we will run out of horses up where nobody lives. Besides it will be winter. Do you not smell the snow tonight? Before the moon is dark again it will be here, as every child among us knows. We must turn to Red Cloud. . . ."

As he spoke, a protest started up against him, but the older Dog soldiers, with here and there an Elk too, moved up behind him in silent agreement, in silent allegiance, and then some young warriors too, these with guns ready, hammers clicking in the rising challenge.

Other young men were moving up behind their man too, behind Little Wolf, making their challenges, and so the Wolf had to rise, his hand lifted for silence around the firelight, his strong, pitted face furious, with the fury that breaks from gentleness, his voice striking out sharp as a Cheyenne battle ax upon the young warriors.

"This dividing cannot be!" he roared. "I will not have the people split. I repeat it: an Indian never caught is an Indian never killed, and only together can we all get away!"

He had more words, a whole harangue boiling up in his scarred breast where the medal of peace from the Great Father hung, but he saw the forward straining of the divided followers, back in the shadows heard the cry of the women, their running for the children as the younger, wilder warriors of both sides moved against each other, knives out, guns up, tempers taut as dry bowstrings worn by the long flight. One finger's slipping and there would be blood in the canyon.

The bearer of the Chief's Bundle saw it and knew that this last, worst thing must not come upon the Cheyennes. So he dropped his hand, defeated. "I am moving a little ways apart," he said slowly. "Let those who would go on to the north follow. . . ."

There was another silence now, one in which none seemed to breathe, none among the men or the women or the children. Then one man stepped forward to the side of Little Wolf, the first to take his stand in this parting. It was Thin Elk.

By the time for the morning light behind the thick white fog, Dull Knife was gone. But on a haired robe, almost the only one left, was a little heap of ammunition and some powder, the parting gift to those people who would still try to fight their way to the Yellowstone.

10

Out of the Blizzard

"WE'LL RAKE THEM CHEYENNES IN AT THE RIVER LIKE
a grizzly rakin' in berries, leaves 'n' all," one of
Thornburgh's mounted infantrymen bragged in a saloon at Sidney. "We'll
toss what's left'a them in with the bunch the Seventh's holdin' down to
the post, let 'em herd the whole outfit back to the Terr'tory."

A wind-burnt trooper of the Seventh moved down the bar a ways, to give
the new Indian fighter room to spread himself. He recalled talk like that
up around Fort Abraham Lincoln the spring of Seventy-six, when Custer was heading for the West, and drank a little to the men who never returned.

But the soft recruit did not get so much as a saddle wolf before the Indians had slipped across the Platte. When it became known that the Cheyennes had eluded General Crook too, there was a roar of anger reaching
from the poorest settler dugout to the domed halls of Congress. There were
editorials, letters, and articles in the papers, delegations calling on the
President, long controversial exchanges over Indian policy between the
generals and the Department of the Interior, and a sour laughing all along
the frontier. Even those who made a career of the Noble Red Man were
silenced by stories of the Kansas border knee-deep in blood, thousands of
horses and cattle destroyed, hundreds of people killed, women and girls
outraged, small children left with their brains dashed out by war clubs.
When the number of the dead was cut down to forty men, to thirty-two
by some, including not one woman or child, it was still a shocking account
of murder, with pilfered garments scattered along the Cheyenne trail from
the Beaver northward: a lace-trimmed wedding gown, embroidered under-
garments, plumed hats—some stained by bloody hands, all dropped in the
fast pursuit, to blow from broken packs and flutter against buckbrush or

plum thicket or browned thistlehead. There were demands for the court-martial of Pope, of Dodge, General Sherman, and even Crook, for a Congressional investigation and for transfer of the Indians back to the War Department. There was a rumor too of a railroad coming through the Indian Territory, so the Indians would have to be moved back, pushed into smaller ground, driven to rebellion.

"Yeh, make 'em bust out so's they kin be eeliminated 'fore the land jumps in value . . . ," an old-timer said.

But now the Cheyennes were caught between the Seventh Cavalry around Sidney and all the troops scouting the breaks of White River. The gallant survivors of Custer's regiment would know how to deal with such bloodthirsty savages. Tilford was heading down from the White. He would catch them.

"Catch 'em, hell! Damn lucky if they don't catch him!" a bearded old trail driver said sourly.

"I hear Tilford has nine companies of the Seventh up there and four of infantry," a trooper replied and turned his back with finality.

But the old cowhand jerked the soldier around. "Nine companies or ninety! Jest so many more bluecoats to run when they sees a feather rise up over some hill!"

Somebody threw a bottle, a bullet went through a campaigner's hat, and the bartender brought up the singletree he kept handy behind the bar. Afterward there were a few more bullet holes in the smoky saloon walls and a soldier carried out to wake up later with a headache.

The Indians seemed to be doing less fighting. Only one man had been killed since they left the Beaver, a cowboy found dead far off the Indian trail, over in range war country. But Omaha and eastern owners of ranches in northwest Nebraska and the Running Water country telegraphed for couriers to ride from the Platte to their foremen, no matter what the cost. Fifty well-armed cowboys could be gathered up at the river in three, four hours, although the Indians would probably pass far west, on the old Cheyenne trail to the Powder.

Bear Shield and two others had stayed back south of the Platte, the Shield creeping up close to Mauck's night camps, listening to the white-man words. Amos Chapman, who had said the Indians were starving in the south, was still along. The soldiers had picked up a worn-out old Cheyenne who slid off in the hard pursuit north of the Frenchman. They wanted to kill him right there in the grass, but Chapman raised his wind-graveled voice against it and then made a talk with the Indian. The old man trembled at this surround by angry, wind-burnt enemies, but he kept saying that he knew nothing. He didn't see anybody killed—just Cheyennes dying from sickness and from the chasing. So they threw him into one of the wagons, but later the soldiers who had been with Colonel Lewis on the Punished Woman bragged they killed the man, and it must be true because Bear Shield got no reply to his Cheyenne signals.

The newspapers told the story of the old man, gratified that at least twenty-four companies were pursuing the marauding Cheyennes. Yet something new was creeping into the stories—admiration. The captured Indian had said they had only eighty men above eleven. Then who were these two men who led this pitiful force so well? Dull Knife was old, long past his active days as a chief. That left Little Wolf, who had brought these sick, half-starved, half-afoot people, old, young, men, women, and children, through 600 miles of open country, cut by three railroads, cross-hatched by telegraph—through settlers, cowmen, scouts, and the United States Army, all in less than a month. Where in history was there another such leader, such a dramatic, masterful, such a noble exploit?

But Little Wolf must not be permitted to reach the already dissident Sioux under Red Cloud and Spotted Tail. During the general removal of Indians last year these chiefs were taken to the Missouri. Refused permission to return this summer, they started back anyway, the two great camps of people moving in dark files over the prairie, the agency beef herds along, to be killed as needed. The troops followed, just followed, challenging no warrior nor firing a shot. Now the two old chiefs were on the south border of Dakota, only a couple of days from Little Wolf and Dull Knife, thousands of well-armed, arrogant young Sioux ready to join the fighting Cheyenne warriors.

General Pope was not the man to take public criticism silently. Mounted Indians could not be caught with infantry, and when the Cheyennes broke out, he had not one company of cavalry in all of Kansas. Indians placed where there was no hunting must be fed. He had written to Washington fifty times in the past two years stating these facts. "In my twenty-five years on the plains in every outbreak the cause was bad faith by the government.

In this outbreak there were no depredations until the Cheyennes were attacked."

Thornburgh, too, had defenders. Newspapermen with the major's column said he had 60 miles of the Platte watched but he could not intercept the Cheyennes because of the ridiculous flood of rumors, reports, and telegrams of Indians along 200 miles of river. All he could do was hold his mixed troops ready. Instead of the pack mules and Indian trackers that he requested he was given wagons and cattleman scouts. The special train, ready on a siding, was delayed two hours starting and then moved very slowly. When Thornburgh got his cavalry and some mounted infantry out and across the Platte, those in the wagon train got stuck in quicksand. Fog came in, the cattlemen could not find the trail, and at daylight the mounted column was wandering in the river breaks; Bourke, Crook's aide-de-camp through his years of Indian fighting, along as observer, was as lost as anybody.

Finally they struck the abandoned camp on White Tail, with the stripped beef carcasses, the bones cracked for the marrow. The gorge was so steep and close that the troops had to ride single file—a dangerous ambush spot, and all the scouts except one left the front. Angrily Thornburgh led them himself, the moisture that gathered on his flowing sideburns glistening as the sun burned through. At last they hit a converging trail, and abandoning the wagons entirely, the ambulance and its four-man escort to get through as it could, they followed into the sandhills at a gallop with less than five days' rations. The column made 50 miles that day in uncharted territory. Thirteen Indian horses were dropped before them, one still under packs, and large quantities of fresh-made meat. But in midafternoon the cattleman scouts went back; the Indians were safely beyond their herds.

That night the troops camped under a ridge of choppy sandhills where the Indians had dug about forty rifle pits, the sand still damp in them, the horses left here still wet in lather. The column had not stopped to eat or drink since dawn on the Platte. Tongues were swollen, eyes and faces burned by sun and stinging sand, the infantry recruits galled raw. The men slept on their saddle blankets with the warriors howling in the distance and calling in white-man distress, "Help! Indians!"

Once some men ventured out to rescue the ambulance from attack. A trooper whose horse played out had to hold Bear Shield off until Mauck came along, close behind now. The Shield let him go. The horse was worth-

less and no one must be hurt up in this country, not even a soldier with
a gun to be taken.

The next morning there was only a fanning trail, the Indians gone like
a handful of feathers tossed on the wind.

Mauck took supplies and the best mules from Thornburgh's stranded
wagons and struck into the sandhills too, followed close by Dallas, his
troops worn by a 300-mile march out of Kansas. Carlton left Fort Robinson
with five companies of cavalry and struck down Snake Creek and eastward
to head the Indians. Sidney had one hour of excitement over a rumor that
Thornburgh had 250 Indians, only to be offset by others: that the Arapahos
with some related Cheyennes were off their reservation in Wyoming, raiding this way; that Dull Knife had gone north past Fort Robinson with a
great herd of horses and that he joined Red Cloud's 5,000 warriors, and as
many more under Spotted Tail only a day's pony ride east. With the Bannocks probably not yet conquered and uprisings in Oregon, Arizona, and
elsewhere, it looked like a general Indian war, a war of Winchester-armed
redskins.

But as far away as California and Florida, troops were entraining against
the Cheyennes raiding through Nebraska, and every man available between
Utah and St. Paul was hitting the field.

Bear Shield remained behind with the limping Black Horse, looking
through the thin sand grass or from behind some ridge-topping soapweed
with the field glass. They saw Thornburgh seek the scattered trail and
finally follow the half-hidden decoy tracks that went west and then turned
around southward, leading the strong soldier horses farther and farther
from both parties of the split Cheyennes, as a quail drops a fluttering wing
and draws the enemy from her young.

But when Mauck came to the place where Thornburgh had turned southwest, he stopped. He had chased the Indians from the far south and had
good scouts, Chapman and Rees, one of the buffalo hunters who was in
the killing on the Sappa in 1875. Black Horse recognized this man and his
face darkened as from a cloud to see him here, very close upon the helpless
ones. Yet too many would die for the avenging shot, so the buffalo hunter,
not fooled by the decoys, was permitted to ride straight north until he found
the thickening trail of small moccasins, with a few horses carrying the

sick and worn-out. They were very close and so the women had to run again, to scatter, losing more horses. For that Bear Shield took the one ridden by Thornburgh's courier back to Mauck, wounding the man but letting him go, leaving the saddle too, and the dispatch that asked for scouts to find the lost trail.

Mauck picked up this message, but no one was sent, and when a courier came up from the Platte, Mauck turned around with all his men and went back. Bear Shield watched this with a smile on his wide lean mouth. Now the good scouts Chapman and Rees were gone, and all the soldiers who had seen Lewis killed. None that the Indians had hurt were left in the chasing now, none except the Seventh Cavalry and these the Cheyennes planned not to meet.

Thornburgh had followed the decoy trail, always finding something dropped, a child's blanket, a woman's moccasin, clear back to a creeklet emptying into the North Platte. The cavalry horses bolted for the water there like a wild herd in a drouth. Afterward the troops went to Blue Water Creek for the night camp. In the morning they rode up along the desolate battle ground where General Harney struck the Sioux under Little Thunder over twenty years ago. Bleached and half-buried bones of man and horse were scattered along the slope, the caving sandstone topping the bluff still plainly shattered by the cannon shots that tore the women and children from their hidings. One of the soldiers discovered fresh horse tracks leading up to some bones crammed into the frost-broken crevasses.

"Perhaps one of the Cheyennes come to visit a relative killed with Little Thunder . . . ," Thornburgh said and looked all around for a feather that seemed like a weed or grass. Suddenly he put spur to his horse and headed north, the way the fleeing Cheyennes must surely have gone.

As the hills became sandier, choppier, the Indian signs became scarce. Perhaps one moccasin track lay beside a dried water hole, or a lone rider stood a moment on some far blue hill, remote as the eagle that circled against the mare's tail cloud of October. Thornburgh's only hope now was to head the Indians at the Running Water, the Niobrara. Without pack train or Indian scouts he was trying to catch a man who had marched his band through the organized force of the Army, much of the way across flat prairie country that would not hide the nakedness of a shedding rattler. Even so, Thornburgh gave the Indians their hottest chase, a newspaperman

with his column wrote. ". . . The whole western army has been demoral-
ized by a few wild Indians, but give Thornburgh just credit." But now
Little Wolf was in a wilderness of fall-dun hills shouldering each other
away into every horizon, hills so close-set that a thousand men could hide
within a mile in any direction and only the wind to see.

From the Blue Water the column struck into this wilderness. Sparse
joint grass brushed the stirrups of the men, and the thick slopes of bunchgrass were orange velvet in the evening sun. But the bayoneted clumps of
soapweed that dotted the hills cut the horses' legs, and the patches that
looked like soft, grayish-green rugs in the lower places were bull-tongue
cactus. Dwarf willows browned the pockets where water had stood in the
springtime, along the lower slopes the prairie rosebushes were frosted to
a russet red, while on the barer knolls drying sandcherries lay in purple
rows on the sand-borne branches, sweet to the hungry troops and purgative
in their profusion. But nowhere was there a tree or even a bush big as a
garden lilac. And no water for the lightening canteens.

The third day out the troopers killed some ranch beef to extend their
dwindling rations of hardtack and salt pork. After that they saw only
grouse and prairie chicken and the curious antelopes, while occasionally a
little herd of wild horses stood a moment at the whinny of some scouting
cavalry mount and then was gone, their bare-hoofed tracks so easily the
cover for the scattered Indians.

Gradually the hills reared their long backs higher, the valleys widened,
and there were lakes, the water only small yellow-gray patches far out in
the alkali-crusted lake beds that smelled like rotten eggs from a mile off.
The horses shied from them although their tongues were swollen as their
dusty riders'. Wearily the men eased their saddle galls and looked along the
high ridges and then down the lengthening alkali flats.

"This shore is a hell of a country! I say let 'em Indians hev it," the farrier
complained, as Thornburgh led his bearding men on, less in pursuit of
Indians now than to get through, out. Their rations were gone, the ammunition only what each man carried, and always there was the possibility
of an Indian ambush around the next hill, any hill. If the Cheyennes had
the ammunition and fresh horses, it could easily be another Custer massacre,
Bourke thought, and wished he were following his cautious, game-nosed
general. Crook was not the man to move without his excellent pack train,

the best to be found in the entire army. But Thornburgh had to go as ordered.

Along the bitter lakes they struck a fresh troop trail, with some unshod hoofs and moccasin tracks at a camping—Indian or breed scouts—Colonel Carlton with his five companies from Robinson. Now even Thornburgh's horses seemed to know they were no longer lost, although nobody knew their position. Somewhere south of the Niobrara, because it flowed across the north for 500 miles, but no telling how far away. Then toward noon smoke began to boil up out of the northwest, pale and opalescent, and scattered in several places, not like a prairie fire. Probably Indians burning the Niobrara ranches—on the warpath. Gradually the wind turned northwest, curling the sand around the plodding hoofs of the horses, trailing the smoke in over the men, the sun red, the nose and eyes stinging.

By now they were crossing broad parallel valleys running southeastward, so long that the eye finally drew the ridges together. The ground was dry, well-sodded, hard under the iron hoofs of the horses. Deer were thick in the buckbrush along the slopes, the strings of hills as high as little mountain chains, and mostly grassed to the top. Then suddenly there were lakes all around, not connected but with underground drainage, for the horses drank well, while in the west ends there were cold currents as of underground springs, with the water sweet and clear. Here the troops cared for their horses, bathed the cinch sores, cooked a lunch of ember-broiled venison, and looked uneasily to the smoke still rolling over them from the north. While the major shaved the stubble from his cleft chin and trimmed his sideburns, the men talked uneasily about the Indians, with every sandpass still a possible ambush and the horses too worn down for a charge or for flight. But Carlton's trail led on, the brush patches on the north slopes thickened, with a scattering of yellow hackberry and boxelder trees growing from plum thickets and from chokecherry brush that was still black and bending with the drying fruit. Deer flushed everywhere and a few cowchips began to show up in the fall grass, the cattle wilder than antelope.

Then suddenly they struck a wide rutted wagon road. Thornburgh stopped, looking both ways. Evidently one of the Black Hills gold trails, the thin sod cut by the heavy freight and mine machinery. They still saw no uneasy game, no Indian sign, only now and then a horsebacker suddenly gone from the top of a far ridge, whether cowboy or Indian it was too far to tell. But suddenly the trail fell to a stream so crooked within its steep little canyon that it must surely be the Snake River of their untrustworthy maps. Couriers from Robinson looking for Carlton came up the trail, with newspaper rumors that the colonel and Thornburgh both had been massacred, two more names added to those of the immortal Fetterman and Custer.

Thornburgh laughed with sunburnt lips. "I think Colonel Carlton is safe enough. From the horse droppings on his trail he can't be a day ahead and we've been chasing him hard. We're reduced to fresh game, and everybody's so loose boweled the saddles are empty much of the time. We need hard tack. . . ."

The couriers pushed on and the next day Carlton sent packs of supplies back from his camp on the Niobrara. He had started to scout down the Snake River for the Indian crossing, but a courier had come with a telegram that there was an uprising among the Sioux. From the smoke rising there ahead of him Carlton assumed the Indians were burning and raiding —perhaps old Red Cloud himself had broken out. Because all possible effort must be made to prevent a juncture of the Sioux with the Cheyennes, Carlton had hurried to the river, to discover that the Sioux were quiet, there was no sign of an Indian anywhere, and the fires were on farther north, probably burning prairie.

By midafternoon Thornburgh reached the deep canyon of the Niobrara. Golden fall timber lay along the feet of the gray bluffs, with patches of blood-red creeper. Great yellow cottonwoods stood alone out on the grassy bottoms, willows and the silver of buffaloberry bushes clumped the river banks, the stream running swift and clear. They had reached the Niobrara, the Running Water of the Indians.

But where were the Cheyennes?

The troops that gathered around the new Pine Ridge agency stirred up great excitement among Red Cloud's Sioux. The women and children were ready to flee and the warriors drew their horses aside, their faces covered with their blankets, refusing so much as the *"Hou!"* given every stranger.

"What are you looking for here?" Red Cloud demanded, while his young men whipped up from all around to protect their chief, faces dark, guns ready across their horses. "If you come for a fight, my men will fight you. If you don't want to fight, go home!" he said, speaking to the officers as to small boys.

But the troops did not shoot or leave. More kept coming along every creek, across the prairie and through the Black Hills. Every morning more bluecoats watched and the women starting the cooking fires were as uneasy as buffaloes lifting their noses into the wind.

"We must wait . . . ," was all Red Cloud could say to his council, to those who would go to Sitting Bull in Canada, even to those who came running from Spotted Tail's agency because a soldier chief was there with many guns and big talk. They had set all the little prairie fires behind them to hold back the soldiers. Now they found them here too.

The young lieutenant Scott who had learned sign talk from the Cheyennes he helped bring down to Sidney was put to live in Red Cloud's lodge. The old chief knew this was a spying, but his people were surrounded. Three days later one of the Sioux from Dull Knife's band slipped in with his family, to ask for refuge for the Cheyennes, hopelessly now that he saw how the Sioux chief was already surrounded.

Although Red Cloud and his chiefs had to ride down to the council called by Thornburgh and Carlton at Camp Sheridan, they came in all their paint and feathers, their scalp-fringed shirts and shell breast plates, their Sharps carbines, the revolvers and cartridge belts. The warriors behind the headmen were armed too, their fingers by habit in the trigger guards.

After the pipe Major Thornburgh spoke of their good will toward the Sioux. They had come to ask help against the bad Cheyennes who only wanted to stir up trouble on the agency here. The best thing would be to turn them over to the troops so they could be taken back south.

The interpreting was followed by a long Sioux silence. Finally Red Cloud spoke, in his deep guttural way, making his graceful gestures. The hearts of his people were good. The Great Father had telegraphed him to stop the runaway Cheyennes, but none had been seen. He was tired of war. The grave wind was blowing around him and he was not afraid. The young men were hot to fight all these white soldiers if he permitted it. "The Cheyennes are our friends; our young men have married their young women. If I see them come, I will feed them and let you know. I think they are already beyond the Black Hills."

To Carlton's impatient question about Cheyennes reported in his camp, a proud shadow passed over the old Sioux's face. "I do not speak with the crooked tongue. I leave that to the whites. I have seen no Cheyennes. If any come, I will hold them but I will treat them right. They have been misused; they have had bad agents."

"Hou! Hou!" the circle of chiefs agreed, and then one after another rose to complain of the thieving whites everywhere. So Carlton had a little feast made for the council and afterward he stood beside Thornburgh as they rode away, uncertain just what Red Cloud had promised.

Thornburgh reached Fort Robinson under the White River bluffs ten days after he left the Platte, his horses so played out it took him two days to make the 45 miles from Camp Sheridan. Near Chadron Creek they struck the trail of a large band of Indians going north, but his men were already walking to spare the horses.

In all the pursuit from the Beaver north only one Cheyenne had been shot, the old man who fell off his horse. Not another Indian was caught by the Army, but cowboys captured a woman and her son of sixteen along Snake Creek and turned them in with Little Chief's band at Fort Sidney. There was a rumor that a Sioux scout for the troops had taken ten Cheyennes, including two fighting men, to Red Cloud. A man and two women captured on Snake Creek by civilians were brought to Robinson. They sat in their ragged blankets, refusing to talk except to say they had fooled all the soldiers. Cheyennes always fooled the *veho* soldiers.

Now the newspapers took up the cowboy's favorite quip. It wasn't, said the Chicago *Times,* that anyone expected Thornburgh to capture the Cheyennes, but there was rejoicing that the Cheyennes had not captured the major, while *The New York Times* referred to the jealousy between Generals Miles and Gibbon, and the common admission that a handful of Cheyennes had outgeneraled the generals.

Antiadministration papers asked if it would not be cheaper to feed the worthless coffee coolers than to chase them all over hell 'n' gone. The handful of Cheyennes could have been fed indefinitely on hummingbird tongues and the taxpayer still ahead. But not the railroads and the contractors, God bless 'em.

Carlton and Captain Johnson took up a wide Indian trail discovered northeast of Fort Robinson, with fresh troops and horses, fully equipped for a winter campaign as General Crook understood the term. With Johnson rode twenty Indian and breed scouts, most of them going because they had relatives among the Cheyennes. Some of the troopers were uneasy about this close tie with the enemy. The first night several came to tell Johnson that one of the scouts was a man who had slipped in from Dull Knife's band two weeks ago and that another was Pawnee, son of Little Wolf.

"We'll be runnin' straight into a ambush!"

Johnson laughed. "There's Chief Young Man, Afraid of His Horse,* at the scout fire. You don't suspect treachery in his presence. Besides most of the scouts are in this for profit, for the Cheyenne stock they can take."

By the next day the weather darkened, turned to fog, rain, and finally to sleet and wind-driven snow—the fall's first blizzard was on the way.

October the twenty-third, nineteen days after Thornburgh took up the trail at the Platte, Johnson's advance scouts noticed vague forms in the blowing storm along the breaks of upper Chadron Creek. Then the captain saw them too, momentarily, between blasts of wind: snow-whitened figures bent almost like cattle before the blizzard, only a few with horses— the lost Cheyennes. Suddenly the Indians ran together and then tried to scatter, those with horses whipping back between the people and the scouts. But it was useless to run, there were too many soldiers. The people crouched down in the snow, almost lost to sight, afraid, while a few of the warriors hurried up to a little ridge between the column and their people and stood there—a couple with warbonnets blowing, visible between gusts of driving snow.

* The Man, Afraid of His Horse family are called the Adams family of the American Indian, reaching in honorable and unbroken line from the seventeenth century into the twentieth.

11 The Rejection

THE MORNING AFTER THAT LAST COUNCIL ON WHITE
Tail Creek a fog came to cover the country like a
blanket pulled over the shame of separation. The fog was thick and wet to
the face, shutting out everything even when the sun climbed high behind
it. The Indians went as fast as they could, but sadly; this dividing seemed
something final, for the years. It was hard, with all the ties of blood and
after the long association, the long living, lodge by lodge around the sacred
circle, the fine happy times of the hunts and the ceremonials made together,
and the fighting too, in victory and in defeat, and now the still closer
bonds of danger and desperation endured together.

Those with old troubles between them were not separated. With Dull
Knife rode Left Hand and Great Eyes, and Little Wolf had Thin Elk
along. Most of the Elks were with their man and with the others of big
reputation in the Crook fight and against Custer, all going to the Yellowstone. But some of the younger warriors like Little Finger Nail, Charging
Bear, Red Bird, and two of the Roman Noses were with Dull Knife. He
knew it was not his leadership that drew them but their relatives with him
or among the Sioux, or the pretty girls along, Hog's and his own, and
Singing Cloud. They were not enough to cheer the old chief for the split
in his people, or for the empty place of Short One when the time came to
own a lodge once more.

But already sharp crane calls came through the hush of the fog, reporting
that soldiers had found the White Tail camp. So very soon.

Little Wolf, with few old or sick and none like the crippled Sitting Man,
had scattered his people immediately and sent them straight for the deepest
of the sandhills. It would be like chasing a new-hatched covey of quail in
a brush patch to get these Cheyennes. Dull Knife, with the helpless ones,

blood Cheyennes with no Sioux ties, to make the gestures of subjugation as to a conquering enemy, begging to be spared. It was a desperate, shaming thing to do, but it too was thrown away, and the men came back in silence, some of those who had gone earlier riding along. Tangle Hair walked, so dark with this bad news that sat like the moldy robe of bereavement, of banishment upon him.

"Red Cloud is surrounded. He can do nothing," he told Dull Knife and the rest at the sheltered little fire, lowering his loud Sioux voice. "The chief has asked that we be permitted to live with his people, but the soldiers and the Great Father say he must give up every Cheyenne found among them. All our friend can tell us is, 'Give up to the soldiers. They will feed you.'"

"He speaks like the pay worker of the whites, not the chief of his great Sioux nation or a man who owns himself!" Bull Hump told his father, shouting it out. "Those soldiers in bluecoats that we fooled all the way now order that it be done and so we have to go back south. . . ."

"We will die first," Dull Knife said, so sorrowful and low it could scarcely be heard by the soft-listening Cheyennes about him. It was a hard thing to see, this man rousing himself to realize that all his plans for refuge had only been a dreaming. They looked into the earth, for no one could speak the comforting words as Dull Knife slowly got up and stumbled away into the darkness. Here and there a woman began to cry softly, and then that too was gone.

Now the Cheyennes began another kind of packing, very slowly, the move put off hour by hour, and then another day because there were still a few people talking to the Sioux. Then word came that those Cheyennes were to be held as prisoners. Besides, Red Cloud had to warn his friends that twenty of his men and a few breeds had gone as scouts. American Horse and Two Lance, both related to the Dull Knife people, would lead them, bringing the fresh soldiers of Colonel Carlton and Captain Johnson from Robinson. The scouts were of good heart toward their friends and brothers, but they would find the Cheyennes. Even their own man, Fool, was along because he knew it was better to have Indians there among the charging soldiers than that they come alone.

Now the Cheyennes must make the last run. The headmen counciled, but it was a decision already marked in the dust. Without lodges, blankets, meat, or ammunition for the hunt and defense, or good horses, they could not hope to get through the soldiers standing across the north, not without the help of Bear Coat Miles on the Yellowstone. Hog admitted this, still not telling Dull Knife that a messenger had been sent there. Help could not come in time now. They had lost two good weeks of fall waiting on Red Cloud, and now the first storm of winter was upon them.

So they must beg help from Spotted Tail. They were not related there, nor were their goods ever promised at that agency, yet Spot's Sioux warriors had ridden with them against the Smoky Hill trail in 1864 and he was along on the great march north after Sand Creek. He was a strong man who had always held the Great Father's agents in his palm like bits of tobacco to be rubbed fine for the pipe.

No one spoke of the soldiers watching Spotted Tail now, or the large band that came fleeing from there to Red Cloud only two weeks ago, firing the prairie behind them. Tangle Hair brought out the big package of tobacco given him by Red Cloud as a guest present. They made a last smoke, drank the gift coffee and sugar, and decided that it was really a very good plan, this going to Spotted Tail.

The women made a busy hurrying with their few packs, but their eyes were dull, their hands dead, and Hog remembered the old Cheyenne saying, "No people is whipped until the hearts of its women are on the ground, and then it is done, no matter how great the warriors or how strong the lance."

By morning the gray clouds ran along the tops of the higher ridges like herds of dirty *veho* sheep. Soon they would hide everything so it seemed safe to keep moving. Only a third of the Cheyennes rode on the worn-out horses—the young men, who must scout, fight if necessary, and hunt, on the best. The poorest had been taken along to better grass by the wood gatherers who went ahead to the last trees, to make enough wood for the night and to carry with them. No matter how fast they traveled, one camp must be made on the bare wind-swept table back to the Niobrara.

The fog turned to graying rain and then froze. The Indians bent before the storm, drawing their rags for blankets about themselves as the sleet began to rattle like shot on the icy ground and then dried to fine snow, the thin white curls running out of the northwest around the feet. It gathered in the low places, moccasin-deep, and then rose higher on the wind, shutting out the warriors scouting up ahead. Hog, leading the long single file of Indians, drew in close to the low ridges of Chadron Creek for protection. The wind quickened, whipping the powdery snow until the air was thick and white and the string of people, humped with the storm and the weight of children and bundles, was so lost that no one could see beyond the snowy horse or the stooping back just ahead. The cold bit the breast and froze the clothing stiff as parfleche, but no one dared stop a panting moment. Like cattle the Indians were driven before the storm, the eyes hooded, those afoot plodding clumsily now, awkward as with the ice that balls under a horse's hoofs. The fury of the blizzard grew, the drifts deepening, apparently to the waist, perhaps suddenly higher, until the little camp waiting up ahead was forgotten, everything forgotten except the people falling in the storm.

Then the Sioux scouts of the Army were suddenly there beside the Cheyennes, their whooping faint in the storm, the men almost within lancing distance. The people tried to run together and then apart again, to scatter. A few of the warriors were back against the scouts, others charging the row of soldiers suddenly there too, like a snowy bank up against the shoulder, with surely many, many more around, and all the guns loaded.

"Nobody could have found us today!" Tangle Hair growled angrily. "We have been betrayed!"

Some around him made replies to that, angry replies. Yes, it must be betrayal, and from among them here, perhaps with signaling last night— somebody who knew where the camp was to be. Ahh-h! Could it have been one of their Sioux, those who might not have to go back south, perhaps Tangle Hair himself?

But at once they quieted. It was done, and already Dull Knife, Hog, and Old Crow were hurrying up to make the signs of recognition, to lift the hand to American Horse and Two Lance and others of the Sioux scouts. Then the soldier chiefs came to a sheltered place and dismounted, awkward in their buffalo coats. While they shook hands with the Indians, Long Joe Larrabee, the breed interpreter, made ready, pounding his mittens, breaking the ice that bound his mustache and beard together with a sweep of his arm.

The man called Captain Johnson spoke. "We are very glad we found you. We want to feed your people and give them shelter—"

"We want no trouble," Dull Knife interrupted. "We were dying in that country south and came back. Now we are going to Spotted Tail, away from your country, so you can take your soldiers back to the fort."

But the captain would not permit the going. Through Long Joe talking Sioux to Tangle Hair, who made it Cheyenne, he said that he was very sorry to see them so poor and cold in this storm. "Nobody will harm you or your people. Come to our camp just a little way from here and we will feed you."

"We are going to Spotted Tail," Dull Knife repeated stubbornly, as though it had been the plan from far down south.

The soldier chiefs looked together and then over toward the miserable huddle of people fitfully visible in a drifted brush patch, perhaps in old cotton cloth like some of the headmen here, their feet wrapped in rags. Then the captain called out some orders and the soldiers moved up close upon the people in a shooting line, the scouts pushing in too.

"Can't you see that your people must have shelter?" Johnson roared out against Dull Knife, making it sound as angry as the blizzard around them.

"We are going on," the chief repeated, and so the captain straightened himself in his buffalo coat, standing there before the little row of Indians with snow in their braids, their frost-swollen hands holding the thin, flapping blankets about them.

"You will have to come to our camp or fight," he said.

Even before it was interpreted, Dull Knife and the others knew the meaning; the people too, already crying their songs for strength, somehow moving a little to the side in the blowing snow without seeming to do this, ready to scatter into the storm, doing it even with the soldier guns drawn down on them.

"We will ask the others," Hog said as quietly as for some little unimportant thing and started away, Dull Knife and Crow following. Almost at once they came back to the officers, the singing louder behind them, the thin high sound of the death songs carried on the storm.

"We go with you," Hog said.

Straight, gaunt now, but seeming even more than his six feet five in the snowy blanket, he turned to lead off in the direction the soldier chief motioned with his fur gauntlet, straight into the wind. The others followed, the few riding trying to whip the horses face on into the driving snow. Mostly they walked too, dragging their horses along through the drifts, panting, heads bent like all the others, the troopers ahead hunched like whitened bears over their saddles, looking back to the Indians as the storm thinned a little and the cold went down far below zero. Several times the Indians stopped in sheltered places, sinking down into the snow. Always Johnson spurred back with a company of troopers, guns ready, and so they had to get up and with the children and the packs bend into the storm again, some of the men loaded too, although their hands should be free for fighting, if help should somehow come, not from Red Cloud now, but perhaps Little Wolf's warriors might break from the storm. But the Wolf had no guns for this, and all that came were the few from the camp that had gone ahead, brought in by the scouts like blizzard-driven cattle.

Finally they reached the soldier camp down Chadron Creek. A big fire had been started in a protected brushy spot where Johnson motioned the Indians to camp. Then hard bread, bacon, and coffee with plenty of sugar were brought. Even a freezing soldier spoke in sorrowful tones to see the people so poor, with so few of the men left in strength, the rest, men, women, and children, thin and worn and ragged, hands, feet, even legs frozen to twice their size in the thawing firelight.

There was fear and heavy weariness, and then a little quiet joy when Two Lance's daughter saw her father sitting there among them for a smoke, and several other relatives. But later troops came closer in the storm and men rode around the camp, riding, riding.

After dawn Dull Knife and several others threw the drifts back from their brush shelters and went out to where the mounted guards passed in the blizzard and motioned to them to go away. But the soldiers kept on, so Bull Hump took a couple of warriors out with guns. A whole company of troops charged up all around, those on the east on a high place overlooking the Cheyennes, ready to shoot down into the blizzard camp. Then Captain Johnson sent for the headmen.

"I must have the ponies and all your arms!"

The chiefs made their best Indian delayings. In turn they spoke of the bad treatment in the south country, although Johnson demanded the arms and horses at every pause. They kept talking so some of the guns could be hidden. Once more Black Bear's wife hung the Custer carbine in two pieces under her dress, and Young Medicine Man's wife and others hid pistols and ammunition. The men put away what they could, but with the women the guns were safer.

When Johnson ordered his men up close in impatience, Hog made the signs and a few horses were led out, Young Hog coming first, shouting, "I give mine to our uncle, American Horse!" others calling out other scouts by name, hoping to get some of the stock back later. A few guns were brought too, Old Crow and Hog going to the place Johnson designated, with a row of soldiers waiting, ready for trouble. Crow laid down the first gun, to the angry cries of the young men, "The agency loafer! The coffee cooler!" Little Finger Nail adding his voice too. "See how the *veho* lover runs to please them!"

But it was as though the wind carried only its own noise. Next Hog put down his bow and quiver and threw back his snow-crusted blanket to show that he was without other arms. Then there was more complaining, going clear back to the goods taken by Sumner in 1857, with Captain Johnson stomping his feet in the cold and repeating, "Bring out the ponies and the guns!"

Soldiers creeping up saw a few horses tied down flat in the drifts and others standing, some of them grayish mules and easier to hide in the winter brush. But Johnson ordered his men back. "The Indians must bring out all the stock!"

So the others were led forward, very slowly, the women making the sad little sounds of mourning to see the last one gone. The horse of Sitting Man was returned to him at Hog's request because his broken leg was still so bad. But when the last rope was taken, the Foolish Roman Nose drew his bow against the soldier. He did it quickly, before even Hog could stop him. The soldier guns jumped up ready all along the watching line, the women cried and ran, falling in the snow. But Captain Johnson charged against the guns of his troops, shouting, "Hold your fire, men! Hold—" the storm carrying his voice away.

From this the Cheyennes saw that he was a strong man, one they would remember a long time. So a few more guns were brought to the pile but thrown down angrily, even by old Blacksmith, long an agency man. Then Dull Knife said these were the last, all. It was a very small pile, only about fifteen—two of them shotguns, some muzzle-loaders, a few breech-loading rifles and carbines—and almost all the bows they made on the way up.

The little pile was carried away, Johnson giving the bows and arrows to the soldiers who held out their hands for them, and the muzzle-loaders and shotguns to the scouts, keeping only the good. Then the camp was counted, Long Joe and Lone Bear going among the Cheyennes, stooping to look into every little brush shelter and hole: 46 men, 61 women, 42 children—149 people and 131 horses and 9 mules. It was all written down in the soldier chief's book: guns, horses, mules, people, all together.

Then the horses were taken away, the soldiers yelling, shooting those they could not move into the wind, the women keening for all these things lost as for a loved one dead.

Now the soldiers came up to the Cheyennes bent together in the storm, helpless, unable to escape or fight. The women began to sing strong-heart songs, not for the helpless warriors but for themselves, to keep themselves from running and getting shot down like the moose or elk that the hunters scare from the winter yards to flounder in the snow. Brave One remembered how it was at Sand Creek and the Washita and Sappa too. She held herself very still, with Lame Girl drawn to her side, wondering when the bullets would strike, as they had struck before. Around her others wondered too, all those from the fight on the fork of the Powder. Always the soldier bullets came flying from the storm.

But nothing happened until it was evening and more food was brought. With the stomach full and fires to warm the ground and the shelters in the brush, the Cheyennes slept easier than in two, three moons. Nothing more could happen to them now except death.

That night still more soldiers came. A Sioux-talking Cheyenne who slipped to the scout camp said that the Colonel Carlton who hunted Indians all through the sandhills was there now, and ordered Johnson to capture the Cheyenne men in the morning, tie their hands, and march them in a string to Robinson.

"Ahh-h!" Black Horse snarled angrily. "It is like the ironing for the prison! We must get away!"

All around him were the *"Hous!"* of approval, but one did not desert the helpless ones. Besides, it seemed that the captain had talked strong against tying anybody. He said the Indians were probably not all disarmed and so everyone would have to be killed to get it done, and some soldiers hurt too. Peace was better.

"Hou!" A good man, this captain, but they were all in bad danger.

In the morning the Cheyennes were told by Long Joe that the soldier wagon train was to stop close by and they could put their goods on top of the rolled tents and ride to Fort Robinson.

"Robinson!" the chiefs roared against him. "You are allowed to come here because you have an Indian mother! Now you betray us!"

The young men pushed up threateningly, so the breed left but returned with Colonel Carlton and Johnson too. Once more the chiefs went out to make a delay, talking for three hours this time. It was behind a little bank out of the wind, with fires to warm the hands, and when the colonel kept saying, "Hurry, hurry . . . ," they always smoked a little more. Finally Dull Knife rose. "It is easy for our friend here to speak of making the hurry-hurry. He decides for the time of one war party; we decide here for all the time of our people, for all those to come after us, those whose grand-fathers have not yet put a foot upon the grass."

Captain Johnson nodded his head in its snowy beaver cap, and there was no more talk of hurrying from the colonel. But they must go to Fort Robinson.

"It is a step toward the south. It was from Robinson that we were taken down there," Dull Knife kept objecting. "We want to go to talk to our friends the Sioux."

So Carlton suggested taking them to Camp Sheridan, and to Robinson the next day.

"Robinson again! Always this starting place for trouble! Take us to the Sioux!"

But that could not be done. Those Indians were not yet settled on their new agency and had no place for the Cheyennes. The Great Father had telegraphed that it could not be done.

So it went, back and forth, a very long and uneasy waiting for the war-riors with the people. Finally a noise and confusion started in the Indian camp, with a drumming on the wind, and dancing and war songs. Then it was as if there had been a message, a signal, for the headmen got up together from the council fire.

"We will die before we go south," Hog said. Dull Knife and Left Hand and the rest grunted their approval and together they started away, walk-ing in single file into the blizzard wall, Hog ahead.

As the excitement grew in the camp, Long Joe refused to go down to quiet the Indians. "It is dangerous," he said, nervously pulling at his black mustache. "The Indians they say they will be fetch' out to move where the soldier can see and then they all be shot. Some they dig the many hole in ground, and I have see the gun they got. It is dangerous to go there. . . ."

Tangle Hair was called out. "Tell the Indians they have had their chance to choose," Colonel Carlton said. "Now it is too late to move. In the morning they must go to Robinson, but nobody will be hurt." He stopped a while, looking down into the storm where the drum still rose and fell. "Tell them too that there will be nothing more to eat until they get to Robinson."

Slowly Tangle Hair went back, giving his bad news only to Hog and Dull Knife. Hog went out to make one more talk. "Our people are worn out and very cold and hungry," he said gravely. "There are many little children hungry among us. . . ."

"Nothing for anybody until you get to Robinson."

Darkness came with troops camped in the snow on both sides of the creek. The Indians worked all night. With little rows of fires shielded from the storm so the ground could be thawed, they dug breastworks facing the soldiers. Then they cut down trees to lay along the top, with notches chopped for gun barrels. If there must be fighting, they would all die here together, and as Little Finger Nail had said down there in the south, their names and the places would always be remembered.

Two Lance had asked that he be given his relatives from the Cheyenne camp and Carlton agreed, but first he must sleep with the Indians this night, he and Lone Bear. They must watch that no one escaped and could have all the guns they detected.

As the white snow dawn came, more soldiers moved up, enough to make a frozen ring around the Indians, a wall, with a Napoleon, a wagon gun, and another cannon later. This time the men of Custer would get into the Indian camp behind bursting cannon balls.

So the Cheyennes sent the scout Lone Bear back to say they would agree to go to Sheridan, but it was still too dark and no reply came, and the Indians felt really cut off, like a small bunch of buffaloes in a tribal surround. There was nothing from Spotted Tail or Little Wolf either, or from Red Cloud. Not even to the desperate call that Young Chief Little Wolf carried as he slipped away into the storm when Johnson first found them. Truly the Powers had forgotten the Cheyennes, and some thought of the Sacred Buffalo Hat left back there in the south.

In this trouble Medicine Man tried to help. Ever since the soldiers came, he stayed off within himself, without food or drink, and had lain unsheltered in the snow until Bridge and the others could not bear to see him die this slow freezing way and went to build a fire beside him. He grieved that they had done this. What was the small price of death if the Powers would show him how the people could be saved?

Now it was morning and the strengthening storm winds brought the smell of coffee in the flying snow. Everything was moved back and rifle pits dug for the soldiers too. Plainly it was to be a fight. Some of the Indians were a little glad. Better that it be done quickly now. The sickest and the hurt ones like little Lame Girl were put into a hole dug for them. Sitting Man took his place at the few guns, the arrows and knives, as good as any man now that nobody could run.

At last Carlton sent for the headmen. He showed them the two cannons, both ready to drop their bursting shells of fire into the camp in the brush. "Be ready to go to Robinson in one hour," he said, pulling out his big gold watch, showing its face to Dull Knife in the storm, his finger pointing. "It is twenty-five miles. We will start on time, or we shoot."

"We cannot go until we know what is to be done with us," Dull Knife still protested, but gravely, without heat and stubbornness now.

"I can make no promises. I can only say that my troops will not harm anybody if you go quickly and without trouble."

But this was so hard that the interpreter, easygoing old Long Joe, could not say it so bluntly, not to his own Indian relatives. So he softened it a little for Tangle Hair's Cheyenne. "I promise to do what I can . . . ," he made the words of the colonel say, and the Indians were so desperate for a little hope that they believed it, and more. Yet they had to go ask the people.

Just then a Sioux came riding through the storm. He was a courier from the soldiers at the new Pine Ridge agency and said there was very little to eat there yet. No rations had come, nothing except the beef they brought along when they moved—thin, and very few. The Cheyennes better go to Robinson and be fed until the Great Father decided what was to be done with them.

Red Cloud—hungry too!

Now Dull Knife seemed really whipped. The colonel looked into the old man's broken face and pitied him. "I have decided not to fire the big guns into the women and children," he said, "but I can give you no food except at Robinson. . . ."

So Hog led the chiefs down to the camp and in a little while they returned. They would go, but it would be difficult. The people were very frightened; the soldiers should be careful. It was true, and several started to run when a soldier tried to help a frost-crippled old woman up over the wheel. They were uneasy too, that Two Lance had taken his daughter and her family on good horses, wrapped in good soldier blankets, and started away toward Pine Ridge, riding sideways to the storm that was rising even sharper. Why did Two Lance risk this freezing ride for his daughter instead of staying with the warm wagons until the storm cleared, perhaps even tomorrow? What was going to happen?

But at last everyone was loaded, the men walking, all except Sitting Man and a couple of others with feet frozen thick and dark as buffalo bladders of pounded meat. The colonel went ahead with his three companies breaking trail. Johnson's troops who had found the Indians were given the honor place along each side and behind them, with the Sioux scouts there too, those who had not slipped away to get some of the better Cheyenne horses from the captured herd. In the middle of the moving column the wagons creaked over the frozen hoof-cut snow, pushing out into the storm like sullen buffaloes going with heads down, driven by winter from the only range they knew.

About ten miles on, the storm had lifted to a low gray ceiling, the cold sharper, the wheels creaking more. But the followers could see now and so Hog climbed up into the tail of a wagon and stood there, a snow-caked, powerful figure, looking tall as a great winter pine while he made a harangue to the men walking behind and beside the wagons.

"Hear me, my brothers!" he cried into the wind, lifting the Cheyenne words loud as the *veho* commands. "Where we are going we will all be locked up. Irons will be burned on to our legs; we will be taken away to the stone houses, the prisons, our people driven back to the sick country. The soldier chief says we will not be hurt, but he speaks with the crooked tongue of the *veho*. They all lie. We were told we could come back and you see what is done. And Black Horse heard them promise no one would be hurt down in the south country and then they were ironed and dragged away. Good men like Grey Beard never returned, and many died trying to get away north from that place. Perhaps it would be better for us to make a break at the next canyon. You will remember it. Our fathers stood off some Crows there, many Crows, a long time ago, and on the bottoms Bull Bear made a very strong Medicine Lodge when the Pawnees had to be driven from our buffalo ranges. We will lie in a good place, for many of us will fall on the ground, my friends, but it is better to die fighting." Then he lifted his voice in a clear, high song:

> Eyia-ah-ah, Powers help us!
> Powers that live in the winds of the storming!
> In all the Great Directions, and in the earth and the sky,
> Help us!

And when he made the thin cry that was the end, the walking men sang back to him, led by Bullet Proof and Bull Hump:

> It is a good day to die!
> Cheyennes, it is a very good day to die!

Captain Johnson did not understand the words, but he knew it was trouble and sent a messenger ahead, his horse plunging through the drifts. Another company of troops hurried back. Guns out, they charged their horses in to separate the walking Indians and cut them away from both sides of the wagons. Cheyenne faces grew dark to see this done, but Tangle Hair brought his right hand out flat and then gently down, twice in the sign of "Wait, wait!" to his Dog soldiers. Even Hog spoke it in quiet words. "Not now! Do not throw yourself away so cheap!"

Farther on one of the wagons turned over on an icy, wind-bared place, the load spilling the women and children and goods down a drifted gully. They were gathered up and hurried into another wagon, not given time to collect their bundles from the snow. But the soldiers opened them, showing the big silver rings that Bear Shield had sent home from Florida, rings given him by a white woman for his children. They were to hold the white cloths used by the *veho* to wipe the mouth during eating, as the Indian did with the blade of the knife or the back of the hand. The children had worn them for bracelets a while, until the sickness killed them. Now the soldiers had found the rings and were making angry words for the Indians because there were white-man names on them: Frankie and Jessie.

The Indians were uneasy about some of the other things in the bundles, and some they had left behind in the rifle pits at Chadron Creek—the boy's saddle from the big black horse taken in the canyon near Beaver Creek, some white-woman garments, and a couple of their blankets of silk pieces sewed together.

Toward evening the wind died and the cold grew until it bit the nose as in midwinter. The men, their feet cut by the ice and hoof cakes of the trail, were glad to get into the wagons. Here and there soldiers walked too, even some with the buffalo coats and muskrat caps, moving cumbersome as grizzlies ready for the long sleep, but ordered off their horses to keep from freezing in the white dusk.

So the long column of double troopers wound down into the White River valley, the flag flying ahead, and in the middle of the long line the Indian wagons with guards on each side. At the crossing of the stream just before the fort some Sioux scouts came crowding in between the wagons and the soldiers. The drifts were very deep here and the only trail was the one made by the troopers riding two abreast, the road through the banked willows little wider than the wagons. So the soldiers had to fall back in the pale night. Here Bull Hump's wife, the daring Leaf who rode the wild horses, rolled herself into a ball, and as the wagon lurched at the icy approach to the stream, she threw herself into the deep snowbank in the brush, the Sioux crowding their horses around her, taking her like a bundle behind one of the saddles in the darkness. Then the scouts moved back to let the soldiers past.

The Indians were taken through the white darkness into the post and up to the open doorway of a long barracks with light spilling out into the frosty night and glistening through the rimy windows. The smell of pitch-pine fire and coffee cooking brought a murmuring of anticipation from the Indians. One of the women began to sob aloud in her relief, and choked herself into immediate silence. But as the Cheyennes got stiffly down from the wagons, fresh soldiers with guns in their hands came out of the night to stand guard around them, their warm breaths smoking in the light.

"Drop the packs in a line here," a soldier chief said, making the motion of a row. "All of them will be searched."

For a moment every foot stopped, every eye. Several warriors tried to back away into the night, hands moving swiftly under their blankets, but the naked bayonets of the guard were against their backs.

"Hold yourself," Hog said, very low and soft. "Hold yourself for the right time."

12   Stepping Aside

WHEN THE SCOUTS SIGNALED THAT ALL THE SOLDIERS were gone beyond the Niobrara, worn out and tired, and not chasing anybody around here for a while, Little Wolf's Cheyennes began to come out of their scattered hidings, cautiously, almost afraid to be seen by the sun. Silently they moved through the broken, choppy sandhills west of the head of Snake River, one from here, another there, toward the place of meeting. Then suddenly, in a little well-sodded pocket already shadowing with the lowered sun, they were together, the first time since north of the Platte.

Suddenly their chief was there too, on his spotted horse on a golden bunchgrass slope. Quietly Little Wolf looked down over them, seeking out any missing, counting them all. Then he lifted his hand and started away, his people following around a hill and down into Lost Chokecherry, a valley so small and sheltered it seemed held within the cupping of two warm palms. Yet there was a lake clouded with fall ducks; muskrat houses rose from the evening water and many sweet rushes. In the northwest end of the valley, a steep hill lifted itself against the winds to come, with a scattering of boxelders standing in their fallen leaves on the steep slope. Lower hills made a wall all around, rising well-grassed from the bottoms. At the south a wide strip of brush lay brown and russet along the slope, with hackberry trees, some almost naked cottonwoods, and higher up, the dark green of a few little cedars.

The Cheyennes trailed into the valley in a weary, bedraggled line behind their chief, the women still led by Buffalo Calf Road, the small children balanced in the hide sacks swung from the saddles, the larger ones riding behind the women and clinging tight to their gaunted waists, even some

grown people riding double, for there must be no betraying track of a moccasin anywhere.

Gratefully the Indians dropped their bundles, the women making it as for
another fast stop, looking back uneasily over their shoulders, always looking
back. But there was only the shadowing western hill that seemed close and
comforting as the folds of a blanket. Some looked around in the other
directions too, watching, no longer hoping, not noticing one among them
who wavered in her saddle, clutched at a bundle, and then slipped down
under the horse that did not move, head sagging in weariness. There was
a cry and Spotted Deer ran to pull his grandmother away from the hoofs.
The medicine man came and spoke quietly to her, "My sister—"

"Let me die," Old Grandmother moaned softly. "I am played out—"
as a chill of the southern fever shook her again.

But Spotted Deer built a little fire and accepted the blanket that Feather
on Head brought, one of the few left whole. Gently he wrapped the old
woman in it, stroking her thin gray braids, but his eyes strayed to the young
Yellow Bead hurrying to the lake with a waterskin for the grandmother.
It was fine to have the girl help, even for a moment.

Slowly the other women had returned to their work, trying to move
faster now, clumsily hastening, for it would soon be night. Only one long
streak of yellow was left. It cut across the sky to a hill rising over the crowding ridges far to the east and the lone pine tree on top, very small in the
distance. The Cheyennes knew a scout was there, watching the white man's
trail that cut deep as the Overland roads along the Platte. But this one went
into their old country, into the Black Hills after more of the gold that made
the whites run so crazy.

There were some, like Thin Elk and Black Coyote, who thought it was
foolish to camp so close to the trail where two columns of soldiers had just
passed and where bull trains and faster travel could be seen every day.

"It is the best place," Little Wolf said, and they let it be done, doubtfully,
yet remembering that he got them away from the soldiers who rode so
close from the Beaver clear across the Platte. Now for the half of a moon
they spent coming through the sandhills most of the people here had seen
no more of the soldiers than if none lived. Here the smell of their small
fires could be from campers drawn off the worn trail for grass, their horse
tracks from the wild herds or from meat hunters chasing deer and antelope
or shooting the big gray wolves.

As the valley shadowed, a cold wind seemed to rise from the water and the sky turned gray and dark. But almost no one had time to think about the storm that was coming in perhaps a day or two. There were fires to build, small against the hill and shielded by sod or piled brush so the red light could not travel to an enemy. The water was close, and the meat put on to roast as soon as the hunters came in with arrow-shot deer and antelope across the horses. As the Indians ate at the little fires, licking fat from their fingers, they looked uneasily away into the darkness, although they knew that Little Wolf was out riding around the closer watchers. No camp in charge of him and his Elk soldiers had ever been surprised, and none would ever be, if he could help it. The people were worn out, barely stopping to draw the fire spots over the ground to heat the sleeping places. Here and there one smiled a little to another as the love flute of Young Eagle started up on the hillside, softly now, and for the first time since the Lewis fight. It was good to hear his sentimental pipings for still another girl, the third since Blue Fringe in the south. It was good that some could still be young and flighty in love.

When Little Wolf returned and Quiet One went to take his horse, he found Thin Elk at his fireside, bragging about the hunts and his war deeds around here as a young man. Across the fire sat Feather on Head and Pretty Walker, the women listening a little, as they rested and warmed themselves, and smiling to this big talk.

At the next fire Spotted Deer fed broth to his old grandmother who had been so homesick for the north that his southern parents sent him to take her there. He was doing it well, a very good thing in a young man of sixteen. When the old woman slept, snoring a little in her weariness, he went softly away toward the fire where Yellow Bead crouched beside her aunt. He knew the girl had heard his step and felt him standing at the edge of the shadows, his blanket around him as he would have stood waiting at her home lodge. But she gave no sign and he returned to his own fire, wondering if her thoughts were following Little Hump, away with his father Dull Knife, as her eyes had followed him all the way north.

So the Cheyennes settled to their first night of sleep in the place where Little Wolf thought they might stay a while, if everyone was careful. He had 40 men here, including the boys like Spotted Deer, 47 women, 39 children—126 people. There would be one less when Thin Elk took the two good horses Little Wolf offered him for his return to Fort Keogh on the

Yellowstone. Tomorrow, perhaps, or the next day, before the swift hard storms of a Cheyenne autumn.

At the first light of dawn there was a bawling of cattle through the little dip in the hills to the north. Whetstone, Woodenthigh, and a couple of others brought in half a dozen young beeves. Others ran for their horses to help hold them on a sandy slope where it would be easy to cover the butchering with earth to keep the betraying buzzards out of the sky. As the bowstrings twanged, the women ran with their knives in the old, old way. Before the sun came, the meat lay on the skins, fat and fine from the seed-rich grass, the dividers working fast. Old Grandmother, who had wanted to die yesterday, was busy cutting a drying string from a hide, cutting round and round, keeping the strip the width of her little finger, exactly even. She was very good at this, and at working sinews for the arrows, the moccasins, and the beading and other useful purposes.

But there was a sudden signal from the watchers and a low warning of alarm from the Crier. Instantly everyone vanished, some young warriors slipping into the gully that led to their horses, the other Indians gone like the striped young quail in the grass, only the frightened eyes moving, searching the rim of the little valley and the hills that crowded away eastward to the black little tree against the sky. All the sun-yellowed hills were empty a long time, and yet without a signal of safety, nothing more than one flicker of a mirror signal, swift as the glint of sun on a bit of bottle glass, or on splashing water, far off. Then horsebackers rose out of the far hills, two, no, three, abreast in the white-man way. They stopped on a ridge, surely looking down toward Lost Chokecherry, and now everyone held very close to the ground, old Arrowmaker singing his medicine song:

> Earth, hide me, hide my people,
> Grasses of the earth, hide our flesh. . . .

while more of the Elk warriors moved like snakes up the brushy gully southward. If these whites came close enough for discovering, they must be stopped with the silent song of the arrow, if possible. But if there were more, then the people must scatter, crawl away into the rushes, into the chophills —all those who could not get to horses that were strong enough to run.

Finally the riders up there started to move, slowly, as though watching someone, until they were out of sight. No more came and after a while the strong eyes up there signaled for replacement. The new ones were sent out, Spotted Deer among them, for these agency boys must be taught many things before this winter was done. No one could tell who the three men had been, the watchers said, or what they saw before they returned to ride on up the Black Hills trail.

It was lucky that the beef had been found so very soon, and to know there were more cattle in little bunches in the hills up here, with many that had no white-man brands to bring cowboys looking. Too, it was proof that cattle lived here over the winter, even if thin. They would be easier than deer and elk for the arrows, now that ears always listened for guns along the trail.

The sun was out warm but with a whitish look that spoke of a coming snow. The last sandhill cranes made their crooked, honking flights south, and the snowbirds flocked together to whirl and dip like dead leaves. The bit of smoke from the little cooking fires that should have been lost to the eye hung in thin blue layers along the hills and brought uneasiness to the watching Little Wolf. The chief was in council below the boxelders to hear Little Hawk, back from Red Cloud, quiet, heavy with the shame of bad news. He brought the Sioux gift of a cup of coffee for them all and tobacco for a pipe, but he had to admit that Red Cloud was truly surrounded by soldiers, squeezed so that the chief had to refuse even Dull Knife's plea for refuge. The Knife's camp was up near White River, with soldiers very close there too, and a big storm on the way.

Little Wolf made the sound of gravity and the women brought up their work to listen. Last night the northern lights had danced and the horses ran in restlessness. But today there was still sun and the girls were going their pretty way on the water path but making it long. They laughed at the teasing things called out by the watchers riding in from the hills. But Yellow Bead carried her waterskins with her eyes modestly down as some of the others pretended, a slight girl, graceful, and neat as a curlew settling to a spring knoll. Sometimes on the way north arrows had flown out of the grass to puncture her waterskins and then Little Hump had jumped up roaring with laughter at her confusion. But now he was far away with his father, and Spotted Deer only stood and watched her pass, eyes soft as the young buck for whom he was named. It was most annoying.

The young men who followed the soldiers as far as the Snake River crossing brought back a few stones solid enough to heat and drop into the cooking paunches and skins because not one stone grew anywhere around the camp here. Meat hung along the rawhide strings stretched from bush to tree, the beef hides were staked to dry for the fleshing, and the brush shelters were well started. Feather on Head took Yellow Bead and several other girls out to dig up soapweed, showing these agency young ones how to find the juicier roots and to peel and work them into the milky, foam-topped water that cleaned the calico and left the buckskin soft and supple. She taught them, too, how to sweep away all sign of the digging and of their moccasin tracks so the earth seemed touched only by the wind.

Toward evening the sky grayed again and ducks came in to the little lake in winged clouds, and then geese too, hitting the water with soft splashes, the quacks and honkings like little songs. Several boys hid in the rushes and shot into them with their arrows. They got quite a few and laid them out in a row on the ground to freeze undivided, much as in the old days, when all ate if any did. That night old Arrowmaker found his fire warmed by boys come to sit around him as in his youth, before everyone had guns. Once more they came to watch him as he trued the shafts with his scraper and notched them for the feathers.

In a cleared place in the thicker brush and trees, where some coals would not be seen, a few were singing a little, softly, and dancing too, but not with the drum because that carried far on the night wind. It had been a long time since another such evening. Little Wolf's daughter, Pretty Walker, helped begin it, and even the shy Yellow Bead joined in, the young men waiting until the girls pulled them into the dance, as was proper, a few older people and the old women watchers of the maidens there too.

Little Wolf listened from his fire, with only Feather on Head sitting opposite, bent over his moccasins, resoling them more by touch than by the light of low red coals on her awl. Everyone else was gone—even Thin Elk was over at the dancing.

Little Wolf was a thinking man tonight. Not only about Dull Knife's people, who were also the responsibility of the Bundle bearer, but these here, with the few little shelters hidden in the brush, their holes in the hillsides. Never had the Cheyenne people lived as these must through the winter ahead, without the pride of their painted buffalo lodges, the beaded lining of each one the big work, the masterpiece of a woman's lifetime, a thing of beauty and of far reputation. They must winter without even the canvas tents of the *veho* and without robes or blankets. They must eat only the yield of the bow and the snare and the knife, without the buffalo that they once killed by hand in great surrounds, or any of the things the buffalo bought from the white traders. Only one kettle remained, and no iron for the arrow points, although some hoops had been brought in from the trail where a wagon had upset and several whisky barrels were broken.

Yet they could live happily here, Little Wolf knew as he listened to the quiet little laughs, if there were no chasing soldiers and none of that other thing, the violence that had grown up during the long pursuit of the years past. With so much need for each man to defend himself quickly with perhaps the poorest of weapons, to be on guard every breath against those who lied to him and stole, cheated, and killed, it was easy to forget there was a better way. Worse than the weariness and southern fevers of the body was the sickness in the heart and the mind of some here. These, even more than the old ones like Grandmother or the children in the cradleboards, needed a season of food and warmth and safety.

As Little Wolf cleaned his pipe and mixed the ashes of the precious tobacco with more willow bark for a second smoking, he heard voices raised in anger. It was over among the dancers—Cheyennes quarrelsome even in their play, quick to anger, forgetting the value of the pleasant word and the open face that belonged to a good man in the village. One of these troublemakers was still Black Coyote, with his brother-in-law Whetstone always close on the fringed heels of his moccasins. Out of this grew an anger against Black Crane, who, with a few Elks, had to keep order while moving through the sandhills and was given the policing of the camp now. Crane was selected for this responsibility by the council because he was long known for his coolness, his foresight and caution, his just eye. But from their departure in the south there had been hot words from Black Coyote against him, and the impatient hand upon the knife.

Wearily Little Wolf arose and walked over toward the dance fire. He met the Quiet One and his daughter returning, with Thin Elk walking between them, laughing to them both. The trouble, whatever it was, had passed.

In the morning there was cold rain, speared with ice sharp as needles against the men watching on the ridges. It turned to a long blizzard—hard on everybody but an excellent cover for moccasin tracks. Now was the time to get as many deer as they could for new clothing, as well as meat. The hunters worked on some quick-made snowshoes and then went out with the new arrows, not too well dried, the maker complained, but perhaps true enough for close.

"Remember, you young men who do not know this country—the wind digs himself the blowouts on the northwest side of the hills. This is a bad place to be lost in a blizzard, with no trees and rocks to give you their signs, and very little wood for a fire," old Arrowmaker warned, wishing he could lead them into the dangerous weather, wishing he were a strong young man. "If you get lost, find a blowout to tell you the directions. . . ."

"We have been out in blizzards before," Black Coyote said sourly, although Arrowmaker's advice was plainly for the boys. "We are not burnt on one side from leaning over the women's fires!"

No one replied to this rudeness against an old man, pretending it had never been said. Thin Elk, Black Crane, and Brave Wolf's Brother led the young men out to hunt in threes and fours, hoping to find the brush patches they recalled from long ago. The little parties rode the snow-whipped ridges, pounding the protesting horses along, the men peering from under the hoods of their blankets for lulls in the driving storm, hoping to locate deer yards in the brush patches below.

Black Crane ran into half a dozen deer in a pocket in Spring Valley. He motioned his followers around against the wind as close as they could get in the heavy drifts. Then they tied the horses to the soapweeds and crept down on their snowshoes, Black Crane waiting to approach with the northwest wind. When the others were fanned out and ready downwind in the storm, Black Crane jumped up, shouting. The snow-caked deer raised their heads, got the scent, and plunged away into the drifts, floundering to their bellies, their shoulders, the hunters running alongside to drive their arrows deep, with here and there a quick slash of a knife to the throat, the blood spurting, the reddened snow covered almost at once by the storm.

They came in to the camp on snowshoes, ice-caked, almost frozen, worn out with dragging the loaded horses into the wind. The young men ran out to help, pointing to the trees already hung thick with deer. Twenty-five was not many for the camp so poor in clothing, but it was a start. Now the young women of the village would make new dresses, not the beaded ones with the flying sleeves that young Cheyenne girls should have, but soft and golden. Unfortunately, the one Spotted Deer got must go to Old Grandmother, who had no blanket for her chilly shoulders.

All that evening the men laughed and bragged at their small coals as though there were no soldiers looking for anybody. The women said it was fine they had such noble hunters because they needed more deerskin and a lot of elk teeth too. There were many here who once owned the One-Thousand dresses, those covered with one thousand elk teeth, such as a good man naturally provided for his wife by hunt or trade. Now there were many younger ones who deserved them.

Three days later there was no thought of elk-tooth dresses. The storm had cleared toward night, the frozen snow crackling under the moccasin. Then suddenly a man from Dull Knife was there, but before he could be drawn into a shelter to the fire, he fell, so frozen and hungry and worn out.

When he had been warmed a little and fed hot soup, he spoke his bad news. Dull Knife's whole camp was captured in the storm and taken to Fort Robinson, it seemed. He had been sent out the first night to tell them here what had happened.

Little Wolf and the others smoked late over this, but already seven men with Woodenthigh along as a sign of good will from his father had started on their strongest horses, taking packs of dried meat to hide for the people if they could get away. The men left the valley by different directions, following the bare frozen ridges wherever they could, or else riding crookedly like wild horses wandering. The Cheyennes here must not be found. Some of the people must be left alive.

The next morning the sun came out hot as was common in a Cheyenne autumn before the hard winter to follow. In two days the south slopes were soft and dark with water from the melting drifts, the grass bare for the horses, and soon the only snow patches were along the sunless northern slopes. Then one raw, cloudy forenoon with a chill wind blowing out of the north, the watchers up near the lone pine tree saw a darkening line move out of the horizon. It seemed miles wide, almost like the old buffalo herds, but not so black, and surely there were no buffaloes left here. This must be thousands of soldiers coming in a wide string instead of a long one, bringing many, many wagons and cannons. A lot of the good men had gone to help Dull Knife, so younger ones were taking turns at watching, too, and it was Spotted Deer who saw this first. His heart almost stopped as the dark line was suddenly there, vanished, and then came again, wider, darker, the dust a haze over it. So he got on his horse and made the swift circlings of great danger approaching for those looking from farther down, making the sign over and over, for many, many dangers.

Others saw the line too and made their signals for the men in Lost Choke-cherry who sent Old Crier to run through the camp calling, "Danger is coming! Much danger is coming!"

The women stopped, dropped their hands, looking swiftly all around the bare hills, and then hurried to pack their goods while Young Calf rode for the horses. The children were gathered, the shelter skins fell and were rolled up by the time the Crier came around again. "Let us be calm, my sisters!" he said. "We will not run like the foolish wool sheep of the *veho* run at the wave of a blanket. Be ready but be calm!"

Then there was a signal from Black Coyote out watching too, but another kind. "Hunters get ready!" it said. "Hunters—" and several of the older men who knew these hills long ago began to laugh together out loud, slapping their thighs, roaring.

"Piva!" Little Wolf called his approval to them. "It must surely be the great elk herd. Perhaps this is a year when they come like a wide dark stream through the hills, running before the winter."

So this was a day when they must risk being seen. Yet with the thickening clouds it would be easy for soldiers to get close, particularly some chasing the elk. For the watching now, careful, experienced old men were sent to the ridges while the strong young hunters grabbed bows and quivers, knives and war axes as the horse herd galloped in. Wild as to a buffalo surround, they raced out behind Black Crane to a place he remembered from another such fall, long ago.

At a narrow sand pass through a ridge that towered like young mountains, the hunters waited in two facing rows, ready to shoot from both sides, each man with an arrow set to the string, three held in the mouth, more in the quiver slung to the back. The rumbling shake of the earth neared, the first great dark-shouldered bulls appeared through the little cut, antlers high, panting tongues red, foam flying. The first ones shied from the man smell but were caught between the hunters and pushed on from behind, the pass running full. Now the arrows began to strike as the thunder and roar of the herd increased, crowding, bellowing through the narrow cut under a rising cover of dust. The Indians shot, the elk went down under the beat of the sharp cloven hoofs, the herd running so solid that smaller, weaker animals fell without an arrow, while over them flowed the running brown blanket, the tangled rattling forest of horns.

As the quivers emptied, the hunters tried to drag away some arrows from the dead, to salvage some for a second shooting, until Spotted Deer, overeager, got the flesh cut from his arm by a flying hoof.

"Back, young men! Keep out of the way!" Strong Nose roared out.

So the two rows of Indians sat on their excited, faunching horses and watched the elk run between them, cows, growing calves, old bulls—snorting, panting, bellowing as they funneled from the pass. Finally the crowding began to thin a little, and then there were only a few stragglers. The last, not pushed, shied from the blood and the men and fled back on their tracks, and then came through again, frightened by the scattering of great prairie wolves and the coyotes that followed the herd. These, too, fled from the men but not in panic, perhaps only to slip around one side or the other and take up the trail again, or stop to tear the throat of a dragging cripple.

Little Wolf watched on the crest of the ridge, sitting quiet between shielding soapweeds, looking all around the lowering gray sky, the clouds now seeming to walk on the far hills. He looked hard for soldiers or white hunters, but there seemed nothing in any direction except southward, the way the elk had gone. There only the rising dust showed the progress of the herd, and soon that was lost against the grayness. But below him lay the dead elk thick on the torn sand outside of the pass, fanning away to both sides as the herd had spread into the valley. The Indians were at work on the butchering. It had to be done fast, for there might still be soldiers following the herd for the hunt, perhaps some new to the country eager to see this unusual thing—elk migrating in such a great moving blanket. Yet it seemed worth the risk—182 elk, the skins of some cut up by the hoofs, but many that were good, and a great deal of meat. Besides there were the elk teeth for the women's dresses, to brighten the camp. Too long had their women walked poor as those of the whites.

Although Spotted Deer's arm wound hurt and Medicine Man had to work a blood-stopping chant as he tied the flesh back with a twist of rawhide, the bone was sound and so the youth rode home in happiness. He would have eight elk teeth from his own killing to offer to Yellow Bead.

Little Wolf waited until all were away, still watching for soldiers and looking down upon the line of meat horses led out of the valley, not toward the camp but heading north to leave a path of tracks away from the country of Lost Chokecherry, and then a plain scattering toward the Niobrara, where two good men were riding many times across a rocky ford, dropping fresh bones and a torn hide to make it seem that the Indians hurried a crossing there and headed north. The others, with their meat, would circle around from the hard-sodded scattering place, one here, one there, like aimless wild horses grazing, and so get back to their camp. Even so it was very dangerous, this hunt.

For a long time Little Wolf sat alone on the ridge above the hunting ground, looking down at two old wolves dragging at the elk gut, but he dared not shoot, and besides, there was the watching work for him. Several times he sniffed the gray evening wind anxiously. Even if no soldiers found this place by themselves, all this blood and butchering would draw a hundred late fall buzzards to circle overhead for even the most stupid to see.

Suddenly Little Wolf turned his face back into the moist wind. A soft spatter had hit his pock-marked cheek. Another. It was the snow that had whipped the elk into such running, the snow that would cover the blood and the carcasses for a long time. Now at last the Cheyennes had a little luck.

But Spotted Deer still had none. His arm healed, and in the skunk skin pouch at his belt were the eight elk teeth he had not been able to offer to Yellow Bead. Once he almost taunted her with Little Hump's imprisonment up at Robinson, caught by the soldiers like some horse-stealing *veho,* some very foolish man. Those who were less foolish, whether horse thieves or Cheyennes, got away. He, Spotted Deer, was not to be taken so. But he had seen the flush of shame on the Bead's gentle face when she first heard of the Dull Knife capture, and then the paling fear for Little Hump, and so he could not bring himself to speak the unkind words.

Then one day even Spotted Deer found himself laughing a little and other people came to see. It was the cousin of Bald Eagle, in from a hunt, finding that his wife had thrown his goods outside the shelter. It was not that this was funny. A woman deciding that she no longer wanted her husband and letting it be known to all in this way was her right. What was funny was that the goods had to be thrown out so formally from a crawl-in brush shelter and that they were only an old pair of moccasins and a sleeping robe that came from a very ugly brindle cow. It was funny, and sad too. Once this man had the accoutrements fit to grace the formal stand outside a handsome painted lodge. In those days his goods included a very fine warbonnet with forked ends to trail on the ground, a beaded scalp shirt, an Elk shield, beaded pipe and pouch, and many fine blue leggins and beaded red breechclouts. But all were lost in the fighting and the fleeing. Now with bad face he could pick up only his old moccasins and the cowskin and go to the sleeping holes of the unmarried young men.

Old Grandmother and another woman went to make the usual good words for reconciliation. "Now sister, are you certain?—It is not just for the moment that he does not please you?" They said it knowing what the answer would be and chuckling to themselves at the angry words they would hear. Ah, it was good to laugh again like a Cheyenne over a Cheyenne joke.

In one moon's time after the Indians reached Lost Chokecherry even the second snow was half gone. All but three of the men sent to Dull Knife were back; two stayed to watch and the third was locked up, captured by the Sioux scout Little Big Man with his shooting revolver.

"Always playing bait man for the whites!" Big Man's Cheyenne relatives complained.

"Yes," Woodenthigh agreed. "But we got signs from Bull Hump's wife. She is out among the Sioux scouts and not even the Little Big One dared tell that she got away. She says the people are in the barracks, well-treated, with food and medicine for the sick, but there are no blankets and clothing, and none can tell what will happen."

Ahh-h! That was the thing that made the eyes stare into the darkness of the sleeping time. More meat must be sent to the cave in the White River bluffs, and two or three guns with a little ammunition, all they dared to spare. Perhaps Thin Elk would go along to help with the pack horse, since he was going north soon anyway.

But the men had to go without him. He was not back from hunting in time; got lost, he said.

The night he came in was stormy again, but he did not go to Little Wolf's fire. Instead he talked a long time at the low shelter of Spotted Deer and his grandmother. Once he went over to Black Coyote and then back. The next night the three men, with several others, slipped out on scattered paths, carrying extra fur-lined moccasins and bladders of pounded meat. But they had two guns in the party.

"You will not forget the helpless ones here," Little Wolf had reminded Black Coyote. "There must be no shooting—nothing foolish now."

The Coyote was silent in his surliness today, and so Thin Elk answered, "You need more horses before you start away from here. I saw some easy to get, loose, toward the big herds near the Box Butte."

"Will there be time for the taming?" old Black Crane said, making obstacles.

"It will be easy, this bad winter," Thin Elk said. "Wolf here will remember. . . ."

Little Wolf did remember. He and the Elk got a fine herd of half a hundred there when they were young. The Sioux that were along got many more, but that was after a moon of deep snow and cold. Still, the horses would be a little weaker now from the storms, easier to tame if caught right away.

Yes, and would play out easier too. Just when the people needed to travel fast. But Black Crane saw the concerned face of Spotted Deer and knew he had a purpose for his horses, so the old chief smiled into his face.

"Go, my son," he said, "but do not blacken your gun barrels. . . ."

It was a very uneasy week for Little Wolf and the others before the horse catchers returned. They came whooping in to the dawn with about twenty head of good young stock, already thinning from the deep snow and cold, and very shaggy in preparation for the hard winter sure to follow such a Cheyenne autumn, the manes long, the tails dragging on the ground. But they would be strong when the grass came and the colors would be fine after they shed: two stripe-legged buckskins, a handsome black and white pinto, the rest sorrel, bay, and gray, including two young stallions, not good for the long hard runs, tiring too soon as stallions did. But Medicine Man would tie them for the gelding, using a string cut from elk hide because it lent the elk's speed and endurance.

Tamed, these two would go to the lodge of Little Wolf, Thin Elk announced, his gift to the women of it, and once more the chief could not roar out his anger against him or his gracious guest present. But others whispered, and laughed a little. Twenty years ago the chief had warned this man away from his wife. Now he was back, warm-eyed as a youth feeling his first bigness.

Still there was the luck of twenty more horses, and some of the young mares were already tame enough so the small boys could ride them along the bare slopes. "Spotted Deer worked hard with them . . . ," Thin Elk teased. "They are almost like old drag pullers. . . ."

"There was no trouble with anybody?" Black Crane had asked even before the feast for the success was finished.

No. Too cold, probably. No one was seen except by Thin Elk, and only a cowboy on a far hill then. No trouble at all.

But this questioning brought anger to the face of Black Coyote. "Answer nothing!" he commanded, as though he were a chief given great powers. "We are not Crane's pay workers, like the whites have, to tell him all we do!"

Everybody looked away, pretending nothing had been said, although some of the younger Elks pushed closer. Quickly somebody sent the Crier to announce that there would be a little dancing. So most of the people moved over to the brush-walled circle, standing like a corral to keep the wind out and to hide the row of tiny fires around the inside. The middle was a smooth warm place, large as the great old-time soldier society lodges, except that there was only the sky above, no tall gathering of poles crossed at the smoke hole. Yet it was a good place when there was no flying snow, and tonight Pretty Walker and the others wore their new fringed buckskin dresses, even Yellow Bead, hers the only one with no elk teeth at all. Everyone knew of the eight that Spotted Deer carried, but not whether they had been refused or offered at all. The Bead drew Young Eagle, Young Calf, and Spotted Deer equally into the dance and none could see that anyone was favored, not even when Grandmother brought out the sack of peanuts that Spotted Deer found where some wagons had turned over along the icy Black Hills trail. The sack was a big one, round and fat as a bear cub in the fall, and the old woman dipped out a good palmful for each of the young people with Little Wolf's horn spoon. It was fine throwing the shells on the fire, the sparks leaping up into the cold blue night; fine munching the kernels.

There was a little excitement later when three of the new horses were seen tied to the scrub tree behind the shelter of Yellow Bead—the spotted one and two others.

"It is possible to move more cautiously upon the game," someone advised the young Deer. "First you offer one or two, then the other. . . ."

The shy, serious Spotted Deer shook his head. He could not use such a bargaining way with Yellow Bead and perhaps it was as well, for finally he had to go lead the horses away himself. He did it late in the darkness, hoping long after everyone had stopped watching. But the girl's aunt never came out to take them, and when the youth crept back into his shelter, Old Grandmother was up, holding out a wooden bowl of soup. "Drink, it will warm you," she said.

But Spotted Deer could not be warmed, and before he finally settled to his robe, he dropped his little pouch of elk teeth into the old woman's lap —the teeth that should have started a One-Thousand dress for his bride.

In almost every shelter and sleeping hole there was a whispering over the rejected offer, nowhere more than in Yellow Bead's.

"You are very foolish, my daughter," the aunt said sadly as she turned her old bones to a more comfortable place in her cowhide robe. "Little Hump will not come to a young woman like you, now that you have no family left alive to welcome him as son and brother. . . ."

The girl managed to make the polite murmur of having heard, but there was no heart in it. She would still hope. Little Hump's own father had taken Pawnee Woman, the captive girl, to wife, one with no relatives among them at all. Of course, she had not been his first one. . . .

It was very hard, this growing up without a proper lodge and family.

The Big Freeze Moon was already very heavy with the weight of the young one to come, the Moon of Frost in the Lodge, the white man's January. Little Wolf sat on the dark hill above Lost Chokecherry and looked down upon the faint red of the fires, still very well hidden. It was cold, far below zero, one of the worst winters he had ever seen, truly the winter to be expected after the swift, early blizzards of the fall. Yet always there had been soldiers riding close, coming across Pine Creek and the chophills in the west, down across the Niobrara and the Snake River, where there was often a little soldier camp watching, no farther than a good ride before breakfast from Lost Chokecherry. But the danger had kept the Cheyenne scouts watchful too, in their wide circle of lookouts, crouched in hide-covered holes out of the wind, with little oil pouches of badger and skunk grease to burn for a bit of warmth without the sign of smoke.

All fall the two men always up at the lone pine tree had watched the long bull trains creeping northward, the heavy wagons plowing the snow or cutting deep into the sand passes through the ridges of hills, the drivers riding alongside or walking, their far-off voices hoarse, the long whips cracking like pistols over the bulls, or over the faster mules as winter deepened. In those wagons were many things the Cheyennes could use: tobacco, coffee, sugar, ammunition—many, many things. But in return it would become known where Little Wolf's people were, a very big price for filling a hole in the belly, and yet the chief knew how hard it must be for the young man to remember.

Mostly the scouts watched for horsebackers, men coming alone or perhaps in twos, and particularly for the blue columns that rode from every direction. These the Cheyennes must see while still far off, so the people could step aside from this fine little valley where the chokecherries had hung, drying and sweet, when they came. Step aside not only so they would not be caught, but so anyone looking down from far off would see the valley serene and empty. The little brush shelters and the skin ones, only stooping high, with branches and twigs tied over them, were lost in the plum thickets and cherry patches, the holes in the steep northwest hill hidden behind the few boxelders, with hides for doors, earth-rubbed ones with grass sewn here and there. Even Fire Crow, the Sioux-Cheyenne who came to join them from Red Cloud, had trouble finding their living places although he knew exactly where they were.

So the people stepped aside this winter, either to the place Little Wolf selected for them across the trail to the east, with some wood and water too, and robes and dried meat cached for the need of hasty flight. If they had to run west, there was a narrow little pocket off that way, with almost no wood but good for hiding a few days. Once they did not have time to do more than scatter out into the chophills, careful to move only on horseback or on loose, blowing snow that held no moccasin tracks to itself. If anyone left tracks, he must not return, not until it could be done without bringing the enemy upon them. Better that one or a dozen die of freezing than that all be lost.

They were almost caught that time, with a row of soldiers coming along a ridge not over two miles away. The troopers made a bunch on the hill, stopping a long, long time to look into Lost Chokecherry, surely with the far-seeing glasses. Then they separated into the column of two abreast again and went on, the flag flying at the front. But scouts were left behind at a little fire in a buckbrush patch high up on the ridge. For two days they stayed there, the pale smoke telling the Indians of white-man watchings. None here would ever forget those days after the fleeing into the snow before the troops came into sight. Now, at last, these Cheyennes had been driven into a faceless scattering, to run afoot along the bare frozen places, falling, running again in every direction, to cower behind some soapweed clump, the people as gray and lifeless as the old dead sword leaves about the bottom of each green bayonet plant, or to dig into some snowbank, crusted as hard as glass. None could guide them now, only fear.

The cold was so hard that they found grouse dead as stone in the drifts, and when the Cheyennes could finally return to their camp, there were many so frozen that Medicine Man had to make his frost cures for a whole big ring of people. He had been given the medicine of the snowbird by the Powers, the little bird that can spread his feathers thicker and thicker as the cold increases, until he is almost as round as the pale gray puffball of the prairie. Medicine spread himself so in his snow-dusted robe and made the picking motions with his head, the scratching of finding feed, and the little "teer-teer" song. He was strong in the cure, for not one lost a foot or a hand or more than a few toes, dead, to be cut away.

But there was great uneasiness now, particularly since it was discovered that their best field glass was lost, the one from the Turkey Springs fight down in the south country, with the *veho* words of the troops upon the case. At first the loss was hidden from Little Wolf, but he discovered that the glass was dropped the time the soldiers were so close and left their watching scouts behind, dropped by a young agency relative of Black Coyote's. A strong search was made—all they dared, but whether the covering snow had taken it or the enemy, none could say now, nor predict that the soldiers might not come riding straight upon them here tonight, tomorrow. When the Elk soldiers moved to punish this dangerous carelessness, Black Coyote stood against them, his finger on the trigger, his face thin and wild. So nothing was done, for there must be no Cheyenne blood upon a brother's hand.

And now Little Wolf was preparing himself for something else that might mean blood spilled too, something that seemed to point his Medicine Bundle oath straight upon him: If a dog lifts his leg to your lodge, do not see it. Your anger can only be for injustice to the people.

Little Wolf knew how many noticed Thin Elk always beside the wives of their chief, and talked slyly of it behind the hand, saying that the coal once kindled is truly very easy set afire. Yet the Wolf could give them no ear. He must act only for the people.

But now the ridicule against his lodge and himself was giving power to the man who wanted to go against the council. Black Coyote and Whetstone were hot to make war on the trail over there and against the Niobrara ranches. The bold talk was attracting young men who had their first coup to count and did not know they bore the welfare of the people like a nursling fire to be shielded by the palm. Even a serious young man like Spotted Deer could be drawn. The Coyote knew that one shot might bring soldiers riding against his own fine warrior wife and children, yet surely he would go against the whites if his chief let himself be made much smaller.

To stop this ridicule Little Wolf need only send Thin Elk from his lodge, as he had done so easily twenty years ago. But now to notice him was to admit failure as an Old Man Chief and the bearer of the Sacred Bundle. Not even the valiant Black Crane could help in this, except in the trouble from Black Coyote and the rest when his head chief stepped down from his high place. The Coyote's belt was heavy with the Custer revolver and his prestige heavy with his bravery in that fight, and with all the trouble he made since, in the disarming at Red Cloud, on the way to the south country, and all the way back. Some thought it was the sickness of Bear Rope growing in him, as in the slobbering buffalo who runs in madness to fight everything, the horse who eats the gray loco weed, the wolf who spreads his sickness with the frothing jaw in man's own camp.

It was not to wonder that the evil and injustice of these years brought such sickness upon a good man, but it was a grieving thing that not all the courage of Buffalo Calf Road could save her husband from it as she had saved her brother from the battle on the Rosebud by charging into the bullets and carrying him away.

Once the Wolf thought of stepping aside, but then there would be no head for the people here, none to hold their crumbling parts together, with the violence of Black Coyote certain to sweep over them. No, those living down there had been given into his palm to shield and they could not be thrown away.

So Little Wolf made ready for what he must do, drive out the man who brought weakness to the lodge of the Bundle bearer. By the light of his hidden fire the Wolf had combed his hair neatly, with the one feather up from the back of his head, the little medicine roll tied beside the part, the braids wrapped in the new skin of the otter that Woodenthigh had shot with an arrow in the waters of the Snake River. On his breast hung the silver peace medal from the Great Father, and across his knees was the long pipe. The ornament shot off the stem in the Lewis fight had been replaced by his wives with beads cut from their own dresses.

Cross-legged before the handful of coals, the Cheyenne chief made his bundle medicine. He laid a little silver sage to smolder on the coals and took out the Sweet Medicine bundle from under his shirt. Four times he passed it through the fragrant smoke of the sage and then he offered it to the Great Directions, the sky, the earth, all around, and put it carefully back. When this was done and his mind quiet and composed for whatever was ahead, he called his horse out of the night and started down the hill to settle this trouble.

But a rider was hurrying toward him out of the darkness. It was Woodenthigh, calling softly, "News! Bad news, my father! You are wanted."

In the camp Little Wolf found the people gathered in the brush circle around a man from Red Cloud. They became silent as their chief approached, some falling back a step, silent and angry and helpless.

"Dull Knife and the rest are to be taken back south. Loaded in the wagons and hauled through the winter blizzards back to the sick country," the messenger said, as from many repetitions, speaking his soft Cheyenne very rapidly but smoothly even now, as a stream runs naturally and inevitably from the upland. "It is settled that they are going."

"I do not believe our men over there have agreed to this," Little Wolf said quietly, pushing past Black Coyote and the others who had sometimes stood against him. "Not Dull Knife and Hog! They are Cheyennes!"

To this the news bearer made no reply. He knew nothing beyond the message.

So once more the decision with Thin Elk and Black Coyote had to wait.

13  In the Barracks

THE WHITE RIVER VALLEY LAY LIKE A BENDING, SNOW-covered leaf in the October sun, the midrib the frozen stream, the veins the little creeks and drifted canyons that reached far out to the higher prairie on each side. Along the northward the steep bluffs, usually a wall against the sky, were now almost lost in the snow banked against them—snow blown off the wide tableland above, so deep that even the tips of the pines growing along the foot were out of sight. From there the shimmering drifts flowed away down the slope to the brush-lined little river and out over the open valley beyond, past Crow Butte that stood dark and alone against the morning sky.

Lost under the snow lay the deep-rutted Sidney-to-Black-Hills Trail that cut through the valley of White River, past the encampment of the troops here to catch the Cheyennes, little except the dark stovepipes of the regular rows of tents visible against the white drifts. But smoke began to rise blue here and there with the sun that sparkled along the frozen valley, while high up against the mare's tail sky two eagles circled the cold air, hungry from the four days of storm. Coyotes were hungry too, the tracks of one crossing between the drifted log buildings of Fort Robinson that were scattered like a half-buried prairie-dog town along the bluff slope. There were wolf tracks too, but no closer than the knoll behind the cavalry stables, showing a sudden running, perhaps from the echoing sunrise gun.

In the barracks most of the Dull Knife Cheyennes had slept straight through with the fatigue, the grateful drying warmth, the food, and the little white pills of Surgeon Moseley—quinine for those still full of malaria chills, morphia for those with their frostbite swollen and mottling, gathering to break. The doctor had cut away the snow-softened horsehide cast from Sitting Man's leg. The bone was well set, he exclaimed in surprise,

so well that only the constant jolt and jerk of the hurrying ride north kept
it from healing—the falling as his horse went down, hobbling up to mount
another and go on, always on. It was a wonder the man was alive; more,
that he could hold the inflamed leg steady with his hands as the doctor
probed the wound for bone fragments, and could crinkle his gaunt dark
Indian face in a smile that the doctor's instrument struck none.

"Hou! Hou!" he said, and Bridge was as happy. The medicine man had
made such probings too, but in their hurry to run he might have done it
badly.

"It's a wonder any of these Indians are alive . . . ," the doctor said to
his assistants. They were so starved and ragged and sick, their skin the
color of muddy gray coffee. Even the powerful shoulders of Hog seemed
as naked of flesh as a two-by-six across a post, covered only by a ragged
shirt. But it was the children that hurt the white doctor most—silent, un-
crying children, their round eyes unblinking, their arms thin as willow
sticks, the little bellies swollen, feet and hands frozen, and even their backs
—frostbitten spots darkened and puffed as spoiled patches on a pumpkin.
He wiped his eyes and worked on, unable to look into the faces of his young
helpers or of the other whites around. He examined little Lame Girl too,
the gun-shot ankle thick and almost black, the big eyes fearful in the thin
little face as the doctor inserted a drain. Then he sent the assistants on
errands and stroked the tender foot gently, very gently, until the exhausted
girl slept.

Finally all was quiet in the barracks except the guards walking around
the building and coming in through the door every little while, the coal
oil lantern kept burning high over the sleeping Indians. And yet somehow
a board of the cold rough-sawn floor had been pried up with knives and
the women's belt axes, and things hidden there, things like Black Bear's
Custer carbine with the nailheads and the lizard made from the plugging
bullet, for the day that Hog had promised them.

In the morning the awakening Indians made themselves neat, the men
like Big Antelope and She Bear braiding the hair of their wives in the
friendly Cheyenne way, and Limpy that of his bride, for the first time
doing it quietly and well. The post cooks came. Pounding on the lid of a
great boiler with a ladling spoon, they motioned the Indians into a line
and passed tin plates and cups into their hands. When the Cheyennes were
fed, they settled to rest some more and smoke, with enough gift tobacco

even for the women's circles. But now Colonel Carlton came, standing broad in his buffalo coat among his soldier chiefs. Some of the Sioux scouts were brought too, among them Bull Hump's Leaf, unrecognized, her hair braided like a man's, and dressed and acting like the others. There were no Cheyenne interpreters at the post and so all talk still went through two people, through Tangle Hair and someone else.

"What are you going to do with us?" the Indians had to ask, unable to wait until the proper smoking had been made.

"The fighting is over," the colonel said, "and we are all friendly now. You must stay here until the government decides if you are to go south or to Red Cloud. But nothing bad will happen to you here. You will have the freedom of the post and can even go out along the river and the bluffs for the kinnikinnick and silver sage you like, but at supper time you must be back. If one man of you deserts or runs away, you will all be shut up. All will be held responsible."

Dull Knife rose and spoke to his people, advising them to do as the soldier chief said. "We are back on our own ground and have stopped fighting. We have found the place we started to."

"But there is something still to be done," Colonel Carlton said, and now the headmen sat silent, waiting, eyes looking down before them. "I must have all your guns. We know you have more. They were seen in the rifle pits at Chadron Creek."

Now the women had to hold themselves, but suddenly one among them broke into a low crying. At the second, angrier demand from Carlton, and a movement of the guards with the bayonets, Hog spoke a low word, without moving his lips. A couple of the young men brought out their guns, and then more, for the shadows of the walking soldiers outside passed the frosted windows every few moments and all around here were a thousand more, with the storehouses of ammunition. So finally six guns were brought out from under the clothing of the men, mostly in pieces, and a couple of revolvers, and laid on a little pile.

Afterward they were given a few presents with more tobacco, and before many days a very young soldier chief, Lieutenant Chase, took charge of the Indians. He made himself an office in a room at the end of their barracks and called the headmen in. Without much talk he said he must ask them all to go out to the parade ground, cleared of snow now and warm in the sun. Their bundles and goods would be left in the building and searched.

Dull Knife held himself silent, but Hog sprang to his feet, very tall in the little log guardroom. "We cannot let this be done!" he said angrily, and calmed himself at once. "It would make trouble, taking the women from their bundles," he said. "The young men would get excited; people get hurt."

Finally Colonel Carlton agreed this might be true, so the search was made with the Indians inside, everybody suddenly ordered to one end of the prison room, away from the bundles. While a row of soldiers stood with their guns ready against the Cheyennes, others went through the Indian goods. Even now there were a few fine old things left, like the quilled pipe case of Noisy Walker, very old, and Great Eyes' feather-tailed shield, carried all the days since the Cheyennes lived far east where the oaks grew thick. There were covetous eyes among the officers as such things were spilled out on the barracks floor. But Carlton was after the lead and powder, the bows and arrows that were found, and the many things that seemed to belong to the whites: children's dresses and underclothing and bedspreads, the fringed one of Dull Knife's daughter now muddied and smoke-blackened from the fires. In the Knife's own pack that Pawnee Woman brought was a child's parasol and several family pictures. There were other *veho* things the soldiers did not see, like the canvas-covered account book in which Little Finger Nail drew his pictures, and his friends Roach Mane and Elk also, using the flat little box of colored pencils. This book was still tied next to the brown skin of the Nail's back with two raw-hide strips through it, one around his waist, another up over his shoulder, as he had carried the book all the way from Kansas.

But when the soldiers made a tentative move to search the people, one motioning toward the women, uneasily, not certain how it was to be done, the young Cheyennes were suddenly ready to spring to violence, to throw themselves against the guns. The Sioux scouts roared out angrily against it too. A couple of days later, when moving a bundle around, Young Medicine Man's wife dropped a revolver from under her dress. The guard who saw it hurried away, and the lieutenant came to Dull Knife, demanding the gun. The woman was afraid, but she brought it to the young white man, saying the gun was a remembrance of her dead first husband. So two sentinels were placed inside the building, day and night, with the lantern always burning. But some still kept their revolvers hidden. Black Bear's wife carried his between her breasts, strapped close with a rawhide thong so there would be no more dropping.

But this boy-cheeked young officer Chase was not a bad man. He always carried a little extra tobacco in his pockets and a small pouch of sour balls for the younger children. Sometimes when he saw Lame Girl alone among the grown-ups because she could not run and play, he took her before him on the saddle and rode around the parade ground in a fine racking, the young men running up to watch his good horse run in the odd white-man way. But when Chase examined the black ornament the girl wore on a rawhide string around her neck, he drew his hand quickly away. It was the breechblock of a Springfield rifle. After that he watched closely around the barracks, letting his eyes move over all the chinking between the logs when he sat to visit, looking carefully down along every crack in the floor. Nothing seemed disturbed. The Indians seemed not to notice, but almost at once Lame Girl was wearing a pyrite disk on the string, and when Medicine Woman swept the floor with her bundle of joint grass, she swept across the boards so the cracks would always look full of dust and trash.

When Lieutenant Chase asked the Cheyennes what they liked to eat, they said soup, and so he had it made in big iron kettles from the bones at the butcher's, with the marrow in soft rich lumps for their tin plates. They got mush with molasses too. The first time that Hog's wife stirred it in her plate she broke out into a laughing chatter, showing it to the small children, putting a little into the mouth of one as she made the smacking sounds with her lips.

"She says it is very good, not ground with the cobs, as they got in the south," the interpreter told Chase.

The *veho* made the dubious face. "With the cobs?"

"Yes," Hog said. It was ground for the mules but given to them instead. The taste was bad and the small children got sick. "There was none of the long sweetening, the molasses to eat with it."

The young officer looked into the strong face of the Indian saying these things so quietly and took the liberty of doubling the meat rations for the prisoners. Although it was almost three times the amount issued to the soldiers, who ate more other foods, it still seemed inadequate to the Indians. But no white man had ever treated them so well, and for this the Cheyennes

humored young Chase, made jokes with him and his guards, laughed and
sang and played cards with them. Because it would help him with the
higher officers, most of the men willingly threw off their blankets and let
him inspect them thoroughly for arms.

"It is nothing," Left Hand said when Chase thanked them. "We would
be happy to take off everything, leave it all behind; we will walk naked out
of the door from here if you can let us go to Red Cloud."

"Hou! Hou!" the others agreed. "Say this in the black writing marks to
our friend Braided Beard Crook."

But soon another young man came to watch them, and while Chase still
visited them and they believed his promise that he would write the letter
to be carried away on the Sidney stage, they never knew.

There were other people who wrote about the Cheyennes, in newspapers
and letters. "They will never return to Indian Territory unless tied hand
and foot and dragged there like so many dead cattle," George L. Miller,
editor of the Omaha *Herald,* wrote Secretary of the Interior Schurz. "It
means starvation to them. I implore you for justice and humanity to those
wronged red men. Let them stay in their own country."

But General Sheridan only complained of an unnecessary amount of sym-
pathy for the Cheyennes in the Department of the Platte. He suspected they
had received encouragement to come north, and he doubted the wisdom
of enticing them to go against government policy. "The condition of these
Indians is pitiable but it is my opinion that unless they are sent back to
where they came from, the whole reservation system will receive a shock
which will endanger its stability," he said. Most of the reservation Indians
were dissatisfied, and if they could leave without punishment or fear of
being returned, they would not stay long.

Then it is true that all the Indians are really prisoners? a New England
idealist inquired. Even if it could be argued that they sold themselves into
this immurement, by what law can a people make such a sale?

Bronson, a cattleman near Fort Robinson, became a good friend of Little
Finger Nail. He was the nephew of Henry Ward Beecher, a preacher man
of good will toward all peoples, the Cheyennes were told. Anyway, the
young man talked much of these things to the Indians, and of the time
General Sheridan went down into Texas when the legislature was voting
on a bill to outlaw the buffalo hide hunter as many other states had done.
Sheridan appeared before the lawmakers to say that the buffalo hunters

did more to drive the Indians to reservations and off the land the white man wanted than all the United States Army.

"The hunters who killed the buffalo on our lands—butchered our cattle!" Bull Hump shouted. "The soldiers kept us from driving them off!"

But Dull Knife was throwing his heart back to the time before his son's birth, smoking a long time in silence, guttering his pipe in thought. He had shook the hand of this little *veho* General Sheridan when they went to Chicago to see him for an agency in 1873, with a lot of other men from here along, and Little Wolf too.

"There we asked him about the soldiers. A long time ago it seemed that they were coming to protect the lives of both the whites and the Indians," Dull Knife said. "Always we were told by the officers to keep the young men from hurting the whites along the trails, around the forts and the other settler people coming in too. If these whites were hurt, the soldiers came running through the country after us. Then it changed, and the soldiers themselves started killing people, our people, because they took some goods and property from those whites who shot our buffaloes, although the treaties say we have the right to drive them out. For these few goods taken, brave men have died. Then the whites started to take our land too, and killing the Indians who tried to protect it, killing us to get us out of the way of those who want to steal our homes. . . ."

"Ahh-h, it is indeed difficult to understand," Old Crier agreed.

"The object of the Army is to protect lives first of all, goods and possessions secondly," Bronson objected, but saying it uneasily. Later that evening he talked of this to his friends around Dear's trading store. He wasn't so sure old Dull Knife hadn't bit into something pretty fundamental, really a change in the whole concept of the military.

From Bronson the Indians heard about the Bannocks that General Miles had killed. Hog thought about the messenger he sent up to Bear Coat from Chadron Creek, while others talked anxiously of their relatives still with the general, men like Two Moons and Brave Wolf and White Bull. Bronson showed them a front-page story about General Miles and his wife and party visiting Yellowstone Park, the place of the shooting-up steam.

"Ahh-h, the place of the black glass that the Old Ones used to make very good arrow points."

Yes, but this story was printed right after the news of the Cheyennes

Little Wolf, a chief of the hostile Cheyennes, and his captor, Lieutenant W. P. Clark, U.S.A. From *Frank Leslie's Illustrated Newspaper,* June 28, 1879.

This print was copied from an old stereoscopic view in the U.S. National Museum by the Bureau of American Ethnology. Note the softened effect usual in such views, the obliteration of the pockmarks from the Indian's face, and the addition of the romantic backdrop, which does not appear in the photograph made at Fort Keogh, Montana, spring, 1879.

Publisher's Note: Sandoz correctly cites *Frank Leslie's Illustrated Newspaper* as the source for her caption. Recent research, however, has shown that the seated figure is in fact Little Hawk, a Sioux.

▲ Captured Cheyennes at Dodge City, Kansas, spring, 1879, to be tried for murder. *Top:* Tangle Hair, Left Hand, Old Crow, Porcupine. *Bottom:* Wild Hog, George Reynolds (interpreter), Noisy Walker, Blacksmith. Photograph from Kansas State Historical Society.

▶ Escape of Cheyennes, page from *Frank Leslie's Illustrated Newspaper,* February 15, 1879. Plainly the artist had no conception of Plains Indian dress.

THE IMPRISONED CHEYENNES FORTIFYING THEIR TEMPORARY QUARTERS AT FORT ROBINSON.

FLIGHT OF THE CHEYENNES FROM THEIR PRISON QUARTERS.

THE ENGAGEMENT BETWEEN CAPTAIN WESSELL'S COMMAND AND THE INDIANS—LIEUTENANT CRANE RESCUING CAPTAIN WESSELL.

NEBRASKA.—THE ESCAPE OF THE CHEYENNE INDIANS FROM THE PRISON AT FORT ROBINSON—INCIDENTS OF THEIR PURSUIT AND MASSACRE BY U. S. TROOPS.
FROM SKETCHES BY ALFRED BROOKS.—SEE PAGE 174.

▶ Dull Knife, Cheyenne chief. Photograph and identification from Records, Chief of Signal Officers, U.S. National Archives.

The photograph is either earlier than 1878 or is the one taken at Pine Ridge after the starvation march from Fort Robinson. The accoutrements are not his usual ones but may be loans or gifts.

▼ Fort Robinson, Nebraska, where the Dull Knife outbreak took place, January 9, 1879. The background is White River bluffs, to which the Cheyennes tried to flee. The trees about the buildings grew up after that time.

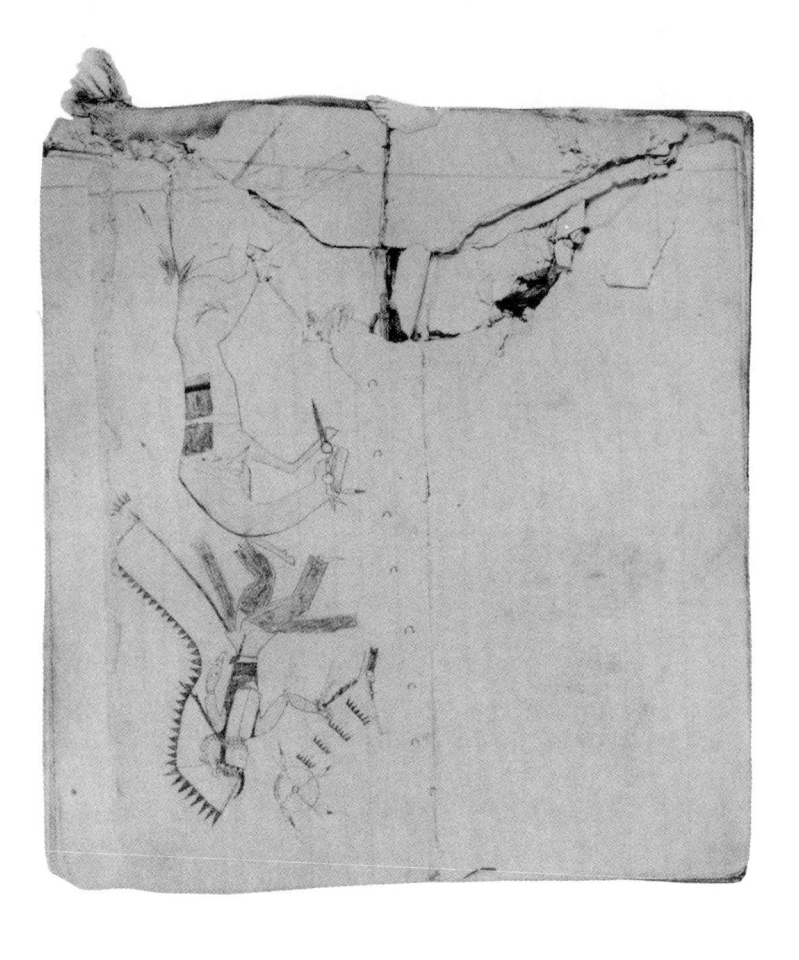

◀ Photograph of the cover of Little Finger Nail's Picture History, showing the canvas pierced by two Springfield bullets. The book is now in the American Museum of Natural History, New York City.

▲ (Left) A warbonnet man counts coup on a fleeing soldier (from the Picture History).

▲ (Right) A great warrior's horse is struck (from the Picture History).

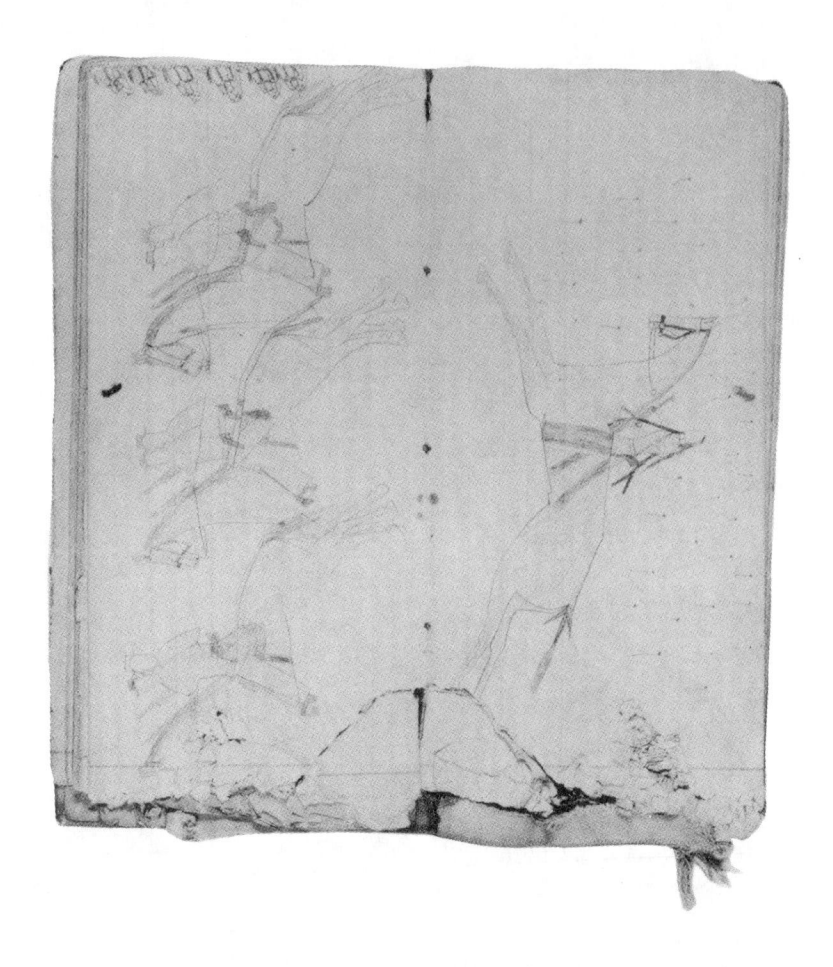

A Cheyenne rides through many bullets from the charging bluecoats
(from the Picture History).

leaving the Indian Territory, and told something more. "It says here that Miles and his entire party have been massacred by the Bannocks."

"Massacred—killed? But that cannot be true!" Hog said.

No. It turned out just newspaper talk, but people got hot to kill all the Bannocks, and the Cheyennes too, and any other troublesome Indians. Everybody got very excited, with all the newspaper stories of the Sioux off their reservations and raiding the Black Hills and the Nebraska settlements or joining Sitting Bull in Canada. Later it was admitted that Red Cloud and Spotted Tail were just moving back to their own country where the land was better and that everybody knew this all the time. But Miles and his scouts did kill the Bannocks who left their agency to hunt.

"We hear from the Little Chief people that they were hungry, like the Nez Perce last year, and everybody this summer."

"Yes, but it seems a dozen were killed just the same, the rest of the forty-six were captured, men, women, and children."

"Twelve dead from forty-six—more than one in every four killed!" The Cheyennes made the figures on their fingers and looked around the smoky barracks. Here one gone, there another out of the little families around them, almost forty people of these here would be laying on the ground.

It made a new kind of sullenness in the Cheyennes and Bronson left early. So the Indians called Lieutenant Chase and asked him what was done with the Bannocks. They were whipped back to their agency without the meat they hoped to get, he said, and read the Cheyennes a piece General Crook wrote about them. "I do not wonder, and you will not either that when these Indians see their wives and children starving and their last source of supplies cut off, they go to war. And then we are sent out to kill them. It is an outrage."

The roomful of Indians sat silent. Those people had been found for Bear Coat Miles by Cheyenne scouts. Indians could always be bought to go against their own people with a few presents, a little dollar pay. Some men here in the barracks had led Mackenzie against Dull Knife's village on the Powder. They had not been told they were going to attack their relatives and made trouble when they found it out on the way. Crook and Mackenzie had quieted them with the promise to work for a good agency for all the Cheyennes. So they led the soldiers with the Pawnee scouts, and the village was destroyed.

Yet Mackenzie seemed a good man, doing what he must, as was the one

over him, Braided Beard. And these men here who were scouts that time
—Old Crow and the rest—they were good men too. What was one to think?

Among the many whites who hurried up to visit with the Cheyennes
were some who came to claim their horses, saying this gelding, that mare
had been stolen from them, several asking for every horse strong enough
to walk, even those captured from the wild herds and without any brands
at all. They brought stories of great Cheyenne killings and other bad things
done, enough for a thousand avenging warriors with a thousand guns. But
one story the Cheyennes heard with open ears—about the Indian boy with
the leg broken by a bullet. He had to be left behind in the draw on the
Beaver because there was no time to make a travois, with the soldiers already shooting. Some cowboys found him two weeks later, eating the
rotten meat of the horses killed in the fight. One was a man called Abbott,
a brother of the boy the Cheyennes had shot to get the fine black, star-faced
horse. So he helped kill the crippled young Indian.

"Ahh-h! Always it is so, one killing makes another!" Old Crow said
softly, under the keening of the women for the boy's warrior death. Everybody had hoped the young men who went back south after the raiding
had saved him and some of the others who never caught up. There was
the warrior and his wife, sent ahead with the young Yellow Swallow. Perhaps they had gone straight north when they saw the running fight below
the Republican, and the troubles since. It would be good to know that the
Cheyenne son of Custer could grow tall and strong in the north country
and see the ridge where his father died fighting. But perhaps the cowboys
killed the Swallow too or took him and the others to the soldiers at Sidney.

One Cheyenne found just below Robinson at an old trading house
turned out to be their own Porcupine. He got separated in the storm, he
said, and was too badly frozen to find a horse. His wife, one of the walking
women, and their children greeted him like a man returned from the death
rocks when he was carried in.

A few nights later two Little Wolf Indians slipped right up to the
scout camp. As always, Little Big Man was working for the whites and
pulled his gun out. He caught one man, but the son of Little Wolf got away.
Next morning Colonel Carlton took the captured one over the region and
saw where he and eight or ten others had camped. They had come to help
Dull Knife and followed the trail from Chadron Creek. But to questions

about Little Wolf and his band the man's face became hard as the butte walls, and so they kept him at the soldier camp, away from those in the barracks.

Hog got the news of this in mirror flashes from the bluffs, and was glad that Little Wolf was still free enough from the soldiers to send help here. Their Chief's Bundle walked with a very strong man.

In a few days there was more news. Hog was out toward Crow Butte, heavy with his responsibilities now. But the day was sunny, the brush of the river brown, with only here and there a tipping of yellow left on some treetop, the bare prairie on both sides as dun as the flank of a young coyote, with the wind blowing chilly over it.

Tangle Hair waved from Clifford's old trading house and Hog sat on a rock to wait for his friend, the blanket dropped about his hips still old and ragged but his broad-boned cheeks filling out, his feet fine in new moccasins, the beading mostly white, a handsome gift from his Sioux brother-in-law, American Horse.

Hog noticed from far off that there was a shadow on the dark face of Tangle Hair. "I have only bad news to bring to your walking," the Hair apologized, sitting down to draw a strip of newspaper from his tobacco pouch. He ran a finger along the margin of the clipping, where Indian pictures had been drawn. "It was left with the trader for us by our relative Rowland at Pine Ridge . . . ," he said. "The pictures tell what the paper says—that we are to be sent back south."

Ahh-h!

Yes, but there was more. The Father down there, the governor of that Kansas country, was demanding that the leaders of the Cheyennes be brought to him to be judged for murder, murdering whites.

Through one slow breath Hog sat like a part of the rock about him, almost as though he had expected this. Then he broke into angry words, his wide mouth curling from his strong teeth. "So that is why we are always asked who did this and that back in the south country by those men of the newspaper!" he said angrily. "That was not murder down there. It was avenging. Nobody judges those who kill our people, not this time or when our women and children were shot on the Sappa!"

"No, but the whites have the guns, and the ironhouses," Tangle Hair said bitterly. It seemed, too, that they often hanged some of their own people after a judging for murder.

"Ahh-h! They do this hanging very easily to Indians, like Black Foot and Two Face. Those men were pulled up on the posts because they brought in women captives to Fort Laramie—the white women others had captured!"

Tangle Hair remembered his heat and his sorrow the time his Sioux relatives were humiliated so in death. Hog was looking down upon the strip of paper that fluttered in the wind, thinking about those two men, and a third beside them, a Cheyenne hanged for something the Indians never understood. Perhaps it was because the soldier chief there was such a drunken man, but the Great Father, like the chiefs, should try to control his warriors. The three Indians hung there beside the Holy Road a long time, drawing magpies and buzzards and wolves to sit and look, the Cheyenne with only one leg because the iron ball and chain on the other had pulled it off to lay on the ground.

As Hog thought of this, his powerful fingers crushed the foolish strip of talking paper, moved to rip it up and throw it like unclean feathers to the wind. But the shadow of its words could not be destroyed so.

Together the two men started back to the fort. They would say nothing of this to anyone, not even to Dull Knife, particularly not to him.

14 The Fasting

BY MID-NOVEMBER THE SNOW OF THE TWO FALL STORMS
was gone. The upper high-plains country smoky
blue in the warmth of Indian summer. When they could forget or cover
their uneasiness, the Cheyennes seemed content in the barracks. For the first
time since Crook came chasing them around in the Powder River country
almost three years ago, they had enough to eat and were not afraid of what
might happen in the night. The women went freely to the river in the warm
noontimes to wash their clothing, to dress the beef bladders for pouches and
the hides given them for moccasin soles. Sometimes they had other skins, a
few deer and antelope, and many rabbit hides to line the children's moccasins and the cradleboards for those like little Comes Behind.

When the ground dried, Medicine Woman took some of the girls far
along the stream and the bluffs and out on the prairie to replenish her parfleche of medicine things, all lost, even the parfleche, in the fleeing. Now
she had a new one, made from the skin of a doe that had reared many young
and therefore carried the wisdom of the life giver. This the woman painted
carefully with her own medicine patterns while the girls, particularly the
shy young Singing Cloud, watched. She showed the girls the plants they
would need to know as good Cheyenne women: cures for painful periods
and the purification, for a good pregnancy and to restore those who lost
their children unborn on the way north, for the easy birth, cooling the
breasts, good milk, and strengthening the children. Soon now the small ones
like Comes Behind who lived through the long run would be plump and
heavy on the back. Medicine Woman pounded a great deal of the mother's
cure, the sweetroot that bloomed in white and rose and purple blankets over
the gravelly knolls of summer. Then she sent a good pouch of the powder

to the bluffs, to be picked up by the Little Wolf people because none grew
where they were hidden.

Medicine Woman knew many village cures too, for the coughing sickness, the fevers and the stinking sicknesses, for aches and pains and gunshot
wounds, and the remedies for restlessness and unease of heart. These last
the young women would need to know in the dark time ahead, and it was
fine to see Singing Cloud develop the healing eye and hand so well. She
would be a great woman to cure the sickened bodies and hearts of her people, and with a fitting husband, if it came to be Little Finger Nail.

The women worked with the few beads they could get, repairing the little
finery left them, making some new, and as many moccasins as they could.
But often even the Bead Woman was idle, although so well known that the
showman Buffalo Bill selected her to bead his fringed buckskin shirt. But
he was angered by the floral design, unlike that of the Indians. He hired
another shirt made, by another woman, and once more it was flowers, because the Cheyenne designs are a sacred trust that comes down the woman's
line, to be used only for full-bloods. Even the traders' sons were given the
white-blood floral patterns.

The Moon of Falling Leaves was a good, quiet time, yet Hog and Tangle
Hair were very silent, the two often sitting against some rock or out of the
wind against the barracks wall. Perhaps the handsome, fine-nosed Left
Hand was beside them and silent too, the power of his hunting arm useless
here as a dying branch. The other older men often squatted along the Black
Hills road where the long bull trains, the mules, the flying stagecoaches with
their fancy people, and the horsebackers all passed, all went to seek the yellow gold that the Indians had seen there with Tobacco fifty years ago. It was
the same gold that drove the whites with the cholera over the trail to California, then to Colorado, up the Bozeman trail to the Idaho country, and
now to the Black Hills. Always they ran after the yellow iron that one
could not eat or wear or use to warm the winter lodge.

Some of the Cheyennes watched in silence, their faces like the dark
granite up there, making no sign to the *"Hou, Cola!"* of the passers. Others
like Old Crow smiled broadly, happy to be noticed, perhaps given a long
burning drink from a jug under the wagon seat, or trading any little trinket
they had for it, perhaps even coming back barefoot, the new beaded moccasins gone. Finally a soldier guard was stationed at the turn of the trail, to
enforce the law of no whisky for Indians.

Mostly the older men stalked in dignity through the fall sunshine to gather red willow bark for the pipe and, on higher ground, the sacred sage to purify them all from the *veho* barracks floor. Black Bear and Bridge used it every day for their little ceremonies, making the packed and unclean log room a more fragrant place.

The younger people climbed over the bluffs, returning with their blankets full of pine cones and sweet plants for the fire, and perhaps a rock rabbit twisted from his hole. There was a great laughing and a fine stink through the post when Charging Bear got a young skunk, but good, sweet meat when well dressed, and the skin handsomely striped for a cartridge belt when they had guns once more.

On warm days the young people ran and laughed in their ball games on the thawing slope of prairie around the post, and in their games with rings and sticks. Owning no horses, the young men like Little Finger Nail and Roman Nose raced those of the officers, the soldiers gathered thick around the ring, even if snow-rimmed, cheering, betting as the Indians whipped and whooped until the track was worn deep and the ground under the betting tree too, where the wagers were thrown in the old Cheyenne way. Some were allowed out on short hunts, chasing antelope with the soldiers or coyotes with the officers' hounds. Some of them cleaned out the old eagle pit up on the bluffs and caught half a dozen with live rabbits for bait when the smaller snows came. Old Eagle and Noisy Walker showed the younger men how to crouch under the brush covering ready to grab the lighting eagle's legs and then his neck to avoid the dangerous talons and beak. But it would take a long, long time to replace all the headdresses they had lost.

Indoors there was no privacy as a people should have, not night or day. No privacy for the women's purifications, or for the married people, when even the buffalo or the wolf and his mate like to get away. It seemed sometimes to Limpy and his Broad-faced One that they had never been married at all.

With nothing for work and little but bitterness for the tongue, the Cheyennes passed the indoor time as they could. The young played the hand game, while the women's circles shook the sweetgrass baskets and wagered the little finery they had on the fall of the marked plum pits. Most of the men played with the *veho* cards, letting the soldiers teach them seven-up and black jack, with which they won much tobacco. In the evenings there was singing, Little Finger Nail's high clear voice drawing everyone, particularly the cattleman Bronson, to the barracks to hear this sweetest singer of the Cheyennes, even when there was no room inside. They danced too, with Cheyenne drums and breed fiddlers, the Sioux scouts and the soldiers always there. Often some of the whites brought feast things from the sutler or gave the girls presents of money to buy ornaments: beads, brass and silver rings, red ribbons, and the yellow powder and red coloring they liked for their faces.

Of them all only Singing Cloud had no eyes for the whites. Dull Knife's handsome daughters, called the Princesses, were the belles of the post. Hog's Daughter was a little more reserved, without the daring that comes to three sisters together. But she had inherited the oval face of her Oglala Sioux mother, the wide dark eyes, the long lithe grace. She made shy talk among the admiring soldiers too, although now and then she remembered the silence of her father and she became silent. Once she cried out in anger, "You make pretty talking words, but you wish to kill us all!" to the young lieutenant, and for that one moment she looked like her gaunt and brooding mother who sometimes broke into wild words here in the barracks and had to be quieted quickly before she roused her young son to foolish things.

The news of the dances at Robinson drew young men from Red Cloud and Spotted Tail, and even a time or two from Little Wolf down in the sandhills, but that was risky, for always there were people like Little Big Man waiting. Once Little Wolf's son Woodenthigh barely escaped after he came out of the bluffs with the girls, laughing, walking right into the post. There would have been many presents for the Big Man if he could have turned the Thigh over to the commander.

Late one thin-moon night there was a sudden shot and a running and shouting over around the guardhouse just behind the Indian barracks. Hog and the others jumped from their sleep, some to the floor place where the weapons were hidden, others crowding the windows to look out. There was nothing except some people moving in the dark, perhaps young men come courting or slipping in with news, but surely no Cheyenne would let himself be caught like that. In the morning they heard another *veho* story of the ghost seen at the guardhouse on nights when the sliver of dying moon rose very late. It was always a silent blanket-wrapped figure that walked the path of the ironhouse. Last night a new sentry saw it and gave the challenge. The Indian did not stop until just outside the guardhouse door, at the place where some Cheyennes had seen the bearded soldier called Wil-

liam Gentles stick Crazy Horse to death with the bayonet.[1] The sentry
fired his gun and the soldiers came running in their underwear.

The Cheyennes did not laugh, although they had no belief for such
stories. They thought about the killing as something that happened just
now, today, because it was here, although a little over a year ago in the
white man's winter count. Crazy Horse had come here after he had been
promised every protection for himself and his people. Dull Knife, Hog,
and the rest had sat beside him in the councils up north and heard those
promises, heard them for all the Indians. No, this story of Crazy Horse
betrayed here was not for laughing.

From the new soldiers the Cheyennes discovered that some of the men
had enlisted because times were very hard for the *veho* too, with few pay
jobs and many of the whites hungry, so hungry that they threatened to
plunder and burn the towns if they did not get work to feed their families,
burn the big towns that the chiefs had seen when they were in Washington.

The first time Dull Knife heard this he asked to have it repeated. "Ahh-h!"
he said slowly over his cooling pipe. "People hungry! Then it seems that
the road the Great Father has asked us to take is not as good even for the
whites as ours was before they killed our buffaloes . . ."

Yes, there was economic unrest, Bronson and Lieutenant Chase admitted.
It seemed that in some places agrarian and communistic sentiment was
causing men to break and burn much machinery. Many of the new reaping
machines were destroyed because they made fewer jobs, less pay work for
those who used to cut the grain by hand.

"It is as if the old arrow hunters had broken the guns when some Indians
first started using them because the game was easier to kill," the whites
tried to explain.

The Cheyennes sat silent to this talk. Guns were a good thing. The
troubles came from bad men who used them to kill more game than was
needed for food and shelter. But when the white visitors tried to say that
it was these hard times that caused the poor food on the agencies, Hog
lifted his voice louder than was good in a Cheyenne. "We do not hold back
part of the land we sold because we need it!"

Yes, and besides, this chasing the Cheyennes cost the government millions of dollars for the thousands saved on agency provisions, and it was
not over.

Plainly it was not over, with the steady movement down at the neat army encampment below the post, the spread of white tent rows growing and shrinking like an April cloud as men rode out in every direction for Little Wolf, or hurried up, weary and dusty, from far off forts to help with the search.

Lieutenant Scott, the young soldier chief of the Seventh Cavalry who had been put into Red Cloud's lodge to watch him, asked the Cheyenne chiefs and some guards to come visit him in his tent at the encampment. With the sign talking he learned from Little Chief's people, he brought the Indians much pleasant news of their relatives still up on the Yellowstone scouting for General Miles. Dull Knife, Hog, and Crow talked a long time, not of the Custer fighting—they were all at the agency at that time—but of happier days for them all, of hunting and guns and about the things they saw when they were in Washington. They showed the peace medals of the Great Father and laughed a little with Hog over his special one, a large metal star with his name on one side and on the other "Newark Industrial Exhibition, 1873, Newark, N.J." They told about a circus they saw, with elephants and the clowns who seemed to be like the Indian Contraries, doing everything foolish and backward to lift the hearts of the people from the ground in unhappy times. Black Bear here among them did such things in the ceremonials.

But before long they had to ask the question that sat on their minds like a watching buzzard on a dead tree. What was to be done with them? Not be sent to the south country!

"We will never go back there; we will die first," Dull Knife said once more, the words already so worn with repetition they had no life, only the stench of something long dead. The answer they got was the same, the old, old admonition to wait, more of the lifetime that the Cheyennes had waited on the Great Father.

Through this Hog held himself quiet, trying to feel if this lieutenant of Custer's regiment knew that the governor in Kansas wanted all the men sitting here for hanging because some young warriors had tried to avenge a great wrong. But nothing was said about it.

The first good weather had brought Red Cloud riding at the head of his subchiefs to talk to the Cheyennes. He spoke angrily when he saw their condition. "The whites have made starved and dying beggars in rags of my friends and relations!" he roared in his loud Sioux. "We are not to be treated like the poor whites one sees, who never have anything. We owned all this great rich country; we are to live well from its selling!"

But there were few words the Indians could say to each other in this first meeting under the eyes of the white officers, with all their failures like stinking old camp bones there between them. The Cheyennes were humiliated that they were caught; the great Red Cloud had to admit that he was too weak to help them.

Afterward the Sioux chief warned Carlton that, if these people had to go south, the knives must be taken from them or they would surely kill themselves. When the colonel was ordered out with a long column and pack train to chase after Little Wolf, he wired Crook that the prisoners would have to be tied and hauled away to get them south.

By now all the Cheyennes knew the sky was darkening for them. The headmen sat up late, wrapped in their silent blankets, planning. Every few days one stranger or another would come to look at them, men in dude coats or in army blue without the sun bleaching of prairie campaigns across the shoulders. Each time the Indians thought that perhaps this was the one who brought the bitter words in his mouth.

Then the man called Indian Inspector came. He leaned his chair back against the wall in the little office of the barracks and talked to the chiefs, seeming only half listening, flipping the gold stone on his watch chain, nodding and holding out his half-smoked cigar as excuse when the long pipe of friendship was offered to him.

But Dull Knife had to make his talk from the beginning just the same: the promises broken, the reservation they never got, the goods that never came, the hunger and sickness, and their coming back north because they had been promised they could. "Now we are locked up like people who have broken laws—like your bad men, your outlaws."

"I am told there is no place up here for you," the chair-leaning *veho* said. "Your relatives are in Indian Territory. The government can't have Cheyennes scattered everywhere."

"The Northern Blue Clouds, the Arapahos, did not have to go south to their brothers. They have their reservation with the Shoshonis. There are relatives of ours with Bear Coat Miles up on the Yellowstone. They are permitted to stay north."

"The Arapahos are a small tribe, but they will be taken south," the man said, throwing the butt of his cigar into the little iron stove and getting up to go. "The Cheyennes with Miles are moving south as soon as Sitting Bull is brought in and scouts are no longer needed."

A dozen officers had led their columns out of the White River valley after Little Wolf since the October storm, some going eastward along the Niobrara, some northwest as far as the Belle Fourche, to join the route of those from Forts Meade and Keogh and Laramie; some to the Platte and out around through the sandhills again, with Sioux scouts along. But nobody found Little Wolf, and now Scott was ordered out. Because he was friendly with the Cheyennes he tried to get someone from the barracks to go along. Old Crow agreed and said he would not run away. At first the colonel refused permission, but Rowland, long married into the tribe, said that any Cheyenne would certainly return if he gave his word.

So Lieutenant Scott took a detachment out in a big swing around the post to pick up the trail of the Indians that seemed to be communicating with the Cheyenne prisoners. As Crow was leaving the barracks, Hog followed him out, away from the rest.

"This time do not forget that you are a Cheyenne!" he said softly, in quietness, but his eyes were as when he struck the Pawnee who had killed his brother.

"You are the forgetful one, my friend! A Cheyenne never tells other people what to do."

"*Piva!*" Hog acknowledged, smiling a little, "but remember!" as Crow kicked his horse into a lope.

One good day's march northwest of Robinson, on a wide rising prairie that was cut by a fan of dry washes and little branches joining Hat Creek, they struck the old-time Cheyenne trail from the Platte country to the Powder. Stopped beside the weedy travois path, the garrulous Crow was suddenly quiet.

"We lost one of our young men here, a very good young man," he said, pointing his long brown hand toward a little gully. Finally he added the name, reluctantly, as always with those killed defending the people. "Yellow Hand."

It happened two years ago, by the *veho* count, when the Indians were going from old Red Cloud agency at Robinson for their regular summer hunt, as the white paper said. That year it was mostly families and old people, the warriors gone north earlier with Little Wolf and even before that, in time for the fights with Crook and Custer. The old man stopped, his lined, gentle face saddened as he rubbed a bare hand down his graying braids. "We were not used to hunger then, and the few young men left were very excited because they heard that Custer was killed. It seemed they were missing something."

So the Cheyennes started away on their hunt, going openly along this old-time trail, the young men scouting ahead as always, although this was still their reservation. The second morning out Yellow Hand, Buffalo Road, and Beaver Heart saw very many troops suddenly there around that little ridge. The Hand and Buffalo Road stayed to watch, the Heart went back to signal the camp, and was sent with some others to see what the soldiers wanted to do. They started shooting at the Indians. Beaver Heart's horse was killed, and with only a six-shooter, he worked his way along the rough ground toward the head of the blue column, where he could get closer. Yellow Hand rode along to help, saying they would have to do some strong work to hold off all the soldiers until the women and children could get away. He pulled his warbonnet from its saddle case, clapped it on his head, and slowly rode down along the line of soldiers to stop their marching approach. The guns came up and fired, the smoke puffing out in sudden blue rows and then blowing away together, followed by another row from the booming guns.

With bullets flying all around, Yellow Hand reached the end of the column, and started back, but his slow-moving horse was hit; it ran a little and went down. He took the bridle off in the cool, old-time warrior way, pushed his warbonnet under his belt, and began to walk back quietly. There was a great cheering from the watchers as he came, bullets throwing up dust all around him, the women singing the strong-heart songs to see this. But he was finally hit, and fell. The soldiers quit firing and one dismounted and got the warbonnet. Lifting it, he shook it in the air. Another man, not in blue, came and squatted down beside Yellow Hand and then the grass there began to burn.[2]

The Cheyennes had to run, fleeing back to the hungry agency as fast as they could, the smoke of the prairie rolling behind them. Afterward some of them went out and found Yellow Hand scalped and naked in the great patch of black ground from the prairie fire.

Old Crow slouched on his horse a long time thinking of that bad day.

Then he drummed his moccasin heels and turned his horse toward White
River and the Niobrara beyond, where Crow knew and Scott suspected
that Little Wolf would not be found.

Little Finger Nail gradually lost his reticence and showed some of the
white men the story pictures he and his friends made in the gray book:
warriors in their regalias, with medicine shields, lances, and arms, the
horses decorated with the medicine things, the feathers, scalp locks, and
paint. Many in the flying, long-legged herds had the burnt *veho* brands on
them, and some of the pictures showed whites who were not soldiers being
killed, some struck down while running, some shooting and falling, some
on the ground with blood flowing, while warriors counted their coups.
From the accoutrements the names of the men killing them could easily
be told.

The rancher Bronson said good words about these pictures. They were
the work of native artists and should be preserved. They told stories of the
Cheyennes and what they did. He would like to buy the book.

There was a sudden grunting of concern, of anger from among the older
men—Hog, Tangle Hair, and Left Hand particularly—and some low angry
Cheyenne words. "They will use it to hang us all. . . ."

Quickly the surprised Little Finger Nail wrapped the book in the rawhide covering he made for it lately and strapped it behind his back, as always. Before the suspicious watching eyes, the angry silence, Bronson,
nephew of a man of the *veho* God, left and went straight home, riding
away toward the ranch through the clear, low-starred night. He never saw
the book in the Nail's hand again. Fortunately he had never told the
Indians that he was a cousin of the man for whom the Beecher Island
fight of 1868 was named—another nephew of Henry Ward Beecher. Their
noted warrior Roman Nose had died there.

Often now the Cheyennes were unfriendly, particularly the younger men,
usually sitting by themselves, backs to the room, sometimes suddenly ordering the singing and games stopped with such angry, snarling words that
the guests hurried away. It seemed the Indians had heard disturbing stories.
First there was the news that Little Chief had been taken south by Mauck,
the man with Lewis and who had chased the Cheyennes clear past the
Platte. The Chief's people were out in Kansas when the blizzard struck
them, with no wood, almost no lodges for protection. At Robinson they

heard too that Rendlebrock, the red-faced captain who went back from the fight at Turkey Springs, was in trouble with the Great Father, for running away, it seemed, and being a drunken roaring man at Sidney.

Then the Indians heard what Hog and some others already knew—that, while the people here in the barracks would surely have to go back south too, the chiefs and head warriors would be taken out and turned over to the Kansas courts, to be tried for the murder of the settlers on the Sappa and the Beaver.

For a long time all the people were silent; even the women stopped their soft little songs to the children. The first to speak was Bull Hump. "Those the white man thinks did what he calls murder are hung up."

Hog nodded. Then there was only the roaring of the fire in the stovepipe.

The next day the cook found a cup too many. The man looked down the line of the people he knew so well by now and saw that Bull Hump was gone. It was said that his wife was with Red Cloud and so he had probably gone there, and not to Little Wolf. Maybe got homesick for her, as a man would. So the cook held up the report until after three meals. Then the soldier chiefs came marching through the door with armed guards along. Sternly they counted the people, and then a second time. Without making any talk about it at all, they took the liberties from the Cheyennes and had the doors locked on them. Now all the people, even the children, were shut in the one room all day. The boys and girls of six and seven too, Lame Girl, the two younger Red Birds, one seven, and his cousin the thirteen-year-old one who had showed himself fit to stand beside his uncle Great Eyes in the Chadron Creek camp. Once more sentries with the guns on their shoulders were walking around the barracks all the time.

In two, three days Bull Hump was brought back and his wife too, the people sorry to see her here after her escape by rolling from the wagon into the snow. So Bull Hump was back, but not the liberties and the freedoms.

In the cold white-man month of December a new soldier chief came to take Carlton's place. Captain Wessells was a short, light-haired, very busy-busy man, in and out of the barracks a dozen times a day, as though that were all he had to do. He even came in late at night; any time. Before, the Indians had had no privacy from each other, living all together as open to the eye as the buffalo, without hill or brush patch. Now they had no privacy from this grasshopper *veho* either.

The little Flying Dutchman, as the soldiers called him when he could not hear, liked to see the Indian women work, so he sent them out to clean up around the post in their old cotton dresses and ragged blankets, to pick up trash and paper, shovel the frozen horse droppings into the wheelbarrows, unload grain wagons. It was healthy exercise, he said. But they managed to hide a little grain in their blankets as they ran back to warm themselves at evening. Besides, they got a present here and there from the pitying people of the post, a few cookies perhaps from some woman, a string of beads, a ribbon. The busy little white man did not like Sioux visitors to the barracks either, not even the scouts when they were around the post. The good days were truly past.

Several times he came to see what warm clothing the Indians had, and always he discovered once more that they had none, nothing of the red woolen dresses and the flannel leggins and tails that the Cheyennes liked, only worn calico and old canvas. Even Bull Hump, usually the dandy with his breechclout of good red flannel handsomely quilled or beaded, had only old tent canvas for tails now. Each time Wessells said that the warm clothes were coming soon, the Cheyennes heard it with two ears, one glad for warm covering in this cold winter, the other uneasy, for it must mean they were to be taken away before the spring.

This matter of clothing for the Cheyennes kept the mail and the telegraph busy. Crook had wired the Indian Bureau, and when none came, he asked if it could not be issued from annuities of Red Cloud and Spotted Tail agencies. "Very cold near Robinson. Inhuman to move Indians as ordered. . . . Carlton says men must be handcuffed." Finally, when nothing arrived, he ordered Wessells to outfit the Cheyennes from the army stores when they started south, but that would help the sixty women and the forty children very little.

Now Red Cloud was called down for one last council. Perhaps he could make the hopelessness of the situation clear to the sullen Cheyennes. The council was in the barracks room, the women and children along the back, not a child playing, not one running to stand between the knees of its father as Cheyenne children sometimes did, even in the great councils.

The soldier chiefs came into the gray, dusky log room and seated themselves in chairs, Wessells, Vroom, and their officers, with Red Cloud, American Horse, and related subchiefs cross-legged beside them on the floor. Around both ways from these men, making a tight, close circle, were the Cheyenne leaders. Wessells spoke through Rowland, one of their breed relatives. He told them what all knew now: that the Indian Bureau had ordered the Cheyennes back to Indian Territory. Then, before Dull Knife and the rest could rise in protest, Red Cloud was up, and no one spoke against this, for he was the guest. He felt sorry to see his friends in this trouble he said, but all he could do was counsel submission. He was an old-time friend of the Cheyennes. His uncle, called Red Cloud too, had married into the people and lived with them all his life, his blood in some of the men sitting here before him.

"But the white man's government is very powerful. They tell me I cannot take you into my lodge and feed you," the Sioux chief said. "The ground is covered with snow, you are almost naked, and it is very far to that north country. The soldiers are everywhere up there too. It is very foolish to think of resisting."

Through this Dull Knife sat silent. He seemed buried deep in reverie, a watching newspaperman wrote, his face as smooth and as classic as any ever put in marble, and much like Secretary Seward's was in thoughtful moments. The old Cheyenne was without adornment, nothing except the old otter wrapping of his braids and on his breast the little beaded lizard worn for the Powers to see when help was needed for the people.

Finally the old Cheyenne chief arose, looking his full mid-sixty years, bleak-eyed from all the things that had been done. The blanket he held about him was very old, yet he stood remote as a mountain peak within its raggedness.

"We bowed to the will of the Great Father," he said, "and we went far into the south where he told us to go. There we found that a Cheyenne cannot live. We belong here. I knew this country before a one of your white men set his foot along our rivers, before he brought his whisky to our villages, or your bluecoats spurred along the trails, north and south. When you first came, you were few and we spoke well to you, made you our guests, and gave you our game to eat and warmed you in our lodges. Even after you began to push in everywhere, to kill the buffalo, bring sickness to our villages, and come shooting our people in the winter night, we still tried to hold our young men to peace, the peace you had promised us so many times. Do this one more thing, you said. Sell us some of your land and we shall have peace. We gave you our land, and the things you promised did not come, not to eat or to wear or a place to live. Many times you promised us an agency, but you only took us far to the south country, saying 'Go and see. You can come back.' Then when we were dying there, and sick for our home, you said that was a mistake; that we must stay because everything was changed. It is true that now everything is changed. You are now the many and we are the few, but we know that it is better to die fighting on the way to our old home than to perish of the sicknesses. . . ."

And as Dull Knife spoke, one man rose from the circle—Bull Hump, the old chief's powerful elder son. Aloof, eyes burning in the duskiness, he stalked back and forth behind the Cheyenne chiefs, the knife at his belt naked, the ends of his canvas breechclout the only thing that seemed to stir in the anger of his lithe steps as he turned back and forth across the narrow room.

And when Wessells again urged the Cheyennes to go, to save themselves, Dull Knife remained firm.

"No," he said in his soft Cheyenne. "I am here on my own ground and I will never go back."

Now none of the men or boys was permitted outside of the barracks, not even for their necessity, but had to line up, use the little indoor facilities like some very sick and dying old *veho*. The women and children were taken out, ten, fifteen at a time, down past the stables and then marched back by the guards with bayonets, the Indians walking one behind the other, shivering easily, now that they were always shut up. In the barracks the Cheyennes seemed so sullen that Captain Lawson decided his wife and daughter must not go visit them any more, as they had often done. There was no singing, no laughing in games, no moccasin beading. The people just sat, now and then a warrior rising to stalk back and forth, back and forth.

It was almost like the days back south when Mizner and Agent Miles kept telling the Cheyennes they must move in to the agency or the cannons would speak. The whites had worked more cautiously then, but now the Indians were locked in the log barracks with bayonets all around and five companies of troops waiting to take them away—five companies armed against the forty-six male Cheyennes, from eleven to eighty years old.

The third of January they were told they must now pack up to go south.

Wessells was ordered to start the Indians no matter how cold the weather, but to provide everything possible for their comfort. He replied that they were resolved to die rather than to go. The next day Crook telegraphed to Washington for an agent from the Indian Bureau to superintend the move. He was unwilling to let this responsibility rest on the military. The seventh of the month he wired once more about the warm clothing that never came.

At Robinson it was truly the iron-hard winter that comes after the swift storms of the Cheyenne autumn. The windows had been deep-frosted for three weeks, the shoveled paths like stone between high dirty ridges of snow, with little white skifts of new fall running before the feet in every wind. The sun was out only once in three days and then with fires on both sides to warm himself. The busy little Wessells, his eyebrows frosted, his face red and raw, had come marching into the barracks in his buffalo coat. Through the interpreter he told his last orders. Once more the Indians said they would rather die. So he had their rations all cut off, and the wood too. Then, turning, listening to no cry from woman or child, he went out into the cold past the dark Indian faces at the window. At the corner, Wessells and his men bent as the wind hit them, the shoulder capes of their blue coats flying up. The captain strode rapidly ahead of the others, to report what he had done and to say he anticipated early submission.

But several days passed in darkness and gloom inside the waiting barracks without capitulation, and then Wessells ordered the water shut off too.[3]

"Yes, even the drinking water," he said sharply to the hesitant messenger. "But say to them that, if they will let me have their women and children, I will take them out of there and they shall be fed and warmed."

The Indians made no word of reply to this, or seemed to hear, not even the women. And when the soldier stammered it out a second time, they rose and drove him fleeing from the building.

Still, the Cheyennes would surely have to give up soon now.

15  The Ordeal Begins

IT WAS A CLEAR, COLD NIGHT, THE MOON SO LARGE AND shining on the snow that it seemed one could see to the horizon, to the circle of the four Great Directions. Only once before had a moon seemed so much like day—the time these Cheyennes had slipped out of their guarded camp in the North Fork of the Canadian. Now, exactly four months later by the white man's figures, the ninth of January, once more Dull Knife's people were preparing to flee, this time to fight their way through the log walls of a prison house and the soldiers and the winter cold.

At first when everything was shut off at the barracks,* there were still the benches and floor boards to be burned. The women had a little grain and tallow put away, and when they were taken to the brush below the stables, they managed to hide a little snow in their blankets for the thirsting children. Not too much, for one woman had looked so suddenly fat that a soldier bumped her with his gunstock and the snow slid from the folds of her blanket around her feet and she stood there, her sunken eyes down upon what was lost.

Now almost everything was used up, and the below-zero cold that sat among them like a wolf grew stronger from the frost crawling in between the logs, the women huddled together, the children crying out in their cold and hunger from the troubled half sleep as they would not have dared if awake.

The young men had long planned for this day that Hog promised them the night they were brought here. The council chiefs were pushed aside

* Last food and fuel, Saturday, January 4, 1879; last water, January 8, Captain Wessells told Board of Proceedings. Other military and Indian sources put both at varying but earlier dates.

even more now than usually happened in warring, this time by younger leaders like Black Bear, Little Shield, Bull Hump, and the southern Pug Nose. There were older men among them too, like Great Eyes and even Bridge, who had never gone armed except by his healing power, and the wilder young sons of the chiefs, Little Hump and Young Hog, following Roman Nose and the Little Finger Nail, the one who had grown so strong these few moons past.

Behind the blanket-covered windows the plans were approached with the old formality now. In the prolonged desperation of the barracks the killings down in Kansas by any avenger seemed suddenly the work of a foolish and faraway time, like the things of hot youth seen from the responsible years of the council fire. Here everyone must work together for the surprise, the power they did not have in guns or numbers.

Little Shield, the leading warrior of the Elks, the lesser and so the guest society here, was given the place of bravery. He would head the outbreak on his end of the barracks, be the first through the window there and upon the walking sentries with loaded guns to be taken, every gun possible. Those on the opposite side would be led by Little Finger Nail. The work of all the others was well planned too, who would step into a man's tracks as he fell, the younger women also in it this freezing night that was like day. Always the weather was against them now, with storms to hide the attacking soldiers, moonlight to reveal the fleeing Indians. Truly the Cheyennes had lost the sacred way somewhere, long ago.

With the moonlight and a cold to freeze the grouse, they must go very fast, and for that the ropes and the few elk-horn saddles and pads must be taken along. Two good horse catchers would run ahead to Bronson's ranch on Dead Man Creek, the nearest herd. Some day their friend would be paid for what they must now take, and if not, no man would grudge the taking less.

Dog soldiers, experienced in this duty, would guard the rear, fight to hold the soldiers back while the other men ran with the children and helped the women get away. Some were to carry a few things of the old times, old medicine objects, although the best they had brought, the Chief's Bundle, hung under the arm of Little Wolf. But they had the stone buffalo horn sacred to the Dog soldiers, the lance heads of their tribal bands, a few pieces of fine old quill work—something to hold to, to remind those who might be left after tonight of the greatness of the past time; to remind them that they must always be Cheyennes. It was in this planning that Great Eyes took out his fine old shield, with the triple tail of eagle feathers and the claws of the strong-hearted grizzly, and called his nephew, the thirteen-year-old Red Bird, to him.

"You have no weapon, not even a broken knife, my son," he said. "You have grown too small in the hungry times to help other people much in the fast fighting of this night, so I give you this shield to care for. You know how old it is, how many arrows and bullets it has turned away. Take it, my son, and run hard. Pay no attention to anything, do not stop for a drink from this long thirsting or for mercy for anyone. Run very hard and keep hidden, and if you must die, die with your body protecting this. . . ."

The tall, thin boy stood shamed by this honor, feeling foolish and weak, unable to reply. Gently the man passed his long hand over the shield cover once more, as if to remember all its form and feel all the greatness of its power. Then he put the wide rawhide band of it over the boy's shoulder, and turning quickly, he went to stand at the blanketed window, looking for a long time where one could not see.

As evening neared, the young men became restless, some walking up and down, their moccasins soft on the bare earth where the boards were gone. Some were like drunk with firewater, talking, talking, staggering a little; some cried out suddenly, "Open the door! Let me charge against the soldiers! I want to die right now . . . ," until older men led them away. And if one young man here in the barracks now wished to give up, he did not put the words to his tongue. Not a young man or any one.

So it was like lying on the hill for the vision, the dreaming, the exaltation. None had eaten or drunk or warmed himself; none had been with a woman for a long time, or the women with a man. Now they were prepared for the ordeal in the old, old way, and it was as if all the foolish things had fallen from them and ahead was the greatest thing in their lives, the greatest test of all.

That morning Wessells had sent for Hog because he was the one the warriors had seemed to follow at Chadron Creek. Hog refused to go, thinking of the hanging post where a man swung from a rope. Besides, no one chief could speak for the Cheyennes, and whatever was said someone must be there to hear it, so the whites could make no lies of it later and his people never know.

"I cannot go alone," he said. "I must talk where all can hear."

When he was told he could bring a man along, Old Crow consented to walk beside him to the adjutant's little building, but the warriors cried out "No! No!" and stood against them at the door. Only Hog's growing power kept them from actually putting their hands upon him. Even his own son, Young Hog, shouted against him. "Those two blinded men will never be allowed to come back!"

"Wait!" the father said again, as he had two days ago when Young Hog drew his foolish knife against a sentry and had to be held back so he would not die right there, heavy on a bayonet.

But now Hog's sick wife saw he was going and she began to moan, rocking herself back and forth, and so he had to stop and go to her with a few quieting words.

"They will kill you!" she cried.

"We have these other people here," Hog said, in the long-known chieftain's reply to such protestations. "They are given into my palm to care for now, to shield. . . ."

So with Old Crow beside him, he went slowly through the blinding glare of sun on snow to the little adjutant's building that was full of whites, several officers sitting around the chunky red-faced Captain Wessells, and many of the soldiers packed in there too. When Hog said once more that they could not go south, the guards sprang upon the two Indians from behind, with irons ready for their hands. Old Crow was subdued first, and easily, but the still powerful Hog, grunting, with soldiers hanging to him all around, managed to bend and twist and get a hand to the knife in his belt as he lurched himself halfway out through the door, his old shirt torn away, his naked shoulders heaving to throw these puny whites from him. One of the men was cut a little in the struggle, as with a great roar to those over in the barracks Hog got his hand up. But as he drove the knife quickly downward against his own belly, the jerk of the panting soldiers deflected the blade, and the iron rings were snapped upon the Indian's wrists.

It was done very quickly, and perhaps even Hog's cry would have been lost in the blowing wind, but a Cheyenne woman was out talking to her brother from Red Cloud trying to get her released to him. She saw Hog burst out with soldiers on him like dogs hanging to a grizzly, and the irons on his hands. She threw her head back and gave her penetrating woman's cry of danger, high and thin on the wind.

Immediately there was great excitement in the barracks. Some of the Indians made a rush for one of the doors and broke past the guards, but were driven back by a company of mounted troops charging in around them. Young Hog, with his sheet blanket over his head, shouted for everybody to get out of the way, for he was coming to get his father. But there were so many guns against him, their bayonets meeting together over his gaunt belly, that he was pushed back and finally the door was closed on them all.

A long time Hog looked where his son had had the sharp steel of the soldiers pushed against his flesh, so close to the place where their relative Crazy Horse had died of the lance-pointed gun. With the water of sorrow jumping down his dark, stony cheeks, Hog held out his manacled wrists. "Take them off," he said. "I will go back and tell my people it is hopeless. They must give up and go back south."

But the little *veho* Wessells gave no such order. Standing silent before the powerful Indian, he stared up into his face, the soldiers who came from the barracks stopped by the long looking. After a while the officers around Wessells began to move a little, uneasily, making noises with their boots on the frozen ground.

"I cannot let you go in there," the captain finally said. "You would not be permitted to come out again."

So the two Indians stood together beside the shoveled drifts, their old blankets whipping loose, now that their hands were ironed, waiting for the ambulance to take them to the soldier prison down at the encampment. Once there was a disturbance at the barracks door and Left Hand came hurrying out. "I cannot see my brothers taken away with the irons on them and stay behind," he said, as he held out the hands that could fell a buffalo with a thrown rock.

At the barracks the roaring increased; the noise of boards ripped off somewhere and hammered across the doors; the sound of digging, breastworks thrown up, holes made to protect the women and children even now if the soldiers charged the building. Then there was drumming, dancing, and singing, singing that those who knew Cheyenne said were songs of war and strength and death.

"We have quite a powwow started now," Wessells said casually, as another company of troops came up on the trot to take over the guard. He had the inside doors from the barracks to the cook and guard rooms boarded up too, and then he rode after Hog and the others to see that they were manacled foot and hand, safe, in the tent that was the encampment's guard-house.

At the prison the three Cheyennes were turned over to Lieutenant Chase.

"I am grieved to see what has happened," their young friend said, when water had been brought them and he saw the men drink cup after cup, jerking themselves back harshly now and then, as they would long-thirsted horses, and then drinking deeply again.

"Ahh-h, it is a bad thing that has been done," Hog finally agreed. "They all want to die up there now. They will break out tonight and die fighting."

This was repeated in the presence of Wessells at Chase's request, with Rowland interpreting and many soldiers around to hear, so everyone could know and be prepared and there would be no excuse to butcher the people like fleeing buffalo. Then the three Cheyennes were fed and told they could go back up there and call their families out.

There was talk of Wessells taking the handcuffed men into the barracks but Hog was against that. "No! Then the warriors must make a fight and everybody will be killed," he said sternly, as though in command here.

And truly it was dangerous to go in to the Indians now. That morning before Hog was taken, a Cheyenne living with Red Cloud came into the barracks room to talk to his relatives and he would have been killed if his friends had not hurried him out. And when the Sioux scout, Woman's Dress, came in, even Tangle Hair shouted against him.

"You want to get us killed like you helped kill Crazy Horse! We have been told how you did it, coming to spy, sneaking around, then telling lies!"

The young men lifted more than their voices against Woman's Dress, and he ran from the door with his arms about his head, the Cheyennes quirting him clear out to the guards, even though he had relatives among them here, and they knew that this would not be forgotten.

When Hog would not go shackled into the barracks, they talked through cracks where the chinking was gone from the logs. After a while the wives of the prisoners and some of their small children were allowed to come out, and two very old women, but only after much angry talk and noise. Young Hog stayed, and the elder of his sisters, the one called Hog's Daughter. She would not leave her brother.

"Tell them all to come out," Wessells urged. "They will not be harmed."

Hog said this, but held his hands out before him, showing the iron that bound them together. He received no reply. Rowland talked to Great Eyes through the blanket-covered window and asked him to let his nephew, the young Red Bird, come out. The boy's angry voice answered for himself. He would stay and die with the rest.

Once Wessells tried it himself. "Dull Knife! Dull Knife!" he called. "Why don't you come out?"

Without waiting for the interpreter, the old chief answered that he could not, and knowing that this would not be understood by the whites, who would think it was the warriors who were against it, not the strong wall built by his own heart, he said it once more: "I will die before I go south. . . ."

But it was the captain's request that Tangle Hair come out that brought the greatest excitement, a roaring and shouting against his going that was unusual, coming from the soft-spoken Cheyennes, who were suddenly as noisy as Tangle Hair's own born brothers, the Sioux. It seemed very strange to the white men who knew that the Hair had said little in the troubles at Chadron Creek, and then was not heeded.

Finally Little Shield made himself heard outside. "It is plain this man cannot go out," he called to Wessells. "He owns us now like a silver dollar in the *veho* palm, and he can do with us as he likes! Most of us are Dog soldiers and he is the leading chief of the society. With Wild Hog taken from us we now must follow this Sioux. We cannot let him go!"

When it was night the Indians in the dark barracks saw the post black-smith come over the moonlit snow dragging heavy chains and make a hammering as he fastened them across the doors that led to the cook and guard rooms of the barracks. The outside doors he fastened more securely too, one with an iron bar screwed down. Now the Cheyennes were shut in tight, not in a stone house as in Florida but in wood that could be fired, burned to the ground. Some of the warriors said this among themselves, whispering it over a little glow of fire to warm their trigger fingers. The women had heard the hammering and huddled closer together in the dark-ness, their eyes where the doors were—watching for the coming of the guns. Perhaps no one would be allowed out any more for any purpose. Perhaps they were meant to die here, humiliatingly, in the smell of imprisoned people who had no privacy and no room for it. They were to die of thirst, trapped together like antelope in the pits, with no one coming to slit the throats, none to make it quick and easy.

But one woman back in the dark could think only of the chained doors. She began to rock herself, "We are to burn!" she moaned, softly at first, then lifting the words louder and louder as she repeated them. "They will put fire to us all here!" she finally cried, thin and high, like a hunting panther, over and over.

The others tried to stop her, to quiet her, doing it gently, remembering that she had seen her baby thrown into the flames at the Sappa. But suddenly the woman sprang up and felt for a sleeping child in a mother's arms, those around trying to hold her back, take the knife from her hand in the darkness.

"No, no! Help me!" she pleaded. "Quick, your knives—let us help the little ones here to die easily, before the burning soldiers come!"

Now the old men hurried to the woman, Dull Knife speaking so harshly to her that she crumpled down, sobbing. Quickly Red Feather and Brave One forced her helpless against the wall and twisted her wrist back until her knife dropped in the darkness, while Bridge started his sleep chant and his slow rattle to quiet her. Gradually she settled down to the floor, her head in Medicine Woman's lap, and seemed to sleep, but the fear she saw was still there in the night and the silence.

So Little Shield called the warriors together. "You see how the people sicken. They cannot wait longer, not even to midnight," he whispered. "While some watch that the building is not fired, the rest will dress in our best clothing. We will die outside, fighting."

Stooped over the little fires that had been saved to light this preparation, they painted their faces and put on the few good things left. Dull Knife drew the beaded lizard outside his shirt, and Little Finger Nail put on his shell-core collar and tied the watchful, clear-voiced bird in his hair, the bird that brought him the sweet singing. Most of them had new beaded moccasins that the women had made, or were presents from the Sioux. Then they tied their blankets at the neck and around the waist to leave the arms free, but they took no other notice of the cold that made the smoky logs creak and was a sparkling of frost along every chink and knot in the light of the little fires.

So the 130 Indians prepared for the going, only 44 men, including the

eleven-year-olds, and with very little in their hands. They brought out the
five guns hidden in the holes and the pistols too, nine of these, and one more
that worked part of the time. Then they divided the cartridges as well as
they could, and the lead and caps and powder. It was so pitifully little; one
man had only two cartridges and one of those so poor in powder it was
only for the noise. Dull Knife sat down by himself when he saw how it was,
brooding alone. But Black Bear had his lucky Custer carbine that his wife
had carried through the searches, and others the two good ones that had
been found in the brush of the White River by the women where the warriors from Little Wolf had signaled them to look. Now even the knives were
divided, those with broken blades whetted to points these last few weeks.
Four men had war clubs to use in the Sioux way, clubs made from wood out
of the barracks with spikes from the floor driven straight through until the
points stuck out of each club head like spines from a great cactus.

As silence settled over the post and there was only the far howl of the
coyote and the slow clump of the sentries on the stony winter earth, one
man after another went quietly to the women's end of the room, whispered
a name here or there in the darkness, touching a braided head perhaps, or
a child fretting for water. Then at the signal they took their places at the
windows, with Little Shield and Little Finger Nail to lead, but good men
at the other windows too and one ready to get into the guardroom for a
gun or two, if possible. Behind them waited such men as Singing Wolf with
his Sharps rifle, the powerful buffalo gun, to stand against the soldiers when
the first warriors went down. Next there were a few men without guns but
carrying children. These were the fast men. Whatever happened some of
these little ones must get away, some must live as seed so the people here
would not be lost forever. With these a few women were to run too, strong
women like the wives of She Bear and White Antelope, to rear any children
that might be saved in this pitiless light of the moon, teach them the Cheyenne way. Perhaps somewhere they could find the good path, walk with
the Great Powers once more.

Older men like Dull Knife and Noisy Walker, without guns, would go
with the women to help them, as was always their duty, someone to help
Lame Girl too, for this last one of her family must not die easily. Behind
these would be Sitting Man, where his healing leg would delay no one.
Two young warriors would come last of all, to get everyone out, out and
running.

Piva, so it was planned, and if it was not good, it was the best they could do, with so little, and so many against them here.

When the stars that the white man called his drinking dipper were turned past the ten on the *veho* clock, there was a single shot from the dark barracks, the explosion like fire in the night as the guard at the corner of the building fell. The boom rolled loud over the snow in the still cold moonlight, followed by three fast shots, so fast their echoes came back together, into a scattered firing. Two more soldiers went down and two in the guardroom were wounded, but truly the Indians had thinned the powder too close or there would have been more than the two guns they got before other guards were upon them and soldiers poured out of the company barracks doors, looking white as the snow in their underwear from the sleeping.

The first Indians through the windows were followed by the rest in close file, like a string of bulky antelope leaping a bank, some of the last ones falling from shots inside the barracks. Then there was faster shooting from outside, dropping the Indians as they ran over the snow toward the river, the men shouting, herding the people together, hurrying along those with children under their arms, and the women with the saddles and the little food somehow saved, heading them all toward the bridge. Below the stables five Dog soldiers led by Tangle Hair dropped in a line behind a snowdrift to hold the soldiers back. They were coming fast now, many of them still not dressed but shouting and yelling, a trumpet blowing, the horses neighing and running, and the powder smoke stinging the eyes with the breath-biting cold.

When all the people were past the stable, all who would ever come, the five rear guards started jumping around, whooping, firing into the faces of the soldiers to hold them back a little longer, just a little longer. But finally the last of the five Dog men was down, dropped in the old-time honorable way—covering the flight of their people.

One of those who never came by was Sitting Man. His leg had broken again as he jumped through the window, so he sat there against a high drift singing his death song as a soldier put a gun to his head and blew his brains out, splattering them dark against the moonlit snowbank. Nine men were killed before the Indians reached the river and twice as many wounded, one—Tangle Hair—injured more than his feet could carry away. So he dragged himself out of sight and called to some soldiers who knew a little pidgin Sioux. They recognized him, took him to their quarters, and sent for the doctor. No other man was left wounded in the stretch of snow to the river. If they could not run, they died and were shot many, many times by the trigger-hot soldiers. Two women and some children lay back there too, and so many were wounded that the fleeing path was plain as far buffaloes scattered to sleep along their trail, many dark things on the crusted snow, the powder smoke creeping in white clouds along the ground, a stink on the biting air.

The Indians that were left struck for the bridge of White River, with thin, snow-drifted brush along the banks, the water low in the little ice-locked center channel. Some had to fall flat there to drink if they died for it. The rest crossed and, turning up the south side, ran toward the sawmill on the second bottom, the faster men getting far ahead of the foot soldiers. But now more came on horses and a few Indians stopped near the sawmill to make a little stand. But when they were charged by a wide line of cavalry, the warriors broke and scattered, all except three men. These fell back a little and held again, desperate, wounded, but firing so long as they could lift themselves. After that no more stands could be made, without the ammunition and against the hundreds of soldiers plunging through the crusted snow almost upon them, and more on the gallop from down at the encampment, the trumpet blowing there.

It was plainly useless to try to get to the horses of Bronson's ranch, so quickly had the Indians been overtaken, so many shot, and there were no shielding bluffs close along that open road. Instead, they dropped their saddles and turned toward the river again, and the cliff-steep bluffs beyond standing in a dark wall for miles against the north. At the frozen stream the swift center channel was open, but the people plunged into the icy water, through it, and on, their clothing frozen at once and hammering like iron against their running legs. The soldiers overtook fifteen, sixteen more on the deep-drifted slope toward the bluffs. All the wounded men were killed with pistol shots through the head because they might rise up with guns. The women were to be captured, but it was not always easy to tell them in the blankets, fallen, sprawled out, or fleeing like shadows over the moonlit snow.

A few, very weak from hunger, had hidden in the narrow tangle of drifted brush and grass along the White River, slipping down the stream a way, or up it, but only a few, the men driving the rest out and on, one woman crying, "Run, my sons! You can save yourselves. I am played out."

Others were found by the soldiers there, the troopers plunging their horses after every moccasin track, with everything so plain on the bright snow.

In the first half mile, half of their fighting men were lost. The women and boys grabbed the guns and ran, not stopping to make any stand now. A little soldier chief who slipped down into a snow-filled washout near the sawmill stumbled upon two Indians hidden there. They attacked him with knives against his revolver and went down. Then he saw that they were women. Another one was shot to pieces. She was without hope or will to live, with her man dead there on the ground, and so she stood up, but she was behind a stump and a line of troopers charged her, thinking it was a man. The bullets tore the blanket from her as she fell.

It was along there that Dull Knife, Bull Hump, and their families struck off across a hard-crusted drift away from the others, with two warriors and the young Red Bird, still carrying his shield, close behind. Because one of the Knife's daughters was hurt and had to be left, Little Hump had dropped back to help make a delaying stand. Another daughter stayed with him until it was too dangerous and then she picked up one of the children of those already on the ground and ran with the women toward the bluffs.

The young men had fought bravely with what was in the hand. Dull Knife's son had a pistol, and when he was hit, he threw it to another as he went down. Later some civilians came along and he lifted himself from the snow and made one lunge at them with the broken-bladed butcher knife from his belt. Then Little Hump too, another of the Beautiful People of Dull Knife, lay dead on the ground.

By now there were many civilians following the Indian trail, some from the trading stores, like Dear and Clifford, and cattlemen, Bronson too, all going close past The Enemy, who had walked north with the Brave One. She was hidden in weeds and brush under a snowbank, cramped and freezing, not daring to move. Some of those passing were afoot, others horseback or in wagons, all with guns, shooting the wounded, the children too, stripping them, taking the scalps. An officer who was sending the wounded and the prisoners back saw the white men up on a knoll and shouted against them. But then he went on back toward the bridge with his soldiers who carried two bad-hurt Indians in blankets, and the other whites moved on along the path of flight, taking everything, their guns making bright flashes, the report rolling over the broad moon-hazing valley. After the looting men were past, The Enemy had to come out, too, or freeze and die. But

perhaps it had already happened, for she seemed cold as the snow over
which she moved from body to body and looked at them all, dropping like
a dead one among the others when anybody came past. She looked into one
face after another of her friends and relatives, seeing them as she saw her
loved ones at Sand Creek and the Sappa, but somehow these seemed strangers long dead and scalped, some of the women too, their skirts thrown up
over their heads, and indecent things done.[1]

Although the soldiers were very close, most of the Cheyennes had to
stop a little when they reached the drifted pines and rocks at the bluffs, resting in their weakness, their clothing frozen and their eyes turned anxiously
back upon their trail that bent down the valley of the White. Even in the
hazing moonlight they could see dark blurs along it, unmoving, with many
troopers hurrying close and spreading with the scatter of moccasin tracks.
There were several quick shots along the bluffs, first the flash and then the
sharp report of the carbine, where soldiers overtook the played-out and the
wounded. It was hard to endure this, when those too were very close to the
rocks where no horse could have followed.

White Antelope was one who fell before the hurrying troops. He had
stayed back to help his wounded wife and some other women, the baby
like a sack under his arm. None of them could run any more, even with the
soldiers charging, and so Antelope left the baby and turned upon the pursuers with his short knife. He fought there a little while before he was
brought down, the women he was trying to protect all wounded now, two
of them dead.

But White Antelope was still alive, and when the soldiers went on, he
crawled to his wife and saw that the baby was dead and the woman dying
too. They spoke a little, a few words in their soft Cheyenne. Then he
stabbed her twice, very fast, with the poor knife, and himself, too, six times,
but his strength now was too little, for when the wagons came to collect
the wounded, they were both still alive, although their clothing was frozen
to the bloody ground.

"The will to live runs very strong in these people," Dr. Moseley said at
the post hospital as he stooped to listen for a beat in the man's torn breast,
but now suddenly White Antelope was gone, and an hour later his wife
also. Their names were added to the surgeon's list, the wounds tersely de-
scribed: "GSW in thigh and knife. . . ."

Then they were taken from the wounded that stretched in a double row across the hospital floor, for others needed their places.

As the soldiers spread along the bluffs to search out the hiding Cheyennes, Little Finger Nail gave his gun to another and slipped back, silent as the tufts of powder smoke that clung to rock and bush and tree. He kept behind the soldiers, trying to find everybody he could, particularly old Bridge, the man who could slow the bleeding wound, bring healing sleep to the paining ones and the afraid. In a dusky place the Nail discovered five hurt women together in some rocks and pines, with three dead children on the shadowed, bloody snow. Among the women was the daughter of Dull Knife who had stayed behind to be with her brother, now down there at the river, his face turned to the moon. She was leaning sideways against a tree, somebody's baby tied to her back, hit too. The girl was still alive but unable to answer the whispered question: "Sister, sister—Are you bad hurt?" But the warrior's propping arm felt how shot she was, almost falling to pieces as he lowered her gently to the snow and smoothed back her hair once. To this one Bridge need not be brought.

A mile farther along the band of bluffs he saw a lone man afoot in a buffalo coat—the little Dutchman who had shut off the food and everything from the children, the *veho* who had killed all those helpless ones back there. If there had been a gun in his hand, the young Nail would have shot. But it was good this way, for the captain had a small Cheyenne child in his arms, carrying it until some soldiers came along to take it to the post.

Carefully Little Finger Nail watched Wessells and a few troopers follow the tracks of two more Indians up to a high rocky place. There six soldiers were sent in. They found a Sioux woman that some of them knew, and an old Cheyenne warrior. To the call for surrender the Indian charged out with his revolver, right into the firing guns. When they were empty, he still came on. The soldiers dropped back to reload and this time the Cheyenne fell, and Wessells and the rest went to stand around him in a dark little circle.

"A man so resolute should have lived . . . ," one of the soldiers said, and went to bring back the woman who was climbing away. But she turned on him with a piece of stove iron from the barracks, fierce as the dead Cheyenne had been.

There was nothing the Nail could do here, and too many more soldiers were coming, their voices very close on the frozen air, so he had to turn back. His feet were senseless with cold and he would surely slip on some icy spot, perhaps set a loose stone rolling into a foolish noise, and be caught. But he must look just a little more, up very close along the bluffs, moving from shadow to shadow, making the little winter-mouse squeak signals. But no one seemed alive any more to hear. Then he saw that many of the injured up here would have to die because their medicine man, the one who could heal them, was lost. Bridge lay dead, face down, a reaching arm out ahead of him. It seemed he had been crawling toward the women where Dull Knife's daughter lay. With his rattle out and ready, he had left a trail of blood stretching far behind him on the snow.

For a while Little Finger Nail stood in the still shadow of the pines, his breath making a cloud around the blanket drawn up around his head. He looked down to the pale frosty points of light at Fort Robinson and to the lanterns moving here and there over the trail of the fallen Indians, and suddenly the Nail knew that his warrior days were done. No longer could he think of this as a fight, unequal, but still a fight, one in which he and the other warriors would gather honors for boldness. Now he saw only that he must get the people away, hide them and himself with them, creep away like frightened mice into the crevasses of the frost-cracked rocks, hide and hunt for meat and shelter and healing—do anything now that would save lives.

Truly it had happened that he was no longer a man of the warpath. He broke the frosted breath from the blanket around his face, and holding a fold up over his stinging nose, he stumbled away to follow those who got up into the bluffs.

With a few fresh soldiers Captain Wessells was moving farther up the White River valley, scouting afoot for a place to get troops over the bluffs, the horse holders following below. Several miles out they found three Indians in a drifted pile of rocks and brush, with only the sheer cliff wall behind them. The men charged down at the soldiers, whooping, swinging war clubs, one with a Sharps carbine that he used like a club too, the frozen walnut stock breaking like glass when it glanced from a dodging soldier and struck a rock. But the Cheyenne would never need it again. He was already down, and then the second man too. The third escaped and no one followed him because the recruits had let the horses get away in those first whoops that broke into echoes along the bluffs, a stable-wise old bay gelding leading them in a run for the post. So Wessells had to walk back several miles. But some Indians hidden along the bluffs tried to stop the horses, and then shot after them, hoping to crease at least one to catch it. Snorting, the horses had turned back, and were finally cornered by the troops in a rocky washout, miles away.

Once Wessells passed the crippled Stubfoot and his nephew. They were dug back under the drift in a pocket, very cold but afraid to have even a handful of smoldering grass for warmth because the smell would carry far tonight. The Foot had his revolver down on the soldier chief once, for the wounding of his wife on the run to the bridge, but he never pulled the trigger. His hands were very cold and there was too much killing already. Later the two followed the trail into the bluffs and ran into their friend Lieutenant Chase coming around a rocky point alone. The Foot and the young white man stopped almost against each other and all three could have died there in one beat of the excited heart, but Chase spoke *veho* words in a friendly tone and held out an empty hand. So Stubfoot put his revolver into it, butt first, in surrender. Then they waited together for the troopers. A man who had been in the sandhill fight down south and lost his first wife in the Sappa killings waited, a prisoner.

"Enough have died . . . ," he said to his angry, protesting young nephew.

Many soldiers were already dismounted and skirmishing along the bluffs wherever there was a snow track or a drop of blood on a rock. One place they were close enough to Pug Nose, Bullet Proof, and a dozen others to see their darkish figures creeping like bears up through a snow-filled crevasse in the 75-foot cliff that had looked impassable to anything except the soaring eagle.

"Look at 'em mountain goats!" one of the soldiers shouted in astonishment, and in admiration, but already the others were sending bullets that kicked rock upon the hurrying Indians. Instantly the graying light up there was empty, and several shots came down upon the soldiers from the top of the bluffs compelling them to fall back.

By now the civilians had reached the bluffs with their wagons and the buckboard that carried the mail on the Sidney-to-Black-Hills stage line.[2] They were taking everything from those on the ground, even robbing the ones Vroom and Chase's troops had covered with their frozen blankets until the six-mule death wagons could gather them up.

By the next day thirty Indians, twenty-one of them warriors, half of all the men Dull Knife had, were laid out in rows down near the sawmill, and probably some frozen ones, particularly children, not found. The post hospital was filled with the wounded, mostly brought in by their young friend Lieutenant Chase. He had shot Indians—killing people for pay was his soldier work in the curious *veho* manner—but they were glad to see that he did not shoot the wounded. For that, and his gentleness with the hurt ones, the Cheyennes would remember him.

By daylight the scouts signaled of soldiers riding everywhere: up and down the White River, on the roads from Camp Sheridan, Fort Laramie, and Deadwood, out past Crow Butte and around northwest on the Hat Creek road, the road the Indians must cross if they would reach Red Cloud or even Little Wolf, although without the horses from Bronson they could never hope to get to the one they still called their Strong Man. The herd down on the Dead Man ranch would be watched now, and no signals came from the two men who still tried to get there.

But it was almost 6 miles around by a place where the soldiers could get the horses up on the bluffs in the snow, so those on top were safe for a little while to bind the bleeding and build fires for the frozen hands and feet—safe for a little weary chewing at the dried meat left in the rocks for them by Woodenthigh. There was not much, for the Little Wolf people were poor too this winter, and with the soldiers watching they had to travel very light. Yet the meat helped put a little hope into the starved stomachs here, helped to keep some of the bereaved ones from running back to die against the guns.

Little Finger Nail and Roman Nose went several miles along the top of the bluffs to see who was at the fires. There were some old people and even some small children, and the young girls like Singing Cloud and Hog's Daughter, with perhaps some others still hidden. Everyone at the silent little fires thought of those down there on the ground. No one asked about Dull Knife and the ones to go with him or spoke of his dead son and daughter down there and another daughter shot, perhaps dying too.

The day divided the Indians in their hearts between welcome and anxiety. The sun might warm their freezing a little, but it would light up every moccasin track, show it from far off, lengthened and curled and darkened at the edges in the thawing. Always the Cheyennes had to think in these two ways, between the warmth of day and the shelter of night. Before the bloody path out of the barracks here it was the trail from the south, and all those other trails. But few had seen a night as bad as this one, or such a morning.

And now there were signals of new soldiers coming close, many more soldiers out, to reach for the Cheyennes like a great grizzly clawing at the rocks for hidden mice. So the people had to rise and start over the broad white glare of tableland, without a stone or a tree, before they struck the breaks toward the north and the sheltering stream beds that led away. Bent from their wounding and lamed by frost, leaning on each other, some carried, one man with crutch sticks for a broken shin, the thirty-four Cheyennes—children and old and all—moved out toward the timbered breaks of Hat Creek, the far pines a black smudging on the snow. The Indians went in a dark straggling file, winding around the softer drifts, their weary moccasins driven faster and faster as they left the protection of the broken bluffs behind.

16 This Is the Place

THE MORNING OF THE TENTH, WESSELLS TELEGRAPHED
Crook that in addition to the thirty Cheyennes
killed they had captured thirty-five, and he would have many more before
dark. The snow was deep, trailing was good, and five companies would be
out.

Vroom's column from the encampment led Wessells' buffalo-coated
troops westward over the shimmering heights between the White River
bluffs and Soldier Creek, the moccasin trail plain as a main-traveled road
through the snow, with now and then a little blood from the injured, perhaps where one had rested, and the steady pinkening from bleeding feet.

"Only thirty, maybe thirty-five, many women and small ones . . . ," the
Sioux scout Woman's Dress said, but he fell back to the column as the trail
led down into rough country. It passed close around the narrow foot of a
hill topped with drift-filled old timber, and on over the rise far ahead. But
the Cheyennes had swung back on their tracks like the jack rabbit watching his trail. When the last of the troops had wound single file past the hill
and down into the creek bottom, bullets came from the timber of the ridge,
and puffs of smoke rose very blue into the sun. A couple of cavalry saddles
were emptied; two soldiers left on the ground like Indian bundles, very
dark on the snow. The horses shied and stampeded, throwing a new West
Pointer into a drift. Clumsy in his buffalo coat, he had to dodge from banked
weed to drifted sagebrush while the troopers, quickly dismounted in the
bottoms, covered his escape with a hot fire. They did it well, but some of
Crook's old Indian fighters laughed aloud to see this commissioned green-
horn run with bullets spitting up the snow around him. Several horses were
killed, one by the soldiers themselves as it fled from the volleying into the
Indian entrenchments. Bullet Proof was hit in the shoulder trying to get

the horse, a big thing now. Even one horse with which to find others was bigger than the life of any man here among them.

When the fight settled to a watching and sniping, Wessells ordered Woman's Dress up as close as he could get. "Find out if Dull Knife's there. . . ."

The scout stood with blank face before the officer, and when he was urged to go, he said it would be too dangerous. The Cheyennes were very angry. Some had wanted to kill him yesterday when they threw him out of the barracks, before a one of their relatives was killed. But finally the Dress did go to a high place far out of rifle shot and built a little fire, perhaps as much to warm himself as to make signals. If he got any reply, he did not report it, but the troops heard a singing from the Cheyennes as the measured puffs of blue smoke rose from the fire into the lazy sky.

At last the grateful clouding of night started to come to the hill of worn people. Wessells had been so certain he would capture the Indians easily that he carried no rations and no blankets, so he left a row of decoy camp fires and the column returned to Robinson. Pug Nose, out watching, came back to say that everybody had gone, and it seemed that the soldiers valued the Indians here very little, thinking them so weak and foolish that they could be held by a few deserted fires.

"They know we are too hurt and played out to run without horses, and that our leaders are all gone. Now even Bullet Proof is bad wounded. . . ."

"The whites did not ask first to talk to Dull Knife, but to find if he and Bull Hump are here. How can they think that they might not be, unless they have found some tracks, or believe they could be killed somewhere?"

"Yes, unless someone told the plans," Pug Nose, the southerner, said.

No, that could not be. They must have found tracks. If the Powers would send another storm, a man could go looking for those people. But not without new snow covering.

Some of the men had butchered the dead soldier horses, and the weary women moved about the fires roasting the meat for the hungry. The rest was stripped and hung on brush over the coals to dry for the carrying. The skins were dried too, some stretched over fire pits to harden for quick-made moccasin soles. Other Indians tried to ease the hurt and the frozen ones as well as it might be done here, with the girl Singing Cloud helping from the things taught her by Medicine Woman. Many needed it, with even Lame

Girl hit once more. But the pain could keep few awake now, crowded close together on earth warmed by the fires.

Little Finger Nail, suddenly forced toward leadership, talked with Roman Nose and Bear about the horses they must have, at least one, somehow, to search for more. Without horses no one here would live to get away.

"It will be very difficult," Bear said, looking into the clouding sky of night.

Yes, everybody would be watching now, and there were only two places left: the herd at Bluff station far to the west, on the Laramie-to-Deadwood trail, or perhaps some foolish people traveling the Hat Creek road, over north. The Black Hills trail would be soldier-guarded, they knew.

"There have been few tracks on the Hat Creek way this cold winter, and now all will be watching there too, with soldier guns riding along. . . ."

Still, it must be tried. But when Little Finger Nail took up one of the drying horse skins set aside to protect the watchers and started to go, some of the others wanted to stop him. It was dangerous to try this alone; besides, the soldiers might come to attack them here in the night and their strong men were so few.

The young Indian looked past the firelight to where Hog's Daughter was singing the west-wind lullaby to a wounded little girl. She was making the "Woo-o, woo-o-ee!" sounds of the wind through her frost-swollen lips, her breath in little fire-reddened clouds about her head and then drifting away into the blackness of the night beyond. No man could see this and sit here doing less than he might.

But before the Nail got very far, he was suddenly overtaken by three of the Cheyennes coming upon him from behind, swiftly over the creaking snow.

"You are not running away?" the wounded Bullet Proof demanded.

The young man brushed the detaining hands from him in the darkness. "Am I not a Cheyenne?" he asked, and walked on in the night.

The 4 miles to the road was very far under the clouding that would have been a gift from the Powers last night. Most of those who were back there in rows at the sawmill or had crawled away to die of wounding in the rocks could have been saved by one cloud no bigger than two good lodge skins against the moon. With a little darkness they might have found horses and now be hidden with Red Cloud or Little Wolf. The Nail thought about this as he walked wearily over the hard snow, his new-soled moccasins feeling out the strength of the crust, treading softly. Why was it that both times in this flight northward there was the bright moon to send the search upon them? It was not just the absence of the Sacred Hat as some said. They had the Hat along and the Medicine Arrows too when Dull Knife's village was destroyed on the Powder. Nor did Little Finger Nail believe that all these troubles and the buffalo's vanishing happened, as the soured old ones believed, because the women of the Cheyennes had lost their virtue, given themselves to the whites that Sweet Medicine had warned against, to the men who killed their people, as Monahsetah had. To those who said that she was a helpless captive, they replied that a good woman knows how to avoid marrying the man who has killed her father. Comes in Sight had not hesitated to use the knife.

But Little Finger Nail believed there must always have been a few such women, and the men for them. Who could look at Singing Cloud back there, or Hog's Daughter and the rest, and think that their women were less now than the Great Mother of Tobacco had been, or any of the old-time ones. But if not that, then something else had been done wrong.

The Cheyennes must try to discover a new path.

It was as though a voice had spoken, and the young warrior stopped to look all around the darkness that was black as a mud-hen's feathers scattered thick over the earth. It was as though from a medicine dream, as the Nail remembered it in his puberty fastings, long ago.

This new path the Cheyennes—a Cheyenne—must try to discover.

The Nail walked faster now, much faster than he should, here where a man could not see the place of his tracks. But the thought that had come to sit on his shoulder would not be left behind, no more than a thorn in the moccasin can be escaped or forgotten. So there must be a reason for this thing that had suddenly pushed into his troubled mind. In the great expanse of earth and sky and all the things between there was nothing without a reason. But he, Little Finger Nail, was only a young fighting man, a warrior.

"—Only a warrior," he said aloud in his soft Cheyenne, as though defending himself.

Yet somehow this seemed no excuse tonight, when he had to remember that a vision in a warring time had made a peace man of Black Kettle, and a holy man of the great Medicine Arrow. Perhaps when this troubled time was over, he should give himself into the care of anyone left who knew of

the old-time holy ways and try hard to learn the good path of the Great
Powers. He would go up to the Medicine Lodge mountain, Bear Butte, off
beyond the Black Hills, where Sweet Medicine went to dream and was
given the Sacred Arrows of the people, and the shields that turn away attacks. He would make all the fastings and the ceremonials as well as he
could; he would vow a red blanket of his blood spread upon the ground at
sun-dance time in humility and suppliance, pleading for a path of wisdom
for even the feet of the foolish young warrior that he was, pleading for the
gift of the eyes, to see what must be done.

It would mean that the gay and bedecked Little Finger Nail must become
a plain man of the village, without the paint and feathers that pleased the
young women; without the display and rivalry of the soldier lodge that
pleased him so much, or the parades, the racing and gambling, the accumu-
lation of horses and honors. All the wise ones of the Cheyennes had been
simple men, and modest, their far-seeing eyes not blinded by the brilliant
prides and vanities close before them. They were humble men, wanting
nothing for themselves, so their hands were always empty and ready to receive the gifts that came for all.

Suddenly the young Cheyenne found himself singing a new song:

> Help me, Powers of the wind and the sky,
> And the earth in the cold nighttime.
> Help me get my people away!

He chanted the words over and over as he waited in the new horse-hide
robe whose harsh folds the women had not yet taught to soften, to yield. He
was squatting on a rise along the Hat Creek road, close up under a bank
where the sounds of any movement would find him from far off. As he
made the thin sweet singing, he knew this song was a dangerous boldness,
when he had never been named any kind of chief or taken any oath of duty
beyond the warrior's: to fight well and honorably, and to protect the helpless to his death.

Stiff and frozen, Little Finger Nail was half glad for the cold that kept
him awake, even if he had dared risk the smoke of a fire. With finger bones
pressed close against his head he listened until every heartbeat seemed an
ice-clumped hoof. Once he did hear something more. Hopefully he put his
ear to the cleared ground before him, but by the pattern of sound he could
tell it was only a cow; far off, she seemed, and walking old and poor. Several times he heard wolves back in the direction of the White River bluffs,

drawn by the blood and meat, yet meat with the man smell that would keep them off for many days.

Toward the clearing of dawn he returned in emptiness to the camp. Most of the people were still as he left them, scattered every way, like rag bundles dropped carelessly, but feet toward the fires and warm, and with water and food and clean air at last. He walked among them, seeing the children asleep, Singing Cloud with two besides Lame Girl under her thin-spread blanket, the young woman so pure-cheeked that his weary heart jumped in his ribs. Only watchers and the bad-wounded ones heard the man's return; heavy sleep was upon all the rest.

But soon the soldiers would be back to their foolish little fires burnt to white ashes down below there. "Come, my friends. It is time . . . ," he said, now the leader of them all.

In the prison tent down at the encampment Hog had watched the morning come after the night of shooting and cries up the river. He held a new dark blue blanket with the handsome white border about himself now, awkwardly, the folds of such a garment not made for the *veho* handcuffs. When the blanket was first given to him yesterday, he had thrown it down in anger, despising what had been withheld so long. His daughter must go out there half naked into the snow, his son too, and the old ones and the babies. None had new blankets.

"We only have half a dozen . . . ," the soldier who brought it had said seriously, knowing what was in the Cheyenne's mind.

So Hog, with the Indian's need for gracious acceptance of a gift, finally drew it up around him. Then, wooden and silent, he waited for what was to be done up there in the barracks. Left Hand sat beside him, and Old Crow and Porcupine, with their braids unkempt upon their breasts in the sign of separation and sorrow. None of them spoke or smoked through the night although there was plenty of good tobacco in their pouches now, and food and water for the taking, with a round-bellied army stove red from burning pitchpine. But every step that came between the sentry's steady tread on the frozen snow brought Hog to his feet, ready to make the sign for talking if anyone should enter the prison.

The first one was Vroom, stopping in soon after sunrise, before he left with the troops on the fleeing trail. A large man—larger in his buffalo coat —he brought frosty air into the tent, to hover like fog a moment at the wooden door casing. He shook the manacled hand of Hog vigorously and hoped that the Indians would help him by telling all they could of the plans made for the outbreak. It would hasten the capture and shorten the suffering.

By now Hog knew that this man had been in charge of the soldiers at Red Cloud's agency up around the Missouri last summer, and when the Sioux decided to move back near their old place down here, he had followed, but he had not charged upon them, roaring as their Captain Rendlebrock had done, shouting that they must go back or he would start shooting. Now this good soldier chief, Vroom, was here, wanting to know the plans made in the barracks. Hog stood before the officer, the top of his neatly parted hair higher than the big man's beaver cap, and had nothing to say. The others were as silent around the stove, looking before them. So Vroom started to pull on his fur gloves again, the stomp of the impatient horses loud on the frozen ground outside, and still Hog could not ask what had been done in the night of shooting to their sons and daughters, to all those people out there to whom they belonged. But before he left, Vroom said the rest of what he had come to tell Hog. He said it with difficulty. "Thirty-five Cheyennes were recaptured during the night, and thirty found dead, so far. . . ."

When there was still no Indian word spoken, no asking of names, his face turned even redder than the cold had left it. "My God, man!—do you think I like this butchery?" he shouted. "There's a small girl not over six months old up there with her hip shot to pieces, and so frozen she will surely die, and she doesn't even whimper. . . ."

Then suddenly the officer jerked the door open and went out of the silence. Once more the frosty air that came in clung to the casing. When he was gone, the Indians did not look to each other. Now and then one got up and walked back and forth across the little floor a while, his feet soft on the earthen floor, walking with urgency, as though even this short span of steps could hasten the moccasins out there in the snow.

The day of the tenth had not been a good one for the few Indians who were still hidden in the snow of White River valley. Lieutenant Cummings was out early in the morning gathering up the bodies missed in the night. He saw Clifford going among the dead again and was angry, but the trader found an unwounded old man called The Sioux, with a baby tied on his back. The Indian motioned to a washout and went there with the soldiers, calling in his guttural-spoken Cheyenne. A woman and three children came out slowly, crying and afraid, clutching at their ragged blankets. These were sent to the post and The Sioux questioned. No, he knew nothing of anybody except this little party. They had run in any direction they could to get away from the soldiers. He knew nothing at all of Dull Knife, but that the question had to be asked brought a little softening to the man's bleak face. And perhaps now the women and children would be warmed and fed.

Several more little trails could now be seen in the daylight, with lost blankets, lariats, and moccasins marking the flight over the wind-bared rockier slopes, and blood too. In a narrow ravine a few soldiers found a cave with two Indians on guard. They were Dog soldiers and would not surrender or retreat and had to be shot. One, with a good Springfield carbine captured on the way north and thirty-eight rounds, tried to shoot very fast so he might use up all the cartridges before he finally rolled over on the sunlit snow. Behind these dead men stood Little Bear, the thirteen-year-old son of Tangle Hair, his young face defiant and desperate, his hands empty except for an old half-bladed butcher knife, trying to keep the soldiers from his mother, his sister, and a little orphan back in the cave, all three hurt.

"Give up, my son," the woman pleaded softly behind him. "Your father must be dead, and all the others. Let yourself and your small sister live. Give up!"

So the weeping boy threw the stub of knife into the snow in surrender.

His mother came out keening for the dead ones who had tried to protect her as a chief's wife, and all the way in she keened until she saw the dark, still rows at the sawmill. Then she was silent, but at the hospital she could no longer be a proper Cheyenne woman. Crying with joy and concern, she ran to her wounded Tangle Hair stretched flat on the floor, but able to lift a hand to her. Then she seated herself at his head and drew her blanket over her face.

Toward sundown another troop of cavalry had come upon the tracks of five Indians and followed them into a broken bluff full of caves and holes. They shot into the place until everybody there was dead except Pumpkin Seed's Son. When the firing stopped, he crawled out over the bodies and walked toward the soldiers, holding himself straight and steady in the bloody, bullet-pierced blanket of his dead cousin Charging Bear, for the one more shot.

But it did not come. Instead an officer rode up to shake hands with the boy and then went to see the dead in the hole, the boy's bleeding and torn relatives. Outside Pumpkin Seed's Son waited, standing still as the rock around him until he was taken up behind one of the troopers, hanging to the ribs of the man whose gun still stank with smoke in its scabbard.

At Robinson the boy was asked what the plans had been.

"We were to make for the big point of bluffs overlooking all the country. 'That is a good place for our bodies to lie,' the young men said to us."

"And where was Dull Knife to go?"

The boy lifted his head in surprise that such a question should be asked of one only thirteen years old, with no dreaming, no buffalo killed, no coup counted.

Another detachment of troops followed the trail of four Indians, probably women, traveling openly in the day, trying to catch up with those in the far shooting over on Hat Creek. When the soldiers overtook them on the dusky tableland, they huddled together in the snow, as for warmth. Then suddenly they started to run and could have lost themselves on the shadowing plain, but old Meat Woman called sternly to the others to hold themselves. Then she came toward the young sergeant, making the motions of surrender and the signs. "Have pity, we are freezing and hungry. No man is with us."

The soldier nodded and so they were brought in too, and had to be held from running out against the guns of the guards when they saw all the captured and the wounded and frozen under the smoky kerosene lanterns of the hospital. There was a little keening, soft and hopeless, that did not stop when an officer came with the interpreters to ask what they knew about others who went out. And where was Dull Knife?

They said they ran to save themselves and knew nothing of anybody, the same thing that Dull Knife's wounded daughter here, and all the rest, had told.

Once there was real excitement at the post, when a little smoke was reported up toward Bronson's ranch. It must be a large party to dare a fire so close in the bright noontime. Perhaps Little Wolf himself, to join up with the fleeing Indians, or even Red Cloud and his warriors, waiting.

A column of sixty troopers went out, their horses throwing snow as they charged through the drifts, an ambulance following, and a cannon ready. Cautiously the soldiers surrounded the bluff where the smoke hung pale as graying breath-feathers along the rocks, and some went up over the top to cut off escape that way. After a lot of shooting into the hole, where a thread of smoke still rose, and a careful crawling to look over the edge, the pocket was found to be empty except for a deserted little fire. A lone Indian was finally discovered in a washout nearby. The sixty men charged him. One trooper was shot in the belly and the Indian was hit many times. But with his right arm hanging worthless he kept firing while the bullets spattered around him and sang in thin ricochet from the rocks. He was a hard man to kill, and when he finally went down, he was ripped and torn as a charging grizzly stopped by many buffalo guns, the snow bloody all around. They found a bridle and lariat around his waist; probably headed for Bronson's horses, but his unprotected feet were so frozen he could not walk on them at all, so he had built a fire to be warm; built it openly that he need not suffer long and starve. The body was loaded into the boot of the ambulance, but dusk came on and somewhere through the drifts to Robinson he fell out and so none would ever know where this man lay.

Troops scouting twelve, fourteen miles up the White River found the trail of two more Cheyennes. One got away, but the other's tracks, made by small narrow moccasins, led up the river on the ice. The soldiers found the little Indian, a girl of seven or eight, sitting on a snowbank playing with a pack of cards, all alone. She cowered down when the troops rode in close, flattening herself to the snow like a rabbit, her face hidden, the cards clutched to her breast. She was lifted up gently and taken to the post, but even there they could not discover where her people had gone.

"I was afraid . . . ," she kept sobbing in her soft hopeless way to all questions, and those around her were so dulled that they did not seem to remember. None of those lying here or sitting hunched over themselves seemed to know who her people had been or that they had ever known this small girl who lived one of them all her life.

Once the child looked up for a moment. It was when two boys were brought in from around Crow Butte. They would not say how they got there or anything else, just stood with their angry, hate-filled black eyes unwavering on the officer's face.

That was the day's fighting in the valley of the White River.[1]

On the morning of the eleventh of January Little Finger Nail's Cheyennes saw the troops coming from far off, a long dark string hurrying across the snow. Some stopped at the hill where the fighting was yesterday and then found the new position, with better shelter. There was some shooting all day, but nothing was done. The Indians watched the little Wessells creep up with an interpreter, close enough to ask that the women and children be sent out to him. For that Roman Nose put a carbine bullet close to his head, but not hitting. With all those helpless ones down there at the post, and scattered everywhere, no soldier chief must be killed.

Part of the day a bluff west of the Indians was occupied by the troops, cutting off the direction of flight if the Cheyennes had to run. But all that the troops could do was keep the Indians down in their holes. One soldier was killed accidentally, while putting his carbine into the saddle boot. Vroom's horse was shot under him, and that of another. Toward evening ten men were detailed to burn the carcasses, the wind blowing the stench over the hungry Cheyennes. Then the trumpet echoed over the snow and the troops started back to the post.

Now was the time to run to Red Cloud, less than a good night's travel for a strong runner, even in snow. But none was strong here, not even Little Finger Nail and Roman Nose, without food for five days until yesterday, frostbitten, worn, and needed to help with the carried ones, and particularly to find horses. But the ranchers around here had gathered up everything that could be ridden. With the thin winter cattle everywhere, and horse droppings plain on the wind-swept ridges, there was not even one sway-backed old mare left now on the range.

The Cheyennes moved as far as they could in the night, and the next day the troops came back. The column took up the fresh foot trail leading toward Hat Creek road, but a small bunch went out scouting and ran into two Cheyennes roasting meat from a yearling that the fleet-footed Roman Nose had caught with his rope while hunting horses. They ran to the rifle pits that Bullet Proof and another man had dug to watch the back trail. The soldiers followed and got around behind them, where the Indians could be hit. Bullet Proof spent two of their cartridges bringing a corporal down. The rest of the soldiers charged and the Proof was killed—the strong leader who had made medicine against the white-man bullets long ago and had it fail because the soldiers who came shooting that time were black. But since then, he had been a humble man who asked no further following, no voice.

And because he became a strong follower himself, a brave man to the end, the others took the time to lay him out in a shallow place and arranged his braids on his breast. It was very little to do for such a man, but even in this Roman Nose was wounded.

The three Cheyennes had to stay hidden there in their holes, with fifteen soldiers left to watch them and to guard the corporal's body. The rest rode off on the fresh trail to fight Indians a while.

So day by day the Cheyennes were pushed westward along Hat Creek bluffs, the edge of the high tableland that extended out of Wyoming in a long tongue between White River and the beginnings of Hat Creek. These north-facing bluffs were much like those that turned southward just above Robinson, where so many Indians had died, except that these here had more timber and were higher, falling in sheer cliffs all the way to the flat plain. They made a great bend around the sources of the creek, the branched headwaters that were like the spreading feathers of a fan or an eagle's tail, the bluffs a band that circled them from the east clear around south and into the west, a dark unbroken wall of perhaps 20 miles standing against the horizon. Below the bluffs were the many snow-filled dry washes that deepened and became frozen little creeks with banks cut straight down into the gray earth and leading northward through the drifted prairie, flat, with several gray badland buttes far away.

The fleeing Cheyennes came out of the bluffs at night to travel on easier ground, with so many worn out now and sick, the children coughing in fever. Somehow they still hoped for help; perhaps Red Cloud had heard what was done, even Little Wolf. But nothing came, no sign, no reply to their smoke columns sent up, and yet they kept going. About 5 miles from the Hat Creek road they reached the winter range of the ranches along there and followed the cowpaths at the foot of the bluffs, their moccasin tracks lost on the frozen ground bared by the sharp hoofs. But they did not dare strike across the wide flatland toward the Sioux and perhaps be caught out there without a tree or a canyon for hiding. In this they needed Bullet Proof very much. He had experience in the old-time warpath ways, in hiding trails from Snake and Pawnee and Crow. They would think of him many, many times before they got across that 60 miles of open snowy prairie between the bluffs and the Pine Ridge Agency of Red Cloud.

Finally the army scouts picked up the deep, round marks of a crippled man's sticks on a cow trail, and the column followed his general direction very fast. When the soldiers were moving between two shallow ravines at the bluffs, the Indians rose from the farther one and fired. One soldier was wounded and a horse brought down. Others were stung by the bullets, the powder so weak now that they only made the horses shy and jump. Lieutenant Chase's big gelding bolted down between the soldiers and the Cheyennes. Little Finger Nail motioned to let their friend go, but a company of troopers dismounted and laid a blizzard of lead over the Indian position to make them keep their heads down while the officer escaped. The fire was so heavy it sheared off the scattered brush and sent earth and stones rolling into their pits. Helpless, the Indians waited for the charge on their weak position, but instead the soldiers pulled back a little and sent a courier riding off in the direction of Robinson. He kept to the high, clear ground and went fast. The rest of the troops stayed, with guards to watch the Indians.

It was a sad night for the little camp of Cheyennes squatting close around their fires, even before more soldiers came riding noisily through the night, with an ambulance and a cannon along. Now Little Finger Nail knew it was time to make an unnoticed escape through the watching soldiers, the kind of escape that Little Wolf had managed so well all those times on the way north. If they had Their Man here now. . . .

In the morning, the thirteenth, Wessells arrived with still more troops, and then they all moved up to surround the place where the Indians had sat so quietly under the mowing blanket of bullets yesterday. The cannon thundered over the ravines, shooting from here and from there into the rifle pits, the balls bursting just off the ground, blowing up snow, brush, stones, and frozen earth, until the forty rounds of shell and spherical case were all gone. But the Indians gave no sign, showed no white flag. Only one or two shots were fired by them all day. They must truly have been out of ammunition and without the will to fight or to live.

Toward dusk pickets were set again so no one could escape. In the morning Wessells went up to see the damage. The Indians were all gone. They had not been there at all during the shooting yesterday. The rifle pits were full of iron and shell fragments, but not a drop of new blood. Then the scouts found more pits farther on, where the Cheyennes had lay hidden all day, their little entrenchments dug into the frozen earth without fires to betray them.

The hiding there was not the Cheyenne way of fighting and hard to do, but the time was past for choosing. "Nobody should get excited and show himself. Nobody ought to fire even one shot!" Pug Nose, the southern Dog chief, had said yesterday, carefully, making it advice even now because he was not of these people except by affection.

"Yes, they can kill us here like stamping on bugs under a leaf, if they find out . . . ," Little Finger Nail had agreed. He was the one who had sent the two bullets over the old rifle pits, making it seem they came from there. He had fired from under a blanket, the muzzle of the gun covered, the bullets making only little holes. In this way the smoke was held together and allowed to creep out very slowly, so none could detect it.

Even with the soldiers firing their cannon and the weather so cold, some of the people had slept, the children warmed a little by the older people drawn close together now as never before. Pug Nose was like a father, helping everywhere. Then he made better stick crutches for the crippled man who must go with them on the long, long escape to Red Cloud tonight or tomorrow night, or never.

By now two men who were left behind in the run through White River valley came in. One had tried to get to the Bronson horses and was shot through the shoulder, the bullet coming out with a big hole in front. He had seen the other horse hunter get killed because his feet were frozen to falling off. This man was finished too, and Young Magpie had helped get him here to die with a hand on the arm of his wife in a rifle pit. The Magpie knew many things that had been done in the valley; he had been with the small girl who was picked up on the river ice. Whole families were destroyed, he said, and counted them out for the sorrowing listeners as he wolfed his meat, the first he had in ten days except a little of the rabbit he caught for the girl and then had to coax her to eat raw because he dared no fire. He spoke of all he had seen, but he put no tongue to the name of his mother, Yellow Woman. He saw her shot at a cave just above him, with the sun shining bright all around.

As he slipped past the soldiers in the dark with the dying man, he heard them say it was twenty-eight below their zero measure. No one here had noticed them as they crept in, all of them so cold and worn out and hopeless. But later every Cheyenne alive rose and followed Little Finger Nail past the soldier pickets because he said the one word: "Come."

When Wessells discovered the escape, he waited for the forage and rations that were to arrive around noon. They never came. In the afternoon a trooper rode in to report that the wagons had upset on the icy hillsides. So the column lined out for Fort Robinson again, this time to get a pack train.

"Bet Cap'd do a lot better with a rowboat," one of the young West Pointers said. The men around him laughed, knowing Wessells had no army training but enlisted straight out of naval academy when the Civil War started.

"Yeh, we got us a duck-pond general . . . ," some of the old cavalrymen told each other once more.

Wessells readily admitted to the newspapermen at Robinson that his position was getting embarrassing: Five companies of cavalry with field pieces to chase something like thirty-five or forty wounded, starved, and frozen Indians running over the snow, many of them women and small children. Six days was a long time, but it could not last now. They had so little ammunition that they fired only two, three shots a day.

"General Crook must be mad as a bee-stung grizzly," one remarked.

"Yes, and Little Phil Sheridan's probably jumping around with some of the same bees in his britches," the man from the Chicago *Tribune* agreed.

Certainly Sheridan would make somebody pay for this, now that the newspapers were turning their attack full upon the War Department, reversing their cry against the Cheyennes as bloodthirsty savages last October, and forgetting their charges of stupidity and graft against the Indian Bureau in September. A Deadwood dispatch to the *New York Tribune* said, "Intense indignation is manifested throughout the whole country, even among the advocates of extermination, over the barbarous treatment of the Cheyenne prisoners at Camp Robinson near here, previous to the recent outbreak and slaughter."

Wessells got the expected telegram from Crook. The general sternly reminded him that he had received no details of the outbreak and so was sending his aide-de-camp out to investigate. Wessells hastened a report of his efforts and the failure of artillery in the natural fortifications of Hat Creek. But the Indians were certainly bound for Red Cloud and would be easy to capture after they got out on the wide open country toward the Sioux. The dead collected at the post had all been buried, those bodies that had not been spirited away somehow. Nearly all the grown Indians were scalped, one in two places.[2]

There was still nothing definite on Dull Knife, reported killed the night of the outbreak but not found among the dead. The captive daughter spoke no word to anyone, replied to no questions. She lay on the barracks floor in her new army blanket and her bandages, making no keening for her dead brother and sister, as though asleep or dead except that her eyes were open, and her gunshot wounds and frostbite healing. The other Cheyennes would only say that old Dull Knife was a sick man when they left the barracks. The southern shaking disease still lived in him, and he had eaten nothing during the starvation time, putting the food into the mouths of the hungry children.

"They must live," he had said. "We are already dead."

As soon as the outbreak news was heard around the Sioux, an angry request came from Red Cloud, a demand that the widows and orphans of the Cheyennes be turned over to him. There was great excitement and mourning all over the reservation at this killing of their friends and relatives, and over the danger that soldiers might come shooting there too, any day. Old-timers advised the whites around the agency to keep indoors, away from any young Sioux who might want to make his bad heart good by spilling a little blood.

Up in the Hat Creek bluffs Young Medicine Man was working as well as he knew for another blizzard, another snow to hide their fleeing tracks toward Red Cloud. But the Powers were still against the Cheyennes, for the sixteenth dawned clear and sunlit and very cold, with more soldiers riding along the bluffs, following six, seven miles of the trail the Indians made since the last attack. After a while they went back too, like the soldiers in south Kansas, but the next morning they returned and this time the Cheyennes sang the death songs when they saw two dangerous men among the scouts, the Sioux Woman's Dress and Shangreau, who knew their ways as well, for he was the breed son of a French trader. These men would make it very hard to get away.

The soldiers had forced the Indians to cling to the protection of the bluffs like game hiding from the hunter, and drove them westward, always westward, farther and farther from the Sioux agency over northeast, and hurting them too, until now there was none left who understood the hiding of a winter trail. Pug Nose was still unhurt, but he knew only his south country and had seen no such winter fighting in all his lifetime. Now truly the

Cheyennes needed their Brave Man, their Little Wolf. Somehow he would still get them away, but he would not have hesitated to scatter them across the freezing snow that first night after they left the White River bluffs. Weak, frozen as they were, he would have sent them out like pebbles flung from the hand, to hide in the snow as prairie chickens do from the coyote. He would have forgotten that people can die of cold and storm, remembered only that those never caught by the soldiers could hope to live.

Some still tried to believe that he must come to save them, but the rest were certain he could not know what had happened, with tracks of scouts on the unbroken snow too dangerous, unless some unexpected one got away from the bluffs. But many among them here were thinking of something else now—that the stronger, the less wounded could run for the Sioux, leaving the others to be captured.

"Captured? Killed!" Young Elk protested. "And we who got to Red Cloud would be given up by the Sioux to the soldiers and we would go to the south in chains with Hog and the others, and our women and children would not be saved!"

"*Piva!* Even if we throw away the weak ones here, we will be taken to Florida or some other ironhouse as my father was," Pug Nose said. "Perhaps even pulled up with the rope and left hanging. Let us keep together and hope to sneak the young ones here in to the Sioux before we are caught, or if Little Wolf could get through. . . ."

Little Finger Nail thought about this and looked toward the gaunt and worn Singing Cloud and her friend Hog's Daughter. Nineteen men were left here, counting the boys, and fifteen women and children. Although they had women like Brave One and others strong with the fleeing children and with the wounded—so strong that their deeds would be sung and remembered—none among them was like the warrior woman Buffalo Calf Road or even Bull Hump's wife. But what could a warrior woman do when there was no ammunition even for the men? Yet here, put into his palm, was the seed that might be all that was left of the Dull Knife people: a few strong young married ones with good children, some young men like Roman Nose, Young Magpie, and himself, the Nail, and the three brave maidens. Perhaps they were really all that was left, and so it fell upon a man who was only a warrior to say how they could be saved.

But the hunter must have his bowstring ready for any arrow. The Nail tried to prepare the people for a storm or a rescue—any saving that might come. They dragged in more beef to be dried, made more moccasin soles and the stiff, quick-cured robes in place of the blankets that were lost like all the other things of the *veho* that their grandfathers had learned to use. Even many things of the Indian were gone from them now—the parfleches, the soft deerskin clothing, the tobacco, all the beautiful beadings and regalias and the medicine objects of them all. There was nothing of the buffalo any more, and except for the few white-man guns and knives they were more homeless and naked to the enemy than any wild creature of the earth.

The shielding storm they hoped for seemed very slow. The weather turned cold, but then warm again, and already Woman's Dress and Shangreau were back, counting the dead fires of the Indians in the morning, feeling the ground with their palms, carefully examining any moccasin track for crippling and sickness, seeing every spot where a forgetful child relieved himself on the frozen ground of night. Finally they came up near the hiding place, not far from some tall chimney bluffs where the Crow Indians once fought off many Cheyennes for a whole moon. But now the soldiers could bring up cannons, so the Indians painted for this fight, the first time since the outbreak. Little Finger Nail tightened the rawhide straps that held his picture book to his back, and was ready.

When the scouts and the advance troops were very close, Pug Nose gave the signal and they fired down into the horses, making them rear and plunge. When one soldier fell dead, Shangreau let his horse go and ducked behind a tree, Woman's Dress too, while the troops scattered back out of range down the slope, their horses still faunching. Because there were only the two scouts left close, Pug Nose started down to talk to them with his signs.

"Ask what would be done with the women and children!" Little Finger Nail called after him, in a desperate, foolish moment, and yet making those words was the hardest of all the things the young warrior ever had to do.

Pug Nose went with his hands empty, one up in the peace sign, the left hand because it is nearest the heart and has shed no man's blood. But before he could get close, Shangreau shot him down. Then, as the anger and the keening arose above him, the breed was suddenly afraid. Turning, he fled like a scared antelope, leaping bush and rock, down past the dead soldier and the crippled horses. With Woman's Dress running as fast beside him, he ducked in among the troopers bunched together in a draw, trying to quiet their horses.

The Indians had not fired at Shangreau at all, not even after Pug Nose fell. Nothing showed of them up there, nothing except the keening that was like a thin, cold wind, high up.

For a while all the troops seemed to be looking toward the Cheyenne position and then they went back a way to camp, leaving their dead man on the slope with his rifle and his revolver and the ammunition belt for the taking. Roman Nose got them and the caped blue cavalry coat and everything else. Then Pug Nose was carried away to a rocky place in the last rays of the sun, quietly, with no time for the mourning ceremonies that they owed this good friend who had come all this long road northward to help them. Now he was dead, shot down with his hands empty, by a man who had an Indian mother.

Through the burying, one of them, Small Woman, had not roused herself at all. She was wounded in some of the early fighting and always worn out from carrying one of the hurt children during the night. Now it was the moving time again and she still slept, so Brave One went to waken her and found the woman dead, a bullet hole in the thin place beside the eye—only a little hole, with no bleeding, probably from a bullet that glanced downward off a rock. There was no time for keening now. They covered her with a few rocks right there—the women who had grown up in the camps of the Platte and the Powder with her, those who married and bore children the same time. Then silently they took up their burdens. Singing Cloud, in addition to her load of meat, lifted the crippled child that Small Woman had carried. They even took her cowhide robe from her shoulders. It was a disrespectful thing to do to the dead, but their need was very great.

That night was not a good one, with the dancing red lights coming up from the northern horizon. Some of the older women muttered uneasily about this, afraid it was a bad omen, as before the attack on the Dull Knife village, and long before that, at Sand Creek. But in this bad time perhaps it meant a change, and so once more they followed the Nail out into the night, a line of slow, bent figures moving to the bottom of the bluffs and along under the northern lights that flamed in great red tongues over the sky.

There were speeches in Congress, editorials in the papers, name calling between the Army and the Indian Bureau, more newspaper controversy between General Sheridan and Secretary of the Interior Schurz, and more telegrams from the governor of Kansas demanding the immediate delivery of the criminal Cheyennes to be tried for murder. When a reporter asked Sherman for details of the massacre at Robinson, the general of the Army shouted, "Massacre! Why do you call it massacre? A number of insubordinate, cunning, treacherous Indians. . . ." But President Hayes was disturbed by the reports of unnecessary cruelty, and so Sherman ordered a complete investigation of the entire outbreak and then escaped on an inspection tour of the Southern and Gulf posts.

Out at Fort Robinson the angry Red Cloud came riding across the snow to demand the story of what had been done. His agent came along, afraid the old chief would flee too, perhaps join Sitting Bull in Canada or turn his warriors to revenge upon the settlers. They found Crook's aide just ready to go to Pine Ridge for some Sioux scouts.

"Your friend General Braided Beard Crook asks you to give him these men to help chase the Cheyennes."

The old chief, still surrounded by soldiers at his agency as well as here in the post, looked grave at this request, eyes on the ground before him.

"My people are very sad, and very angry . . . ," he said at last, slow and earnestly.

But with the shadow of the guns across his own women and children, Red Cloud had to agree. Seventeen men came, the subchief Three Bears, with Cheyenne connections, among them. A mountain howitzer was brought in from Camp Sheridan, and Colonel Evans started down from Fort Laramie with fresh troops and a good wagon train. Over in the sandhills the search for Little Wolf was doubled, to eliminate all chance of a junction with his warriors, while down south the quinine that Agent Miles ordered for the malaria of the Northern Cheyennes last spring had finally arrived, the seventh of January.

Roman Nose of the medicine eyes was the first to see the new soldiers coming from the west. He had been far out looking for a horse—so far he had to use skin from a long-dead carcass to replace the moccasins cut from his bleeding feet by the crusted snow and the ice. There was no sign of horses anywhere now, but from a high point he saw something in the west, a darkening there. While he watched, the blur separated itself from the horizon and moved out upon the tableland, coming fast—soldiers, and from a new direction.

Then he saw another column approaching from the west along the foot of the bluffs, a great row of wagons behind them. And the soldiers from Robinson were riding out of the southeast again too, with the two dangerous scouts ahead. Quickly the young warrior sent his mirror signals in the sunlight. Between these marching troops the Cheyennes would be crushed like rabbits in the deadfalls. They must strike out across the flat country right away and hide their trail completely, or be lost.

Yet reluctant as morning fog to move out into the open, they clung to the protection of the bluffs for just one more day, one more.

Shangreau located the Cheyennes again on the twentieth of January, eleven days after the outbreak. In a little skirmishing an officer's horse was shot under him, but that was all, for the soldiers from the tableland could not find a way down, and after a lot of riding back and forth along the bluffs, above and below, everybody camped. This night the Indians made one more move, a short one, climbing to a high place to prepare for the final run through the surround of watching troops. In the meantime some young men crept down past the watchers to kill a few last steers. One of the hides was cut into strings to tie on the stiff quick-tanned robes made since the outbreak, their only covering against the cold now, the hairside in, their moccasins the same, the people as unkempt as wild men and women now, thin and gaunt but tough as the rawhide. So they waited.

There was still some confusion among the soldiers most of the next day. Finally they discovered the Indians, but soon a wet, cloudy darkness settled down. The Cheyenne fires were little flickering points of light on the high place, the soldier fires big burning stacks, lower down, but on both sides.

As soon as the dusk came everywhere, the Cheyennes piled up wood too, but in long narrow ricks into the little wind, so the fires would burn back slowly and a long time. Then they left, with Roman Nose and Bear at the sides, Little Finger Nail ahead. Between these warriors went the older men with the women and children, carrying all their dried meat along, enough for two weeks, even a month, if needed; carrying a few new-made bows too, and war clubs. There was the soldier gun with its belt of ammunition and the revolver taken the day Pug Nose died, but for the other guns there were only a few cartridges that had enough powder to carry the bullet from the barrel. Although the Indians still had some lead and a little powder, these could not be used until a fight was started and some cartridges emptied for reloading. But Hog's Daughter knew how and several of the older women, if it happened that the men were all lost. It was a pact between them. They would fight to the end together, the end of everybody, and as hard as possible.

This last going from the entrenchments up there was a sad one, the women looking around almost as though they were deserting the lodges of a lifetime. Then one by one they slipped away past the watching pickets. Out from the bluffs the clouded night was so warm that the scattered snow patches were mushy, even the top of the ground soft to the moccasin. The Cheyennes had to fan out and walk carefully, planting the foot on none of the snow and only on strong-rooted grass that would betray nothing of the light-footed passing. The hideout for the day was well selected before night came, a spot all could see far out on the flat plain to the northeast. If any got lost, they must remain hidden all day in some hole or weeds, beseeching the earth for the covering given the rabbit and the mouse.

So they started, but too many of the younger, the agency people, did not know how to hide tracks in the darkness, how to feel out the ground with the moccasin before its mark was left behind. Some had to cross a wide prairie-dog town with the many piles of soft earth and almost no grass to hide the passing track. Before they were half gathered, it seemed very hopeless to Little Finger Nail. Still, soldiers had gone back many times when the people seemed lost.

At dawn the Indians were far out from the bluffs on the north side of a deep dry creek that was sometimes called the Warbonnet. They were hidden in a washout that lay like a scarring wound along the cut-bank, 30 feet above the creek bed. With their knives, Brave One leading, they had dug under the frozen sides while the men made the little breastworks, the sod placed so the grass and brush looked natural. They left a deep place in the middle for the women so no bullet could get in unless fired from right up on the edge. Here, where attack could only come from the ends or one side, lay the last of these Cheyennes that the Army had been chasing for thirteen days, and for almost five months before that—eighteen men and boys here, fourteen women and children—crouching in a hole as wide as the height of two men, as long as four or five, and from the top of the breastworks as deep as a standing one. From a little ways off the hole seemed little more than a shadow along the high cut-bank, with a shaggy scattering of brush and sage at the edge. If no track was seen to lead that way, the place of the Cheyennes would surely be missed. If it was found, one cannon shot could sing the last keening for them all.

As the morning grew, smoke rose from the soldier camps and drifted away, and then the troopers started to ride both directions along the foot of the bluffs and to scatter, looking for the trail. They fanned out for many miles, riding back and forth; they got off and ran from this place to that, so very many of these whites, led by those two scouts that were not easily fooled. After a while the Indians could see Shangreau on his mule wave his cap in signals and then stop to look, probably with far-seeing glasses. He seemed to turn slowly, examining all the far washes and winter creeks leading together out on the Hat Creek flats, the occasional badland butte and beyond, to where the prairie went into the horizon and two winter buzzards circled on angled wings. Because he made no signal of finding, the Indians waited, knowing that all those soldiers could scout every foot of the ground. This day the Cheyennes needed luck.

But it seemed this too was not a Cheyenne day. Soon there was a gathering of troopers in the prairie-dog town and then a separating again, but most of them moving in the direction that the man with the crutch sticks had taken, and the children. So Roman Nose slid down from the little breastworks where he was watching, and without a word or sign, the ragged, half-naked men began to paint themselves, the one who had the blue soldier coat brushing it with his medicine plant, the silver sage. Once more Little Finger Nail ran his hand over the picture book at his back to test its safety there. Then he went from one to the other of his hopeless, worn people, looking down upon their silence, touching a shoulder with his hand, perhaps a bowed head; going around them all, with no more than that now even for Singing Cloud. Gently he touched them as though he were one of the old, old ones in a time far back, when the people wore stiff hides for clothing and lived in the earth, with only clubs for their hand. Not since long before the people crossed the salt sea in their ox-hide boats had anyone seen such Cheyennes as these in the little hole beside a creek called Warbonnet.

Now the soldiers were coming together, as the tracks of last night converged upon this place. Each man in the washout made his little medicine ceremony. The Dog soldiers left here passed around the medicine horn of their warrior society, each man touching the gray stone that had grown like the horn of the buffalo. The women quickly smoothed the hair of the children and looked long into the faces of all those gathered in this last little hole. Then they sang the strong-heart songs, not loud, not to be heard outside of this little remnant, while the men went silently to their places up at the edge of the hole, the women who could help moving ready behind them, the rest deep down out of the way.

By now the scouts were coming along the little creek, already so near the horses were lifting their ears and looking. Certainly the hiding place was seen because the troopers prepared to charge them, and so the Cheyennes fired from the sagebrush bank. Woman's Dress was hit and knocked down; the handle of Shangreau's revolver flew off. One horse went down, the soldier running until he fell too, his feet still going a little. Trumpets blew, more troops hurried in from both ways with Wessells and Chase and the other officers that the Indians knew, until their four companies were all there. So Little Finger Nail signaled the Indians back into the hole.

The Little Dutchman dismounted his troops now, divided them, and tried a hot fire from the three approachable sides for a while. But there was no sign from the hole in the middle of all that smoke, as though only the flying earth and weeds and brush were there to feel the bullets. Then Wessells set a detachment to keep the Indians down with a sharp cover of fire while the troops moved in from the three sides, some down along the creek bank, some up it, and a strong force in toward the hole from the land side. So a half circle of bluecoats pushed in upon the hole, the crawling soldiers only two, three steps apart, moving up here, then there, firing as they came, looking like foolish bugs in their slow and awkward advance through the patches of snow and freezing mud, puffs of smoke spitting from their gun muzzles, with streaks of fire in them.

At first there were a few shots from the Indians, but soon that slacked to silence and Wessells crept up under the bank. From there he motioned the firing stopped, and through the silence he demanded the surrender of the Indians. A corporal beside him, who knew a few awkward words of Sioux, tried to make them understand.

"*Hou! Washte!* Good!" the man yelled out, as though all the guns were still roaring. "Give up! Give up!"

But there was no reply, only an isolated shot or two after the soldiers resumed the attack. A second time the captain called for surrender and there was still no reply, just a few more shots from the Indians, shots that hit so close that Wessells' men tried to warn him back.

"Look out, Cap! They're 'a playin' 'possum!" an old Indian fighter bellowed.

By now most of the soldiers were so close that the Indians had to jump up above the breastworks to see them to aim. In this one Cheyenne was hit, and then another. As they went down into the smoke and dust, others grabbed the guns. The women reloaded as they could, crimping the bloated cartridges to the bullets with their teeth as long as the lead lasted. No one spoke under the thunder of the guns, the sing of the bullets, although now and then a woman or a child sobbed a little, a spasmodic sucking in of air, no more.

"If we die in battle, our names will be remembered . . . ," Little Finger Nail had said in the council down in the south country, six long moons ago. "They will tell the story and say, 'This is the place.'"

So this was the place. To this hole on a little dry creek they had come all that long and sorrowful trail.

The fighting went on for an hour more, with only a shot or two from the Indians, and finally even that stopped. When it seemed they were really done, Wessells and Chase led their troops to the breastworks, firing into the hole through the smoke and dust that hid everything until there seemed nothing there ahead at all. Then the two officers jumped up on the edge with revolvers cocked, ordering immediate surrender where surely none lived.

But there was one more shot out of the smoke of the hole. Captain Wessells staggered, struck alongside of the head. Chase helped get him back out of range, and now, as a foot charge was prepared from all three sides, there rose a clear, high song from among the Indians, the voice that everyone knew was Little Finger Nail, the sweet singer of the Cheyennes singing his death song. In the middle of it there was the sudden cry of a small girl as a woman stabbed the child and then herself, and then more singing, all the others joining in now—the thin, high death chant of the Cheyennes.

At the sharp command, the troops charged the breastworks, firing a volley of a hundred shots down into the Indians, jumping back to reload, and up again, the guns a solid roaring. Finally they withdrew from the blinding, stinking powder smoke and watched it drift away from around the hole as from a great fire burning.

Then suddenly three almost naked, dirt-streaked, bloody Cheyennes leapt out, Little Finger Nail, with a pistol and a knife, in the lead. At the crack of a carbine he straightened up tall, and fell. Roman Nose, just behind, jumped over the Nail as he went down, and fell too. Bear got clear down among the white men before he died.

When the smoke had cleared away, the troops approached the torn breastworks, cautiously, reluctantly, and looked down upon the bodies piled like gray, bloody sacks of earth thrown this way and that upon each other. Lieutenant Chase went down among them and helped lift the Indians out. Seventeen men dead and one mortally wounded, crying that he wanted to die too, be thrown back into the hole with his friends, all that was left to him now between the earth and the sky. Four women and two small children were dead too, among them Brave One who had come through the blood of Sand Creek and of the Sappa to end in this place, and Singing Cloud, the beloved of the warrior Little Finger Nail, with the wounded child still in her arms. Under them seven women and children were alive but wounded, one woman to dying. Hog's lovely daughter was alive, bloody, haggard and wild now, her neck drawn tight against her bullet-torn shoulder. And deep in the bottom, under everything, was a pile of dried meat 3 feet high, standing in a pool of the blood that the frozen earth refused.

"God—these people die hard!" a soldier said when he saw this. Once he stooped to pick up a gray buffalo horn, but he threw it back down when he felt that it was heavy as stone.

At the edge Wessells, looking into the hole, saw one of his officers reaching to a little girl who was peering fearfully out of a pocket dug back under the breastworks. It was the six-year-old Lame Girl, looking imploringly toward the Little Dutchman whom she had seen many times in the barracks. She let herself be picked up and taken to him, holding out her hands as children learn to do, for he was not an unkindly man. But as he took her, his palm felt a stickiness under her arm, a new gunshot wound, this time in her side.[3]

And when they turned up Little Finger Nail where he had fallen face down outside of the breastworks, they noticed something on his back—the canvas-covered book * in which he had pictured the stories of the fights he had and the coups he counted. But two 45-70 Springfield bullets had gone through it, the blood-soaked holes as close together as overlapping finger tips.

* In the American Museum of Natural History, New York.

17

This Remnant

TWO DAYS AFTER THE WOUNDED CAPTIVES FROM THE Last Hole were brought to Fort Robinson, there was a sudden shouting through the post and a running toward headquarters. Somebody, an Indian, was coming down out of the bluffs, indeed was already past the stables and there among them. It was a Cheyenne woman with a child on her back, leading one not much larger by the hand. She staggered a little and let a trooper who ran out take the two little ones under his arms. She motioned that the children be fed and she went to sit down at the barracks door, returned to the only place she knew now.

"Where has she been these weeks?" the interpreter was told to ask when he came pushing through the circle of curious soldiers.

Between soppings of bread and molasses she said she had been in a hole in the bluffs up there. The night of the outbreak the young men drove her through the window. She had no relatives left, and no man, so she carried only her bundle until someone fell. Down around the sawmill she saw these children among the dead ones. With the two she could not run very far, so she flattened down in the brush of the river. She had a little tallow hidden, and after the soldiers quit looking, she took the children up to a hole where they could have a little fire in the night. She knew nothing of anyone else. She would have come in sooner, but it seemed all the Indians were dead and she was making the mournings for a lost tribe.

Wessells hurried up and had the woman sent away to the other captives. She was an embarrassment, just as the board of officers ordered by General Crook gathered to investigate the whole Cheyenne outbreak. Colonel Evans of Fort Laramie and Crook's aide, Lieutenant Schuyler, were waiting, the third member late because he could not get a seat in the coach from the railroad, the stage agent admitted. Too many sight-seers, in addition to all those who drove up or came horseback to stare at the Cheyennes. Some remembered that the stage agent had been seen with the other civilians out along the White River bluffs the night of the outbreak, shooting wounded, and worse. It could be that he was not anxious for an investigation that would list him as guilty of offenses against the dead and wounded, even though the proceedings would never be published.

Officers, enlisted men, civilians, and the captive Cheyennes were all called. But Shangreau and Woman's Dress had not waited. Although they led the soldiers to that last hole below the Hat Creek bluffs, they were sickened and silent over what was done there. Besides, there would surely be Little Wolf warriors, skulking. Shangreau wanted to go home to Pine Ridge immediately, and so Woman's Dress had his wound bound up again and was given the two women relatives from the captives, as promised. Then the four rode away.

Not far from the post they met the Sioux scouts coming from Red Cloud. "Go back! It is all done . . . ," Shangreau had called out.

"There is still Little Wolf," the Sioux replied.

In the investigation the terrified Indian women spoke so low in their soft Cheyenne that they could scarcely be heard, or did not reply at all, and none here could press them. The captive men were brought in too: the four from Vroom's prison tent, Hog, Crow, Left Hand, and Porcupine, and the five taken in the outbreak, Tangle Hair, Old Man or Noisy Walker as he was called here, Blacksmith, The Sioux, and the one sometimes known as Stubfoot—those nine the only men left, without mutilating or fatal wounds, of all the Dull Knife band, unless the chief and Bull Hump were still hidden somewhere.

Hog and the others talked readily enough of everything except the killings on the Sappa and the Beaver. No *veho* would understand that a headman like Hog might actually have no arms except a bow and quiver on the entire flight north, the family gun carried by Little Hog, carried to his death in the snow. It seemed that the officers could not realize that a Cheyenne chief had responsibilities beyond those of warmaking, that he fought only in actual defense of the village, and that vengeance was a gratification denied him by every chief's oath. None of the whites seemed to wonder why the settlers in north Kansas were killed and none harmed in Nebraska. Nobody seemed to know of all the Cheyennes who died on the Sappa three years before. Still it seemed awkward to inquire about the clothing and bedspreads and photographs in the bundles of the Indians, now that so many Cheyenne women and children were scattered over the snow these last three weeks, and no officer pressed the chiefs about their young men now.

When the Indians were asked why they left the south, they repeated the old story—hunger, sickness and death, and the promise that they could return. But when the Cheyennes were asked about Little Wolf's camp, they shook their heads. He had said he was going north the night they separated at the Platte. No one had seen Dull Knife. It was said he died in the fighting in the bluffs the first night.

"Then where is his body?"

The men smoked in silence, their pipes guttering in hidden thought. They knew about nobody except the people here, Tangle Hair finally said. Of the 149 brought to the barracks here 78 people were left, with only a few men among them—all they were certain lived of the 284 who had left the south country six moons ago.

"Now there are so few, we beg you spare this remnant. . . ."

When the investigation reached Wessells, he admitted that he had cut off the food, the fuel, and even the water from the prison barracks, but he had reported what he was doing and received no protest from his superiors, not from Crook or General Sheridan. To prove his kind intentions he told of buying 4 pounds of tobacco for the Cheyennes out of his own savings.

When they heard this, the Indians were prompt with their "Hou!" "Hou!" He had indeed given them this tobacco, they agreed, not looking over to their friend Chase, who was still their friend even though they knew he fired into that last hole up there, and knew too that he had brought the wounded in as kindly and gently as could be through the winter night. The lieutenant had spent much of his pay on the Cheyennes, buying tobacco and candy for them, dolls for the small girls, and enough beads for fifty moccasins for the women to work—the fine new Cheyenne moccasins that were stolen from the dead the first night when they fell on the snow. The Indians had made presents for him too, of course, but even these were from his own materials.

Yes, Wessells bought the 4 pounds of tobacco, and he had carried one of their children at least 2 miles, saved her life that freezing night.

Several newspapermen were around the post and out with the troops in the final annihilation. Their stories doubled the public anger of two weeks ago and brought loud demands for court-martial of the officers who used cold and starvation to subdue these brave savages and then harried them through the winter snow to the last horrible butchery.

The newspapers told too of the wailing when the relatives of Woman's Dress were allowed to go with him, and then of the second dividing, when those who need not go to Kansas for the murder trial were loaded into wagons for Red Cloud—forty-eight women and children, including the boys, a few badly crippled men, and the old ones, fifty-eight Cheyennes in all. It was a sad and horrible parting.

The Cheyennes were in the long prison room when they were told to get ready to move, a room that seemed as narrow in the lantern light as a corral chute where the white man burned and bloodied his cattle. The Indians had crowded themselves closer than need be. Wounded and sorrowing, hair streaming down in mourning, the men and women crouched in their blankets or lay on pallets, silent, staring at each other in the new sadness and fear of the morning and the wagons. Near the door, as would be her place in a lodge where young girls lived, squatted an old woman, one leg out straight before her as no Cheyenne woman was ever to sit, unless it happened that her knee was gunshot and could never bend again. Beside her sat an orphaned girl of seven, combing and braiding the hair of her baby sister and singing a soft humming lullaby. At the end of the room was Dull Knife's wounded daughter, her legs slashed in mourning for her brother and sister, perhaps for her whole family except the small niece beside her, with the long, light-touched hair, the soft eyes—all the shining countenance that was the mark of Dull Knife's Beautiful People. The child cuddled a beaded doll in a little piece of bloodstained blanket, singing to it. Beyond her a woman leaned over a half-grown girl in serious instruction now that they might be parted forever.

After the long waiting for permission to go to Red Cloud, at last the Cheyennes were to be taken there, the crippled remnant of them. There was soft keening for all those who could not climb into the waiting wagons, for the living as well as the dead. Then the wheels broke from the frozen ground and the little queue started down the White River road to the encampment where Hog and fourteen other men were in irons. Here a few more women and children would be loaded in too, all except those who must go south with their men to the trial for murder. These left-behind-ones were gathered on a little hill back of the camp, and as the wagons started away toward Red Cloud, they set up a wild wailing and gesticulation, Hog's wife leading them. Keening in sorrow for her lost son, she threw her bony, shriveled arms in supplication to the Powers whose winds blew her loose mourning hair and her rags as she moved in a sad dance of despair, half a dozen others circling with her, naked butcher knives flashing in the sun.

One of the Sioux scouts was ordered to take Hog's wife to her tent and search her for weapons besides the knife she surrendered. He had the Indian's reluctance to touch a woman not his wife, and when he finally made a move toward her, she struck her breast quickly with both hands, half of a pointed scissors hidden in one and in the other a table fork with only the sharpened middle tine left. She stabbed herself several times more before she could be disarmed, blood streaming down upon her moccasins. Even then she broke loose and tried to kill one of her small children and stamped on another, fortunately with the soft soles of Cheyenne moccasins.

Before she was quieted with morphine, there was a shout from the prison tent. Her husband, the powerful Hog, lay in blood too, unconscious, stabbed four times about the heart although his hands were ironed and he was apparently disarmed.

"It seemed best to him, when he is to be killed by the whites. If he dies here, his wife and children can go to their relatives with Red Cloud," was all even Tangle Hair would say.

That night the reporter from the Chicago *Tribune* went to see Hog. The chief's eldest daughter lay on the bare ground of the prison tent, sleeping heavily from her wounding and the exhaustion of the long flight over the winter bluffs. She had crept very close to the fire, her face almost in it, as though she could never be warmed again. The white man looked down upon the worn and haggard girl who had been so lovely to see only three weeks ago, and then to her powerful father, lying head to head with her. Hog breathed heavily and moaned under the morphine, his handcuffs rattling as he tried to move, the big silver peace medal from the Great Father in Washington sliding on the black kerchief about his neck. The attendant gave the chief another pill and spoke kindly in some pidgin Indian to him. The mother, her eyes wild and tortured, sat at the tent door as protector, an old gash above the right eye swelling her face, her stabbed breast hunching her awkwardly upon herself. Suddenly the wounded girl awoke with a low moaning of pain, and seeing the soldiers through the smoke, she screamed as though she were once more in that last murderous rain of bullets in the hole out from Hat Creek bluffs.

The proceedings of the Board of Officers investigating the Cheyenne outbreak at Fort Robinson closed with two questions: Could not identification of the guilty have been tried at Robinson as well as elsewhere, and did the dignity of the government require removal of these Indians back to Indian Territory without full investigation into the merits of their complaints? In his report General Crook wrote, "Among these Cheyenne Indians were some of the bravest and most efficient of the auxiliaries who had acted under General Mackenzie and myself in the campaign against the hostile Sioux in 1876 and 1877, and I still preserve a grateful remembrance of their distinguished services, which the government seems to have forgotten."

If there was a helpless sort of anger against Woman's Dress and Shangreau, there were those among the Sioux who were not too friendly toward some of these Cheyennes either—Sioux who had lost their relatives and friends in the last fights under Crazy Horse, when the soldiers were led against them by Cheyenne scouts. But when the men who rode out to meet the wagons saw these people now, they whipped back in angry excitement, and so the whites were sent indoors as the young Sioux came roaring up in paint and arms around the building where the Cheyennes were unloaded, threatening the little troop escort. Even some old agency-loafing scouts drew their guns in anger to see the wounded people, sometimes only a boy or a girl or a crippled old woman left from a whole family. The Sioux divided their poor rations with them, gave them blankets and moccasins and ornaments for their hair, making the guests feel welcome as the Indians had made the white man welcome once, long ago, when he first came.

A week later more wagons carrying Cheyennes, with soldiers riding ahead and behind, started from Robinson, this time the prisoners going to Sidney and the special railroad car that would take them to Leavenworth, Kansas. Among these were Hog, stooped and ponderous in his unhealed wounds, Tangle Hair, Left Hand, Old Crow, Porcupine, Blacksmith, and Noisy Walker with their families, most of the men still in irons, Hog holding his manacled hands out at the stop in Omaha and all along the way for the crowds to see, proudly, arrogantly, it was thought. But there was no Little Wolf or Dull Knife to exhibit at any station. The Wolf was reported to be many places between the Platte, where horses were being stolen as always, and the Canadian border, where raiders from Sitting Bull slipped down to hunt and pick up anything they could.

"Dull Knife is dead," the captives were now saying. "He was killed in the fighting of the first night."

But none told where his body lay.

"These here church folks is sure doin' a lot 'a yellin' in the papers about them Cheyennes bein' cleaned out," one of the cattlemen from the White River country complained. "I been corral-feedin' my stock horses over a month now—waitin' fer the troops to round up the last 'a them wily bucks. . . ."

But now the last of the Indians were gone, and most of the soldiers had ridden away from Fort Robinson to look for Little Wolf. Then one afternoon an Indian boy, young Red Bird, came hobbling out of the bluffs toward the house of a man he knew down the river from the post. The boy was so starved he seemed no thicker than the forked stick he used as a crutch for the dragging leg, but on his back was a painted rawhide case. Inside was the shield he must save by running hard and keeping hidden, to protect even in dying if need be. It seemed he was very young for such a trust, and played out, hungry, and very sorrowful, for all the other Cheyennes must surely be dead.

No, he did not know where Dull Knife was; he knew nothing.

By this time the Sioux around Pine Ridge knew. Dull Knife [1] had left the barracks with Pawnee Woman and the daughters. Behind him was Bull Hump with his wife and a child and his father-in-law, Great Eyes, and the young Red Bird with the Eyes' shield on his back. There were three young warriors along to help in the flight, including Calf, the Knife's grandson. Strung out but together, they got through the first run past the river with only one of the daughters hit but crying for them to go on, go on. That was when Little Hump stayed back to hold off the soldiers, close enough to hit now, and another daughter stayed too. The rest could not wait to argue this but had to go fast to get the old chief away. North of the river they turned from the direct path toward the bluffs to a frozen drift that had no friendship for tracks. From there they moved up a shallow gully, stooping low as they ran, keeping to the moon-glistening, the hard-crusted snow. At the bluffs they slipped carefully through the shadows, clinging along the rock face as much as they could so no snow would be touched, no track remain. Once when the soldiers came close, there were a few hasty snow steps that they could not hide and one *veho* shouted, "Here's a trail, leading off this way!"

So Great Eyes, as rear guard, turned back. Stumbling out into the moonlight as though seriously wounded, he made a great whooping and singing as he dodged awkwardly back and forth among the boulders and brush, moving away from the others, firing an old revolver loaded with very little powder, but making his defense last as long as he could, until he was finally dropped dead on his face. By then there was no picking up the tracks that his moccasins had covered and confused. So the others got safely away, except that young Red Bird was hit by a glancing bullet and dragged a leg.

Dull Knife led them to a great hole in the rocks that he recalled from his young days in fights with the far-traveling Crows, a hole that showed no opening at all two steps away. The soldiers never found the trail again and so these Cheyennes were safe as long as they stayed inside. They almost starved waiting for a good time to come out.

Ten days later the soldiers were all moving out in long columns to the western Hat Creek bluffs, as Bull Hump could see from a hidden place high up, with the field glass Pawnee Woman had carried through the barracks. The snow had melted to patches, and before it was all gone, there would be more to show their tracks. Now, if ever, they must start for Pine Ridge. All but Red Bird. He could scarcely walk with his forked stick; he could never get over the long miles of the high open country where they must go very fast.

So the boy sat in the back of the cave alone, singing a strong-heart song to give himself courage as Bull Hump led the others away into the night. They moved very carefully, traveling in the moonless dark, setting no moccasin down in snow or soft earth, keeping to the high, drier, well-grassed slopes, but where the cold burned the breast, and not even a bush offered protection.

"It is better to be very cold than dead . . . ," the blunt-spoken Bull Hump told his little daughter when she whimpered in the freezing night wind.

So long as the sick old chief had the strength to walk, they kept going, and when he began to lag, they hid in one little draw or another little gully for the day, in places so shallow and bare that none would think to look for such foolish hiding. They ate any roots and prairie rose hips and buds they could find, the two rabbits the Hump snared, some sinew one of the women had hidden, and finally the tops of their moccasins, chewing the rawhide like buffaloes working at their cuds. Then one night, half a moon after they left the cave, when Hog and the other headmen were already far on their way to the stone prison at Leavenworth, Dull Knife reached the place of a man he recalled from around the old Red Cloud agency near Fort Robinson. Gus Craven, married into the Sioux, was a man known as unafraid, and so not one to be feared. This *veho* cried out when he saw the bare, frozen, and bleeding feet of his old friends, their gaunt and sunken faces. His wife made the little sorrowful wailings as she fed them hot beef soup and fried bread, and buckets of coffee with sugar in the bottom of the cup. The next night they were taken to their interpreter friend, Rowland. So these people were slipped in with the Sioux, their presence to be unseen, their names unspoken.

Dull Knife was taken to a lodge set up for him under a little bluff off out of the way on Wounded Knee Creek, with wood and meat, and blankets for the long sleeps. When he had rested two days and eaten well at his own fire for the first time since he left the north country, he finally demanded to know what had been done down there by the chasing soldiers. So he had to be told how few were left besides the handful of prisoners taken to Kansas. His wounded daughter was brought to him, and one of the women who had lived through that last day in the hole. Slowly, speaking as with lips still frozen, they told what they had seen.

Once the old chief rose in a towering self-rage. "I am an empty man!" he cried to the Powers. "I have become so weak that I cannot even die with my people!"

Before his sorrow, everyone slipped away, some afraid of a blaming word, afraid of seeming to blame Dull Knife for splitting off from the rest of the Cheyennes down there north of the Platte because he trusted to his old-time wisdom and the old-time reliance upon a man's word, even the word of a *veho*.

After a while Dull Knife went to sit up on the bluff. Almost it seemed like the time foretold by Sweet Medicine, a time to happen here in the north country. Many people were to die, perhaps all the Cheyennes. For that time Sweet Medicine had left one instruction: "The last woman among you must carry the Sacred Arrows to a high hill and lay them down for the time when the people shall return to the earth."

But that was not for now, with the Arrows not here. Besides, the sacred objects had failed when the soldiers destroyed the Powder River village and left so many dead on the ground. Yet how is a man to lead his people when the old holy things, the old, old wisdoms fail?

A long time Dull Knife sat up there, silent, alone, without his pipe, his hands hanging helpless between his knees, as helpless as in the cold iron shackles of the whites.

18

And Now the Yellowstone [1]

WHEN THE FREEZING MOON, THE WHITE MAN'S DECEM-
ber, was past, the cold became heavier, the thermom-
eter dropped toward forty below zero, a time for the fires and the sleeping,
but still the troops rode the hills after Little Wolf.

In Lost Chokecherry the ice holes in the lake had to be chopped deeper
than the length of an arm for the water that crept back to the warm breast
of the earth. The snow was hard as stone; the air burned the lungs and
settled in frost on the cowhide and elk robes, thick about the face. Most of
the time the Indians kept close to their holes in the hillside, squatting over
their little fires, a stick at a time laid on the coals to char before it burned,
so there would be no smoke to cling along the slope in the heavy air. The
few horses hidden in the brush lived on the cottonwood branches carried
to them, the bark so glassy in the cold they could hardly gnaw it. The other
horses, scattered through places like Spring Valley, tried to paw the knee-
deep snow for grass and stretched their necks high into the few cottonwoods. The herders in their holes could not cut anything for them because
the soldiers would discover it in the open valley. Even in this cold weather
those scouts were everywhere, the troops riding in their buffalo coats.

Finally the thaw of January came. It was gradual, the drifts eaten in little
holes by the dryness of the wind instead of its warmth. But it was still no
weather for raiding, the horses too weak to go against the grain-fed ones
of the ranchers, and so Black Coyote and Whetstone held themselves quiet.
But Little Wolf knew their thought and knew he must move his people
before those men started trouble. Yet first he must find out what was done
up at Robinson.

After six moons of waiting, his fire was finally freed of Thin Elk. The
Elk's going was still a little funny to some of the old ones, and it would

have seemed funny to laughing to the Wolf at another time, although his women found their fire a very quiet place now, particularly the Pretty Walker, who liked very much to laugh. After Little Wolf made his hard decision to do so unchiefly a thing as drive out a guest who brought ridicule to his lodge and his person, the Elk went without urging or one shout of dissension from anyone. The messenger who brought the bad news of Dull Knife's people and their orders to go back south had added that the chiefs would be given the *veho* trial for murder and surely the hanging rope afterward. No one noticed Thin Elk's face in this hard hour. When Little Hawk got ready to go up to Robinson again, they asked him for his horses.

"There are so few strong ones left and you are not using the two we gave you for your return home. Let us borrow them."

"I will need them myself," the Elk replied. "I am going north."

"When? We will be back."

"I need them now. I am going with you."

So there was a hurrying to get the three ready with warm clothing, enough for the Elk too, if he really did go clear through to the winter Yellowstone. In a week Little Hawk and Woodenthigh came back. Too many soldiers were around Robinson, and more coming, even with the cold and the snow. No Indian was allowed outside of the prison barracks any more, except when the women were taken to the brush patch for their needs, with soldiers going along to stand with their backs turned, but the guns ready, and watching everything all around, the far bluffs too.

"No men were taken out at all? It is truly an ironhouse!" Little Wolf said. "And they are to be named as murderers!"

Ahh-h, yes, it seemed this would be done.

The council sat a long time, angry and sullen. But they were not strong enough to help the people up there, not in anything, and there was work here. They must move very soon if they wanted to get away. So the horsemen took the stock to the few bare slopes for grass. Spotted Deer and the others rode out to gather the seed from the blackened pods of the soapweeds dotting the hills, and the seed tops from the swamps to feed the horses, give them strength.

Then the news came of the outbreak at Robinson. A signal of the sorrowful news reached the farthest watchers around Lost Chokecherry, a mournful howling signal, repeated over and over, as from an old and worn-out wolf. But when someone took a horse out so the man need not bring his moccasin tracks close, he still did not come, and it was known he bore very bad and shaming news. Finally Little Hawk and some others brought him to the big brush circle, where all could hear. The man sat back from the fire, and those who had seen him walk knew his feet were stone from freezing, and his fumbling hands too. Now even in the duskiness they saw that his face was twisted with a raw scarring wound from a bullet that went in at one cheek and tore a hole out on the other side of the nose, pulling the lower lid down so it seemed the eye could never be closed again.

At last the Wounded One spoke in a hoarse un-Cheyenne voice. Painfully he made his first words since the bullet broke his upper jaw over ten days ago. Several times he stopped and tried to swallow soup from the horn spoon Feather on Head held for him, but it seemed his throat was almost closed from the long disuse and the wounding. As he warmed a little, he began to tell of the freezing, the hunger and thirst in the barracks, of Hog, Left Hand, and Crow dragged away in handcuffs.

"Ahh-h!" the men listening said in their soft, subdued Cheyenne. "Ahh-h!"

Wounded One told what he could of the outbreak too, the bad luck of moonlight clear as day, the running, the falling from the bullets, the women and children like bundles of old rags scattered on the frozen snow.

"Ahh-h!" the listening people cried too, making it the murmur of horror while Old Grandmother's voice rose in a keening and then stopped to hear the man's difficult words, coming slow as stones falling.

He had been one of those sent to get horses from the Bronson ranch, running with lariats and saddles while the rest struck for the bluffs. But the bullet through his face stopped him, made him dead for a long, long time, so he was almost frozen when he awoke in a brush pile in the snow, where he must have crawled after the hitting. When he came out, he saw a lot of people laid in a row down near the sawmill—men, women, and children dead in the snow there, thirty-three, twenty-three of them men, and no telling how many had died since, with the soldiers black over the Hat Creek's breaks, hunting through every snow-filled draw and canyon. So few men and not one horse to get the helpless ones away.

Back among the listeners the mothers drew the children closer to their backs, looked quickly around the circle of darkness, and then pushed in with the others around the man, making a wall tighter than the hills, forgetting the cold of the night, waiting. Slowly he began to tell the dead from that first running, speaking the names with the reluctance that wished to show no disrespect. Here and there a little keening started, low, private, for there were griefs all around now. Forgetting her maidenly reserve, Yellow Bead edged herself in close, but then she became afraid and began to shrink back until she found herself up against young Spotted Deer, always nearby. He was holding his elk robe open to gather around the girl, not as for a few moments of gay talk in courting, but to hold her against the grief when the name of Little Hump came, as it would, for the Hump was a very strong young man.

But when the name was reached, Yellow Bead was steady as a tree. She had no right to make a public mourning for the young warrior, only for White Antelope and his wife and a dozen others who were her relatives to claim. Quietly she went to stand beside her aunt and joined her voice with the old woman's in the soft keening cry for such a time.

So the man told the names that would perhaps never be spoken again, except those taken by some of the living. There was only the faint red fire glow on his swollen, shell-torn face, the standing people pushing in from the darkness, the song of sorrow rising all around, and the fear of soldiers to charge them here, surround them with no canyons and no bluffs for the hiding.

And even before the story was done, Black Coyote had slipped away, signaling others to follow. "We have listened to the Wolf all this time, and now our relatives are dead up there on the ground!" he cried in fury to them. "We cannot wait longer, my friends; sit here like chewing cattle for the guns to start. We must go out and avenge this Cheyenne blood!"

Little Wolf and Black Crane and the others sat late over the sorrowful news and the keening of the women. "The Indian never caught is the Indian never killed," Black Crane said, in the words of his head chief, but tonight there was no satisfaction in them. Many had died and many more would die up there in the snow, yet there was nothing anyone here could do, no help they could bring. "Probably the only saved ones will be those held with the irons," Little Wolf said slowly. Dull Knife and the rest of his family would surely be hunted down. It was a thought to twist the heart as Wounded One's face was twisted.

Before they went to their sleeping robes, Woodenthigh was sent to Red Cloud for news, and carried in his hand all Little Wolf's plans for the time to come. Then at the first dawn of morning the Crier ran through the frosted grass and brush of the camp. "Wake up!" he called. "Make everything ready today. We start as the sun goes to his sleep!"

Perhaps it was well it had to be done so, the hands of the bereaved too busy to gash and slash themselves for more mourning blood, the mind too full of planning and hurry. As the people wound out of the valley toward the low yellow sun, the way they had come in three months ago, they looked back sadly and already nostalgically into that peaceful shadowing place. They were going out to be chased again, and they had the reminder of all those dead up on White River, and yet none here was as terrified as when they came fleeing to this lost spot. It had been a wonderfully healing thing, this quiet good life in a quiet good place—the best three moons of many years. It was true they had been poor in dress and in the kettle, with the shadow of the soldiers always upon them, even to scattering them into the snow, but Their Man, Little Wolf, always managed this stepping aside in time. Then, when the bluecoats were gone, they came back. It had been a poor time but a healing one. . . .

"We are peaceful, my friends!" Little Wolf told his young men before he let them go. Those with Black Coyote had waited for no advice or permission.

Yet peacefulness would not be enough, and the women saw they must be prepared to run when the warrior woman Buffalo Calf Road was sent ahead to lead them, instead of one of the older ones put in the place of honor. Many of those riding behind looked to her in pity because her man, Black Coyote, had become so strange, flying into such angers as no Cheyenne should permit himself unless he wanted to go down the road of Bear Rope. He was always drawing his gun against people, even Little Wolf, when the chief tried to stop him from raiding the soldier herd at the Snake River camp back in the fall.

"You will get us all killed, my son," Little Wolf had said quietly and turned his back upon the gun held against him. The whole camp had been silent as a stopped breath, but the younger man did not shoot. Now, almost three moons later, it was plain that the Coyote, of them all, had found no quiet, no peace in Lost Chokecherry. He was out already, since early last night, avenging, making trouble.

Only one good ride away was the Snake River soldier camp often used this winter, and now with perhaps five well-mounted companies of troops there and surely more coming, so many that they could ride stirrup to stirrup over the sandhills until no one could remain unseen. Besides, with the snow drying off, surely the field glass lost by the watcher up at the lone tree must be found, with the plain mark of the troops in the south country. It could not have been dropped by some Sioux hunting party from Spotted Tail—only by the Cheyennes.

But Little Wolf must have horses, so the foragers were out, Little Hawk leading them, in addition to around a dozen who slipped away with Black Coyote. Of the young men only Spotted Deer asked to remain to help the women and children. His grandmother was so old and afraid. . . .

Black Crane's face remained expressionless as he considered this, looking toward Old Grandmother, with her little bundle ready before all the others, talking with the Crier like a maiden. Yes, they needed some young men along, the Crane said soberly, as though he had not noticed this, or that Yellow Bead was riding the Deer's new spotted horse. Not that it was an acceptance of him as her future husband; one did not make a courting in such a time of grief, not unless one was Old Grandmother.

So Spotted Deer joined the rear guard, the direction from which the soldiers would probably come, although it was hard to give up the chase for the horses or the raiding that Black Coyote had promised.

In a few days news of more Cheyenne depredations filled the talk and the newspapers from frontier saloons to Washington and across the seas, where the red savages seemed a very romantic people. A rider sent with a dispatch to the Platte River from the Niobrara said Indians had chased him 50 miles. He confirmed the killing of two men at the Moorehead ranch on the Niobrara, the twenty-third of January, by thirteen Indians and reported two more white men shot about the same time. All the horses along that stretch of river were swept away. Major Ferris and five companies left their camp on Snake River to take up an Indian trail about ten to fourteen days old, at the head of the Boardman fork of the Snake—going southeast with three, four hundred horses and signs of women and children along. But the trail scattered and he followed its general direction one day down the Loup River in a gathering blizzard and then returned by the west route down Pine and Deer Creeks to the Niobrara. There was great suffering among the troops—the weather thirty below zero, the Indian trail lost under the deep drifts.

There was news too of a bull train surrounded east of Flint Butte on the Fort Randall trail to Robinson. All the extra clothing and provisions were taken, and in return the Indians gave the whackers a silver watch stolen from the Moorehead ranch and laid seven silver dollars into a palm. There were about a hundred in this party, it was reported, but no women or children. Although the Indians carried Winchesters and Sharps rifles, with plenty of ammunition, they were friendly and asked which way was north.

Old-timers laughed at this story. There were not a hundred men among all the Cheyennes when they left the south in September. The Wolf could have told them he had only thirty-nine, and these were split into three parties, with fewer than four hundred horses all together. Nobody said anything about the hunting bows the Cheyennes carried, and surely no Indian had to ask which way was north.

Then a messenger from Woodenthigh slipped in from the Sioux. He brought the story of the last fighting along the Hat Creek bluffs and the washout where so many died. All those strong young people killed! Yes, and at Robinson the leaders and their families must go south in irons to be called murderers, perhaps given the *veho* hanging. Hog, Left Hand, and the others.

Ahh-h! Hog, the big, judicious man who never liked trouble at all. And Left Hand, too, the good brother-in-law, the father of the strong young warrior that Little Wolf had selected to bear his own name—Left Hand, the great hunter who never wanted to harm anyone, not even an enemy Pawnee! Now he was dragged away in irons to die on a crossed pole. For a moment the Wolf was more angry against the whites than Black Coyote could ever be, with the fury of the grizzly that lived under the Chief's Bundle. But because he was the head chief, Little Wolf had to quiet himself. To avenge this would bring death to more Cheyennes, and when those were avenged, still more, and soon there would be none.

The messenger told that the bad-hurt ones and the women and children had been taken to Red Cloud at last, now that the families were broken like a stone under a great hammer. Hog had tried to kill himself so his family could go there too.

Yes, Hog was the man to do such a thing for his sick wife, but these were indeed bad times when it must be so. And Dull Knife?

Of Dull Knife he knew nothing, the Sioux messenger said, looking down into the fire before his crossed knees. Some of Spotted Tail's Sioux were

traveling west to make a visit with their relatives under Red Cloud. It was
said that Little Wolf should come to visit with them at their camp near
White Lake on his way north.

"*Hou!*" Slowly the Wolf cleaned his pipe, put it into the beaded bag, and
arose.

Late the second evening after Dull Knife reached Red Cloud, he, with
Pawnee Woman, Bull Hump, and three young men, left the lodge on
Wounded Knee. Red Cloud knew the old Cheyenne was going and let
him slip away, even though it was forbidden, for the Knife said he would
be back. They were met by Spotted Tail's people going west. While the
Cheyenne warriors went to the young Sioux Dog soldiers, old Dull Knife
was taken to a lodge a little to the side and yet close too, with a horse tied
behind it and a pile of firewood beside the flap, as though this were in the
old, old peaceful times, the owner just visiting somewhere nearby. It might
have been Dull Knife's own home, the one destroyed on the Powder. Inside, the fire sticks were laid, ready, in the center, and a kettle of meat waited
for the spoon. There were warm bed robes, and in the back, the man's place,
were two fine chiefs' blankets neatly folded. Here the old man settled gratefully to his smoking, still loose-haired and in the rags of his mourning for
Little Hump and the daughter lost. After a while there was the sound of
horses on frozen ground, more people coming out of the dark. Spotted Tail,
the managing man of the Sioux, the great diplomat, had arranged it well.
Dull Knife, in his defeat, with his heart on the ground for his people dead
and one more beautiful son lost, was given the good, the proud place of
host.

As the hoofbeats neared, Pawnee Woman slipped out into the darkness
to take the horses. There was a scratching on the lodge flap and Little Wolf
stooped into the fire-reddened lodge. He stood for a moment looking over
to the older man seated behind the nest of coals, to the ragged hair of his
sorrow, his body melted of fat as a hibernated bear's—a poor man sitting
loose within the skin of what had once belonged to him.

"I greet you, brother," Little Wolf said. "It is good to see that you got
away. . . ."

At the old man's silent gesture he went around to sit beside him, silent
too as the pipe was new-filled and the fragrant smoke of kinnikinnick with
a little good tobacco drifted upward through the smoke hole to the stars.

Once more the lodge flap lifted, and Pawnee Woman and the two wives of Little Wolf came in quietly and settled to their place. Pawnee Woman drew some coals closer to warm their hands and passed them bowls of hot soup from the kettle.

After a long time the two men began to speak in their quiet Cheyenne. "Come with us, brother," Little Wolf urged. "Come to the Yellowstone. Our moccasins are already on the path north around the Black Hills. We have good horses ready for you."

"I cannot do this. I have given my word to return."

Once more, as down on the Platte and several times before that, Little Wolf was roused to anger. "What is a spoken word in the world of the *veho,* the spider? We must learn to walk on his road in the white man's way. These are the times of promises written down to show to the liar, to remind him. It is no longer the day when there was no paper and so the liar could not be tolerated. You have not touched the pen to your promise."

"No, yet I cannot go. . . ."

"Not even after all these dead ones from broken *veho* promises?" Little Wolf wanted to roar against this man. But it could not be done and so the Wolf admitted what he had known from the first. Shifting his Chief's Bundle under his arm, he made the solemn *"Hou!"* of approval. "You are a good man, my brother, a lone one left from the old times. It is a hard road for you, yet perhaps even I would not have you turn your good face from it now. . . ."

"But you—what will you do with your people?"

"We are going north, as I say. Some are already encamped toward the forks of the Cheyenne River. . . ."

"You will have to go with those soldiers up there. You cannot hide without the buffalo to feed you. They will find you now anywhere. . . ." Dull Knife said it bitterly, and in this bitterness was the measure of the great loss the whites had cost this moderate man.

"Yes," Little Wolf said slowly, "the soldiers will find us, it is true. I think that grass grows in buffalo trails up there too now. The soldiers must find us soon or we will be very hungry. . . ."

"Then you must accept the word of the one to whom you surrender, take the word into your open hand and clasp it without using the eye that sees too far ahead. You will have to believe he speaks straight when he says the women and children will not be shot after you have given up your guns. . . ."

It took Little Wolf a long time to answer this, the long-gathered sorrow stirring deep within him. It was hard to see this man beside him pushed upon such a path, when four moons back on the Platte he had believed very easily in the goodness of the northern whites.

"I will try to make it so the cost will seem very great to the soldiers if they shoot us. It is the best I can do now."

It was the best, but it was not good. That Dull Knife knew.

Slowly now the Little Wolf Cheyennes moved northward over the new-fallen snow, across the frozen White River far down, and up around the naked Badlands. The camp looked like a war or hunting party, without travois or lodge, only the rolls of hides across the women's horses for the little night shelters. The cold Big Moon Month, February, lay over all the earth as they pushed on, heads bent into the north wind, the reversed cow and elk robes, gray and awkward, tied as close around them as could be, the manes and tails of their horses blowing back.

No soldiers chased them now, and there was little raiding. The bad heart of Black Coyote was apparently made a little better by the cowboys that his party killed on the Niobrara, and although he kept out of the way of Little Wolf and Black Crane, who still policed the moving camp, he was back with the rest. Now and then the scouts saw white men out in the north country, even away from the Deadwood roads. One day Little Hawk and Woodenthigh found a man on the trail, and hoping to get a little tobacco, they called the commonly understood *"Hou, cola!"* and laid their guns down to show they were truly friendly.

But the man seemed too much afraid to realize that they were peaceful. He fired his rifle, the first bullet going between the Indians. They were too close to get away, so they shot him and took the little he had. It was an unhappy thing, for those who killed him were peaceful men, and they hurried back to tell Little Wolf about it.

"We know this was bad and may bring the soldiers running, so we have come to say we go willingly if you must drive us out. . . ."

"That is for the council to decide," the Wolf replied, and because Little Hawk was known as a good-natured and a cool man who would not endanger the people foolishly, they said that the two men should remain but be kept with the moving camp in the future, to help there. Others would be trusted to hunt and catch the horses. No one must start the shooting now.

"*Hou!*" Little Wolf agreed, thankful that he need not see his own son driven from him in this unhappy time. But it was not easy to meet the hot eyes of Black Coyote as the pipe passed in the council circle that night.

At another place a hunting party with young Spotted Deer along found a ranch. There were three men around and one came out to shake hands and make signs that the Indians could have whatever they wanted. Shield, who understood the *veho* words, laughed a little. "*Hou!* Good!" he said, and then they all went inside and looked through the little log house. They were given sugar and coffee and some flour to carry in their hide sacks, besides some plug tobacco too, and several bed soogans. One of the men had a good blanket he had planned to trade for a Sioux warbonnet, but he gave it to Spotted Deer—a heavy dark blue one with the woven white border along one side, very fine.

"Put on, make young feller heap big chief!" the man urged, showing his tobacco-stained teeth.

The Indians laughed, and the whites too, and then the Cheyennes rode away, waving their guns over their heads as they kicked their horses into a run.

"The government will pay, out of our goods," the Shield said. But Spotted Deer did not care how it was made right. Here was a fine blanket for Old Grandmother, even though it was for a chieftain's wearing. Or perhaps he could fold it about Yellow Bead some day, as a man with his bride.

Little Wolf rested his people three fine sunny days near Bear Butte while he went up there to fast and meditate a little, work for the power to see what must be done now. Off by himself on an isolated point the third day of the fasting, the chief looked out over the gray snow-patched prairie for one whole sun's passing, throwing his eyes back over all the long Cheyenne trail to the time when the people first came past here on their way westward to the streams that flow to the Yellowstone, and then around down to the Platte. The Cheyennes had seen their greatest days as a people since then, and now this long sorrowing, with all their hearts on the ground. But with wisdom they might pass this trial also—this hard Cheyenne autumn and its frozen winter that was the time of the *veho* foretold by Sweet Medicine here so long ago. Beyond it must be a new springtime, with grass for the horses, with the geese flying north overhead and children laughing in the painted villages—a springtime when the Cheyennes were once more a warm, a well-fed, a straight-standing people.

After a while he took the Chief's Bundle from under his tattered old shirt, the bundle that was brought by Sweet Medicine from this sacred butte. Then Little Wolf made a song:

> Great Powers, hear me,
> The people are broken and scattered.
> Let the winds bring the few seeds together,
> To grow strong again, in a good new place.

But as he sang, the sky grayed and he knew that there would be more snow and that he must get his camp to a protected canyon before it came. Slowly, stiffly, the man arose and went down to a little stream where an evening snowbird watched him drink.

At first it seemed good, with the storm only a short wet snowfall that left the ground dark for a day after the sun came out. Another whole week they traveled toward the Little Missouri with almost no sign of white men. But the buffalo trails were gray in weeds; the chips rotten and bleached by the snows that had passed over them; game scarce and thin from the bad winter: a very easy time for the soldiers to starve the people on a reservation up here too.

It was then that Black Coyote brought in some army stock, branded with the government US sign. There was a council over this grave and dangerous act, and Black Crane as keeper of the peace was instructed to order the stock taken back.

"We only steal and fight when we have to, because the soldiers have come fighting us," the Crane said. "Do you want the soldiers to ride against us here like those down at Robinson, shooting into our women and children until nothing moves any more? Return the horses in the good way where you found them, my friend."

"I get the stock I need as it pleases me!" the violent Coyote roared in reply.

"You are endangering the people. You must obey commands of the council and take the horses back or you will be whipped."

"No one will dare! I will kill the man who strikes me!" Black Coyote shouted, drawing his Custer revolver as Whetstone came running up with his gun too.

So Black Crane lifted his pony whip and struck the Coyote over the shoulder with it. But this time Black Coyote fired, and the old chief fell, shot through the heart, at once so still on the hard cold ground that it seemed he had been dead a long time—and all the camp still around him.

Then suddenly men from all directions were there, divided into two factions, guns and knives out against each other, with only a finger's slipping on a trigger needed to begin the butchering. But already Old Crier was running up to intercede, the pipe held out before him, the sacred long-stemmed pipe that demanded peace.

"Peace?" Black Coyote cried out, his voice roaring through the silence, and with its echo he shot again. And as Old Crier went down, the Coyote ran over toward him, his dark face gaunt and wild as he fired again and again, his foolish bullets hitting the ground, spurting up little puffs of dust before him as the shocked Indians, even the warriors, fell back. But the old man's two wives and his daughter had thrown themselves over his body, and shots were coming at Coyote from Black Crane's camp guards, so he had to let the Crier live. Blood running down his arm where somebody had hit, Black Coyote walked away, the beaded moccasins stumbling a little on the rough ground, almost as from drunkenness. And none tried to stop him, everyone seeing the sickness that lived in him now, as the keening for the dead arose.

But a Cheyenne had been killed by a brother and there was nothing left but to drive the man out. So while Black Crane's keening women bore his body away, the Coyote was motioned off to one side. All those who would join in his exile could go to stand beside him publicly, for everybody to see. His brother-in-law Whetstone was the first. Then Buffalo Calf Road came running with her baby tied hastily to her back, loose, so it bobbed in her hurrying, the other child dragged by the hand, the young woman seen to be gaunt and sick to falling. The watching ones cried out against it. "No, no, sister! Do not go with him! It can only come to sadness if you follow your man's angry path!"

But the warrior woman had no ears. Firmly she stood beside her husband as others came, until there were seven grown people in the row. Then all of Black Coyote's stock except seven head, one for each, was taken from him, and he was left there on the prairie, with the blood still running a little from his wounded arm, and the six people and the horses.

Now the Cheyennes were nearing the Yellowstone, the place they started
for back in September, in the Moon of the Plums Ripe and Red. Every day
now they went slower. But no one seemed to recall the good times that they
had seen here and in the country west—the fat hunts, the rich villages, the
women weighed down with the finery of beads and elk teeth and rich red
flannel cloth. No one spoke of the fights against the many, many soldiers
that came running across the prairie the summer of 1865 after the Cheyenne march north from Sand Creek, or recalled that the Sioux and the
Cheyennes together drove them afoot and hungry back to the Platte. They
had had George, the son of the trader Colonel Bent, along then, to make
the *veho* talk for the defiant words of Dull Knife, a very strong chief that
summer.

But the next year the Bozeman Trail war came to the north country. Dull
Knife, who had tried to be a peace man as far back as 1846, when Tobacco
was killed, went in to Fort Phil Kearny to talk peace, and was whipped for
it with the pony quirts of the Sioux when he came out. In the meantime
Little Wolf's warriors rode with Red Cloud and the younger Sioux like
Crazy Horse against the Bozeman forts and helped kill the soldiers who
came out to die in the Fetterman fight. When the troops were driven from
all that country, the buildings of Fort Phil Kearny were given to Little
Wolf. With his people he rode down to look around inside the stockade that
he had helped besiege so long. The women picked this house and that for
their homes, Feather on Head and Quiet One running from one place to
another in their excitement, and the rest too, all made foolish as the white
women by the houses. Little Wolf remained on his horse, watching, silent.
And what he saw made him set fire to the fort, the Cheyennes whipping
away to the ridges to watch the hated soldier houses burn to the ground.

"We would have starved staying in one place. We must follow the buffalo
to live . . . ," the Wolf had said that day, only twelve years ago, a time
that seemed ten times the life of one man now.

But the soldiers had returned to the north-flowing streams of the Yellowstone. It was at the fork of the Powder that Little Wolf got the six wounds
a little over two years ago, and all those good people were left on the ground
in the dawn attack on women and children—a thing even more shameful
than killing those white men on the Sappa and the Beaver. He and Dull
Knife had missed the good fight against Crook on the Rosebud because as
chiefs they had tried to be peaceful and gone to the agency at the Robinson

where so many Cheyennes now lay dead. But their bolder fighters rode with the Sioux that day, Black Coyote and his warrior wife among them, the Buffalo Calf Road so brave there that the place was now called Where She Saved Her Brother. The Calf Road charged into the battle against Custer too, riding beside her warrior husband the time the Long Hair was left dead among all his troops over there on the Little Big Horn. Yet today she was a wanderer out with her man.

What sorrowful times had fallen upon them all; how much better to have died as the chief Lame White Man did in his brave fight against Custer on that gravel ridge. He died in honor, in the last fight of strong and honorable men.

With the coming of the Chinook, the ice began to break out of the northern rivers, the sound like pistol shots in the silent night. The Powder and the Yellowstone piled great dams of dirty ice against the islands and brush-choked channels, the water behind spreading over the gray bottoms and rising in the willows, driving the muskrats and the few beaver to the prairie. Then one day the first lance point of geese came over, flying high and fast on the south wind, while down on the ground there was much soldier sign: shod horses, soldier-made fire spots all along the trail from Fort Keogh to the Black Hills, and many troops at the mouth of the Powder under Lieutenant White Hat Clark, with Indian scouts along, Indians who wore Cheyenne moccasins.

"It is well," Little Wolf said quietly over the pipe, once more without tobacco. He had stopped 50 miles up the river from the mouth, waiting for a sign, for something to happen. The hunting was poor, the dried meat they carried from the sandhills almost gone, and the people very silent now, particularly since the killing of Black Crane and the loss of the thrown-away ones. Even Spotted Deer had withdrawn into his old quiet and reticence. No one had seen him waiting along a water path for Yellow Bead. Little Wolf's own daughter, the Pretty Walker, was slow-footed and silent as she had been for some time, although the north was the place of her bravery too, where she saved a life, dragging a man out of the bullets in the Powder River attack, a white man, a soldier. She was silent ever since they heard of the outbreak at Robinson. Or was it since Thin Elk left the fireside that night?

For a moment Little Wolf thought uneasily about this. But he shrugged it from him as he would have dropped a worn blanket in better times. There was no denying that the Elk was full of joking, particularly with Little Hawk there too, a man who was as solid as the mountain when there was trouble. Together around a peacetime village they could be a pair of foolish boys behind the big bellies they had both started years ago. And now they were very near to the Elk once more, and no telling when he would be sitting there at the fire, among a man's women again.

Angrily Little Wolf shook the ashes from his pipe. He had the responsibility of these people upon him, hungry, waiting, none knowing when the shooting might start, and here sat their chief, concerning himself with the business of village gossips.

Down at his Yellowstone camp, White Hat Clark was getting uneasy too. He knew Little Wolf must be somewhere near and that the scouting troops might run into him any time. With the Wolf's warriors nervous and desperate, one foolish thing could bring on a hopeless charge to die on the guns, and his troopers would have to kill them, no matter how they regretted it. So Clark sent to General Miles for a Cheyenne interpreter. He was told that Seminole, the only one he considered suitable, had been discharged and would not be reemployed. Without wasting time, Clark hired him out of his own pocket and sent him with the Indians to find Little Wolf.

But by then the Wolf's young men had discovered two of White Hat's scouts, a Sioux and a breed, and brought them to the camp. The men made big talk about Sitting Bull up in Canada as though they were from there, until the Sioux tried to slip away to Clark.

"Let him go . . . ," Little Wolf said, weary and inert. After a while he had the breed called to him. "I know you and everybody knows me," he said. "Go tell the soldiers I am here."

Then he moved to a strong place where it would cost many white-man lives to kill the Indians. By then the Cheyenne scouts were close, and recognizing their relatives they had not seen in two years. Brave Wolf called to his brother from far off and Thin Elk came laughing as anyone might who had been away just a few weeks. But their chief, Two Moons, looked soberly out of his broad well-fed face upon these relatives in their cowhide robes and awkward skin clothing, such as few except the very old ones had ever seen the people wear. Their shelters were scarcely bigger than the sweat lodge, not one tall enough for a standing man.

Invited to join the council circle for a smoke, Two Moons admitted readily that he and the others along were working for White Hat. They talked too of the hard chasing the soldiers were giving the hungry hunters from the Sitting Bull camp, who had come south from Canada for buffalo to eat.

"It will be difficult to get the people across the ice-flooding Yellowstone now," the Moons said seriously, "if anybody is planning to go on north."

But he got no response to this, no sign of concern from even the women listening around behind them. Little Wolf saw Two Moons' perplexity and knew that these visiting relatives, warm and fed in this healthy north country, could not realize how little a river of floating ice would be to a people often afoot, sick, and half-naked in the winter snow, yet who had come through almost two thousand miles of hungry country and many, many thousands of shooting soldiers.

Besides, the Little Wolf people had never planned to go to Canada. All they wanted was to live here in their own country. "The white man gives you nothing until you already have it tightly in the palm," Little Wolf had said half a year ago, and so he had taken the best grip on this country that he could manage. It was with some satisfaction that he watched the visitors look around the camp to report its strength to Clark: water, wood, and even a little grass in a rocky knob that would withstand many soldier charges and a long, long siege.

"This place is well chosen, my cousin," Two Moons admitted, and turned to talk of the good treatment the Cheyennes had received from soldiers up there at Fort Keogh. The Wolf guttered his pipe and did not remind the Moons that Little Chief was taken south from there or say that the officers who brought him down from the Missouri told Dull Knife that Two Moons and his band would be taken to Indian Territory as soon as Sitting Bull came in, for the Moons was a good man and it was hoped none need go south now.

When the Cheyenne scouts got back to the Yellowstone camp, Lieutenant Clark started for Little Wolf immediately. Now the chief must decide if they would believe even this white man. When the long line of troops came riding out of the haze, he prepared to meet them half a mile away from his strong rocky place that stood out alone over a flattish prairie, a place so small and high that even the cannon balls would fly right over.

"If I do not come back, you must decide what you will do. I cannot advise you now," he said to the little line of men who would have to guard the people, make the plans. They were of strong hearts, but some were old and content in comfort long ago; others had seen only a few short moons of fighting before they were driven to a reservation. Yet all their eyes followed Little Wolf as he started silently away, holding the cowskin robe about him, going poor and powerless as no Cheyenne chief within memory had gone.

But Old Grandmother came running after him. "For you . . . ," she said, holding a folded blanket out to him across her arms, offering it like a child would be offered to the Powers, her wrinkled old face as shamed by her boldness.

"Take your fine new blanket, Grandmother? That I cannot do. . . ."

"Take it! It is the one Spotted Deer brought in from the ranch back there, where it was honorably given. I have saved it for this time. We cannot have you go to meet the *veho* looking so poor. For this even the mourning rags should be set aside. You are our Great Man. You must go in dignity. . . ."

For a moment the look of darkness and sorrow moved from the man's lined face. He put aside the cowskin and took the blanket, folded crosswise as it was. With the white banding to the front, he laid its dark blue length about his shoulders, over the peace medal of the Great Father on his breast. Then, as Grandmother watched and all the rest, he mounted and rode down to meet White Hat Clark, the one for whom he had scouted at Fort Robinson, the man who, it was said, had never lied to an Indian unless it was to Crazy Horse, and the untruth of that unknown to him.

They met on a little grassy place, the Cheyenne alone, without one warrior to watch with a finger on the trigger, and the lieutenant with all his troops behind him. But they shook hands, first one and then the other hand crossed over, the white man seeing the lifetime of age that had come over the Indian in the two years since the Wolf was one of his scouts.

"I have prayed to God that I might find my friend Little Wolf, and now I have done so," White Hat said over the joined hands.

But to the anxious questioning he could only promise that he would recommend that these Cheyennes be permitted to go to the northern Arapahos in Wyoming. Beyond that the lieutenant could say nothing, except that he would not let anybody be hurt if they all gave up their arms and horses.

So it was the same, always the same, Little Wolf thought, and now truly the hearts of his people would be on the ground.

"I will feed you all," Clark added, "and take you to your relatives at Keogh, where none of the people have been harmed."

To this Little Wolf replied the *"Hou"* with the falling tone, meaning only that it had been heard, trying to look beyond the officer here to those who stood behind this man, to bigger and bigger soldier chiefs, a row of them clear back to the Great Father in Washington.

"We will go back and talk it over with the people," the chief finally agreed, "but I ask that you move gently. We have heard what was done at Robinson. My people are afraid."

So, with Little Wolf beside him, the handsome White Hat, called Nobby by his men, led the column close up and camped it. Then, after the chief had an hour to quiet his followers, Clark came to the Cheyennes, leaving his arms on the ground behind him where all could see. Little Wolf motioned his excited warriors back, and the headmen settled to a counciling with the lieutenant, talking a long time. White Hat said he was sad to see his friends so poor. The people standing away, afraid, could not know his words, but the close ones saw the water as of a raining stand in his white-man eyes.

"You are indeed poor, my friends," the lieutenant said, "but I can see that you are very strong now, and you still have a good man to lead you, one wise enough to select this difficult place that would shed a great deal of blood for everybody to capture."

Little Wolf replied very earnestly, telling the reasons they came north: their sickness and hunger, their longing for their own country. They wanted peace, but they could not give up their guns now.

"We told the troops that followed us we did not want to fight, but they started shooting. So we ran away. My brother took half of the people up to where you used to be at Robinson, but you were not there and those other white men promised that no one would be hurt, yet after the Indians laid their guns down in a pile, they were locked up and starved. When they had to come out for water and food, or die, the soldiers killed most of them. I cannot give up our arms. You are the first to make a good talk before fighting us, but we cannot do what you ask. We are very poor, but we are brave, and we know how to die."

So Clark had to wait. The Cheyennes were fed well that night, with plenty of coffee smelling fine in the evening air, the sugar deep as the width of a finger in the cup. The next day they would start toward Clark's wagon train, where there was plenty more coffee and sugar and flour and more meat too, enough to last to Keogh, and some blankets for the ragged ones.

Now Thin Elk came loaded with a great kettle and a sack full of special meat, dried fruit, and some hard candy for his friends at Little Wolf's fire. And who could be unwelcoming toward him now, as the chief's wives and Pretty Walker laughed aloud and ran to give a piece of the sweet rocks to everyone there.

In the morning the Indians came out of their strong place, a few running back for a little while, so afraid to leave this last security, but finally they were all moving toward the wagons down the river. On the way the Cheyennes hunted with the soldiers, challenging each other at every antelope and deer that was flushed. Little Wolf knew that the *veho* officer was encouraging the Cheyennes to use up their few cartridges. But there would not have been enough for even a little stand.

Once the Wolf shifted the Chief's Bundle under his arm and wondered if he were true to his trust, his oath. How could a man know what to do in these new times if the path to the Great Powers seemed lost?

As he rode beside White Hat, the Cheyenne leader turned now and then to look back to the Indians moving slowly behind. All he had left was 114 people now, of the 284 that he watched slip away from their standing lodges in the south country, and those extra ones who came later, the strong young men. Most of those died or returned, and two or three young women with them, perhaps, but none could ever tell it truly now, with the soldiers and cowboys all shooting. He could not even be sure of what happened to the young Yellow Swallow, the Custer son, who was to grow tall and strong in the north country, and was now back in the south too, or dead in the grass somewhere, as his father had died.

Although Little Wolf had only thirty-three men left altogether, counting the boys, and everybody was as poor and ragged as yesterday and the days before, somehow they rode with more ease, with even a little gaiety among those away from the mourning family of Black Crane. The chief watched them as the men whipped in triumphantly, bringing game taken with guns, the first time in many moons that they dared use up ammunition. He noticed the mother of little Comes Behind, the son born in the first shadows of the flight, clear back south there. She lifted the cover from the child's face, lifted the cradleboard too, and showed him this parade of the hunters with meat across the horses riding around the moving village in the old, old way. Little Wolf saw too that Spotted Deer went along the people until he found Yellow Bead. Then he rode proudly, slowly, past her with the buck across his saddle. It was a big one, the antlers hanging low, and now the girl made the trilling of pride, as though for her returning warrior.

Once more the chief had to stop his horse. "You will work to see that a few of us can go to the Great Father, my friend? We must ask him for a piece of land, a reservation of our own for the young people left. . . ."

"I will ask this for Little Wolf and his Cheyennes. I cannot promise that anything will be done, but I promise I will work hard for it," the white man replied, and held his shamed face quiet before the searching, the probing eyes of the Indian who must know.

Finally the gaunt, pock-marked man turned to look back over his people and then ahead toward the north, one hand moving gently to the bundle that lay against his ribs. The movement stirred the round medal of peace that hung on his breast, just a little.

"*Hou!*" Little Wolf said at last, but in the good way, in acceptance. "Perhaps the wind that has made our hearts flutter and afraid so long will now go down."

Three days later, almost at the Moon of Spring, the people stopped along the gray bluffs and looked down upon the tree-lined stream that was the Yellowstone. For a long time there was only silence, as from strangers come to a strange land. But then a trilling went up from among them somewhere, a young voice, a young girl come into a new time. Her thin, clear peal was followed by a loud resounding cry, a cry of the grown, the old, the weary, and the forlorn. But on the spring wind it was a cry of joy, of tears and sorrows too for all those lost on the way, but a cry of joy. It had taken a long, long time, but they were home at last.

In the Aftertime

BEFORE THE LITTLE WOLF PEOPLE WERE WELL SETTLED in the soldier tents at Keogh, there was news of raiding Indians up the Mizpah River. Two soldiers repairing the telegraph line over that way were attacked. One of the men was killed; the other, wounded, had crept away into the brush, and was picked up by travelers on the Deadwood-to-Keogh road. Troops took up the trail and followed it fast for five days before they caught the Indians. It was Black Coyote's little party; the soldier's horse and his revolver were still in the Coyote's possession.

The Cheyennes were brought to Keogh. Black Coyote and Whetstone were locked up with chains on their legs, as the men down south had been before they were taken away to the Florida prison, and here too the people were helpless. During the long months of her husband's imprisonment at the post, Buffalo Calf Road, the warrior woman of the Cheyennes, sickened and slowly died, some said of the white man's coughing disease. The herbs of her aunt, the cures and chants of the medicine man helped no more than the powders of the army doctor. Every few days the Cheyennes signaled her condition to Black Coyote who watched night and day, it seemed, at the little barred window. When he discovered that his brave Calf Road was dead, he became so wild no one could go near him. He did not eat or sleep and had to be overpowered and dragged out beside Whetstone for the hanging. There were angry words over this wherever it was known, even from army officers. Would the two soldiers have been hanged if they had shot Black Coyote or even the whole party, including his wife and children? This was a time of war.

The women keened on the hillside and the men sat dark and sullen in their blankets against the log buildings at Fort Keogh, but the bodies of their relatives were not given to them.

In the south there was a little more to eat, and the warriors who had returned from the Sappa and the Beaver slipped back as though only away on a hunt. Some of the Cheyennes thought that Yellow Swallow died in the Last Hole beyond Hat Creek bluffs, but the boy lived out his sickly way to seventeen at home.

Long before then many other things were settled. In Kansas a commission sifted the claims for damages in the Cheyenne outbreak. Cut down, the total demanded was still $101,766.83—three beef claims for over $10,000 each, one for $17,760.

"Even at a fancy five dollars a head for them Texas longhorns, the Indians'd oughta been fat as badgers—around three hundred Indians eatin' bettern' ten thousand head a beef in less'n a month," some of the settlers said. By 1882, $9,870.10 had been ordered paid from the treaty funds of the Northern Cheyennes to claimants for damages in the flight through Kansas in 1878.

In the meantime ministers, newspapermen, and others called foolish idealists by those who lived along the bloody Beaver and the Sappa had taken up the cause of the Cheyennes. Attorneys came forward to defend them without charge. By the autumn of 1879—a better one for the Cheyennes—Hog, Tangle Hair, and the others taken to Kansas in irons had been tried for murder and released for want of evidence.[1] It would have looked pretty bad for the whites who killed so many noncombatants in the trouble, all those Cheyenne women and children, some said, if these men were found guilty. Afterward the prisoners were taken back to the southern agency, but soon they were allowed to come up with Little Chief as far as Red Cloud's people. They brought the Sacred Buffalo Hat along, and the few Cheyennes left with the Sioux went out to meet them, singing the songs of reunion. Later all except a few rode away north to the Yellowstone country. But not the big, broad-faced Hog. He had sickened with pneumonia, a disease that struck deeper than any enemy's weapon, deeper than the knife he had thrust into his breast with his shackled hands in the encampment near Fort Robinson that cold January day. This time he died, very fast.

At the request of General Miles, Dull Knife had been allowed to go north long before. With his crippled, orphaned band he came to sit in this north country that had cost so much. But the beaded lizard of his medicine dreaming, of his power to save the people, no longer hung on his breast. Soon Dull Knife, the Morning Star of the Cheyennes, was allowed to settle in the Rosebud Valley that became a part of the Tongue River Reservation finally set up for the Northern Cheyennes. Silent, sorrowful, the embittered old man died there about 1883.

Little Wolf's followers found Keogh the good, safe place White Hat Clark had promised, but there was nothing for the Indians to do. A few scouted a little against Sitting Bull, but mostly there was not even much hunting, with the settlers and cattlemen coming in thick ahead of the railroad that crept up the Yellowstone, the railroad for which Custer had marched into the Black Hills in 1874. There were not even hides to dress or many beads for the women's work. So the Cheyennes talked over the glories of the past and played games, gambled, and drank the bit of whisky they managed to get now and then from the plentiful supply around the post.

The first winter Little Wolf obtained a little bottle. Hiding it under his blanket, he slipped away and drank it up fast. Then he went to a trader store and watched his daughter gambling for candy with Thin Elk there as always, looking on, talking and laughing in his bold easy way. The Wolf became angry to see this and tried to stop the girl, take her home. But nobody paid any attention. He was a little drunk, and this telling people what to do was not the Cheyenne way but the white man's, and so was ignored. Little Wolf brooded over this a while, the whisky heating the anger of his youth against this man that had lived in his heart such a long time. So he got a gun and shot Thin Elk. The report was like a cannon blast in his ears and at once he was sober. Slowly he put the gun down.

"I am going to the hill," the chief said gravely. "I will be waiting if anybody wants me."

He sat up there for two days without food or water, while down below, his lodge was cut up by the Elk's relatives and his possessions looted, as was their right. After a while Little Wolf came down and sat waiting beside a building for what was to be done with him. No Cheyenne came near him with the formal banishment; no one came at all, except an army officer.

"Little Wolf," he said. "You are no longer the chief."

The gaunt, bowed Indian did not lift his dusty head for this one small man of the people that he had defeated so long and so well. There was no need for a reply to him.

After the killing Little Wolf never smoked the sacred long-stemmed pipe again or sat with others who were smoking. He kept to himself and went everywhere afoot, often alone. He walked clear over to visit the Arapahos, the relatives of his father, beyond the Big Horn Mountains 200 miles away, his two wives along this time, carrying what they could on their backs, sleeping in the open or in the little brush shelters like those they made on that long flight north.

For twenty-five years Little Wolf lived so, the humblest of a reservation people. When he died in 1904, there were some who still remembered and still loved him. They propped his body up tall on a hill and piled stones around him, drawing them up by travois until he was covered in a great heap.[2] There Little Wolf stood on a high place, his face turned to look over the homes of his followers and beyond them, down the Rosebud that flowed northward to the Yellowstone.

Notes

Only sources of the most important new material or those on very controversial points are included. All Indians in the outbreak, Sioux or Cheyenne whom I interviewed (except Old Cheyenne Woman), requested anonymity because the taboo is still strong against all talk about the 1875 fight on the Sappa and the 1878 killing of the Kansas settlers.

Gone Before—page 1

1. Cheyenne system of chiefs: forty-four, consisting of four Old Man Chiefs, representing all the people, and four from each of the ten tribal bands. Chiefs of the warrior (soldier) societies were not included in the council, although they sometimes remained warrior chiefs after they became band heads. Little Wolf was the only man ever to retain a warrior-society chieftainship after becoming an Old Man Chief.
2. Martin F. Schmitt, ed., *General George Crook, His Autobiography,* University of Oklahoma Press, Norman, Okla., 1946.
3. Commissioner of Indian Affairs, *Annual Report,* 1854.

CHAPTER 1. *Sixty Lodges Standing—page 13*

1. Monahsetah and her son Yellow Swallow: Charles J. Brill, *Conquest of the Southern Plains,* Golden Saga Publishers, Oklahoma City, 1938; Thomas B. Marquis, "She Watched Custer's Last Stand," pamphlet; Wild Hog to Jules Sandoz; Old Cheyenne Woman and others to author.

CHAPTER 2. *Ahh-h, Buffalo—page 24*

1. Number and names of Cheyennes gone north: Reports from Agent John D. Miles to Commissioner of Indian Affairs, Sept. 10 and Nov. 18, 1878, Records, Bureau of Indian Affairs, U.S. National Archives.

CHAPTER 4. *The First Man Killed—page 47*

1. Cheyennes in south Kansas: G. E. Lemmon manuscript, copy with author; Old Cheyenne Woman and others.
2. Whereabouts of Gen. William T. Sherman: *New York Tribune,* Sept. 22 and Oct. 11, 1878; *National Tribune,* Sept. 2, 1886.

CHAPTER 6. *A Soldier Chief Dead—page 71*

1. Lewis fight: Cheyenne outbreak, Reports of Officers and Physician, Oct. 15, 1878, Department of Missouri, War Records, U.S. National Archives; Wild Hog to Jules Sandoz; Old Cheyenne Woman and other Indians to author.

CHAPTER 7. *Sappa—Meaning Black—page 83*

1. Selection of prisoners for Florida: Darlington Agency Records, 1875, Oklahoma Historical Society; Agent John D. Miles to Commissioner of Indian Affairs, *Annual Report,* 1874–1875; Col. George A. Armes, *Ups and Downs of an Army Officer* (no publisher given), Washington, 1900; Old Cheyenne Woman and others.
2. Gen. Thomas H. Neill, *Report of the Secretary of War,* Vol. I, 1875.
3. Manuscript of Sand Crane, Cheyenne Keeper of the Sacred Medicine Hat; Brill, *op. cit.;* Old Cheyenne Woman and Cousin.
4. H. D. Wimer letters to author, 1949–1950, with account by C. H. Carmack, ambulance driver, Fort Wallace, 1875, to Wimer, saying twenty to twenty-five buffalo hunters were in the Sappa fight and that the Indians tried to surrender and were refused; Old Cheyenne Woman and others, including some Sioux.
5. Wimer letters and Sappa notes, with accounts by John and Charles Koontz.
6. *Report of the Secretary of War,* Vol. I, 1875; Wimer accounts of Carmack and Sam Grout; Hill P. Wilson, sutler at Fort Hays, Kansas Historical *Collections,* Vol. X; Adolph Roenigk, ed., *Pioneer History of Kansas,* A. Roenigk, Lincoln, Kan., 1933; F. M. Lockard account; Bureau of Ethnology, *17th Annual Report;* Old Cheyenne Woman and other Indians.

CHAPTER 8. *To Make the Bad Heart Good—page 96*

1. Wimer letters, with several accounts, including that of Frank Janousek, a survivor of the attack along Beaver Creek; voluminous printed and manuscript accounts; inscription on monument erected at Oberlin, Kan., to the memory of the nineteen men killed by the Cheyennes in Decatur County in the fall of 1878; Old Cheyenne Woman and other Indians.

CHAPTER 14. *The Fasting—page 179*

1. *Denver Post,* Apr. 12, 1903. Gentles was an old soldier from the Mormon campaign.
2. *Boston Post,* 1910, Dawson Scrapbooks, Colorado Historical Society; *Winners of the West,* Vol. 2, No. 8 and Vol. 9, No. 12; E. A. Brininstool, Accounts of Beaver Heart and Josie Tangleyellowhair, sister of Yellow Hand, *Northwest Nebraska News,* June 18, 1936.
3. Fuel, food, and water shut off from Cheyennes: Capt. Henry W. Wessells, Jr., Military Division of the Missouri, Letters Received, 1878–1879, War Records, U.S. National Archives; Wild Hog to Jules Sandoz; Old Cheyenne Woman and other Indians, including several Sioux.

CHAPTER 15. *The Ordeal Begins—page 194*

1. Mistreatment of bodies: Richard Stirk, Ricker Interviews, Nebraska State Historical Society; Lieutenant Cummings on Cheyenne outbreak and surrender at Fort Robinson, Neb., *Proceedings of Board of Officers,* Special File, Letters Received, Military Division of the Missouri, Jan. 25, 1879, War Records, U.S. National Archives.
2. Lieutenants Simpson, Crawford, and Hardie, Dr. Moseley and interpreter Rowland, *Proceedings of Board of Officers, op. cit.; Chicago Tribune,* Jan. 16–18, 1879; Old Cheyenne Woman and others.

CHAPTER 16. *This Is the Place—page 212*

1. and 2. *Proceedings of Board of Officers, op. cit.; Chicago Tribune,* Jan. 9, 1879 to February, 1879; Old Cheyenne Woman; Wild Hog to Jules Sandoz.
3. *Proceedings of Board of Officers, op. cit.;* John Shangreau, Ricker Interviews, *op. cit.;* Old Cheyenne Woman.

CHAPTER 17. *This Remnant—page 238*

1. Saving of Dull Knife: Charles P. Jordan, Ricker Collection, Nebraska State Historical Society; *Chicago Tribune,* Feb. 11, 1879; Mrs. Susan Bettelyoun manuscript; Edgar Beecher Bronson, *Reminiscences of a Ranchman,* McClure Company, New York, 1908.

CHAPTER 18. *And Now the Yellowstone—page 248*

1. Little Wolf Papers, Apr. 6, 1879, Special File, Letters Received, Military Division of the Missouri, War Records, U.S. National Archives.

In the Aftertime—page 269

1. Kansas State Historical Society, *18th Biennial Report,* 1910–1911.
2. K. N. Llewellyn and E. Adamson Hoebel, *The Cheyenne Way,* University of Oklahoma Press, Norman, Okla., 1941; Thomas B. Marquis, interpreter, *A Warrior Who Fought Custer,* The Midwest Company, Minneapolis, 1931.

Index